ARGUI

FROM EVIDENCE
IN MIDDLE SCHOOL
SCIENCE

ARGUING
FROM EVIDENCE
IN MIDDLE SCHOOL
SCIENCE

24 Activities for Productive Talk and Deeper Learning

Jonathan Osborne

Brian M. Donovan

J. Bryan Henderson

Anna C. MacPherson

Andrew Wild

CORWIN

A SAGE Publishing Company

FOR INFORMATION:

Corwin

A SAGE Company

2455 Teller Road

Thousand Oaks, California 91320

(800) 233-9936

www.corwin.com

SAGE Publications Ltd.

1 Oliver's Yard

55 City Road

London, EC1Y 1SP

United Kingdom

SAGE Publications India Pvt. Ltd.

B 1/I 1 Mohan Cooperative Industrial Area

Mathura Road, New Delhi 110 044

India

SAGE Publications Asia-Pacific Pte. Ltd.

3 Church Street

#10-04 Samsung Hub

Singapore 049483

Printed in the United States of America

Library of Congress Cataloging-in-Publication Data

Names: Osborne, Jonathan, author.

Title: Arguing from evidence in middle school science : 24 activities for productive talk and deeper learning / Jonathan Osborne, Brian M. Donovan, J. Bryan Henderson, Anna C. MacPherson, Andrew Wild.

Description: Thousand Oaks, California : Corwin, 2017. | Includes bibliographical references and index.

Identifiers: LCCN 2016019918 | ISBN 9781506335940 (pbk. : alk. paper)

Subjects: LCSH: Science—Study and teaching (Middle school)—Activity programs.

Classification: LCC Q181 .O828 2017 | DDC 507.1/2—dc23 LC record available at https://lccn.loc.gov/2016019918

This book is printed on acid-free paper.

Certified Chain of Custody
Promoting Sustainable Forestry
www.sfiprogram.org
SFI-01268

SFI label applies to text stock

Acquisitions Editor: Erin Null

Developmental Editor: Julie Nemer

Editorial Assistant: Nicole Shade

Production Editor: Veronica Stapleton Hooper

Copy Editor: Gillian Dickens

Typesetter: C&M Digitals (P) Ltd.

Proofreader: Gretchen Treadwell

Indexer: Beth Nauman-Montana

Cover Designer: Gail Buschman

Marketing Manager: Margaret O'Connor

16 17 18 19 20 10 9 8 7 6 5 4 3 2 1

Contents

Visit the companion website at https://resources.corwin.com/OsborneArgumentation to access downloadable versions of all reproducibles.

Preface

Why This Book?

What has argument got to do with science? After all, the science that forms the basis of school science has been around for decades and, in some cases, centuries. For instance, Newtonian mechanics, which is the basis of most school physics syllabi, was essentially settled in 1776 with the publication of Newton's *Principia*. Nobody questions this any longer. However, just because the arguments about whether Newton's ideas are correct have long since been settled does not make them any easier to understand or accept if you are a young student. After all, one of the basic premises of Newtonian mechanics—that all objects keep going forever unless acted on by a force—seems contradicted by our experience of riding a bike. Why do we have to keep pedaling if Newton's premise is correct?

The job of the teacher of science, then, is to make the arguments for the scientific ideas—however crazy these arguments might seem to your students at first. Science is founded on the idea that evidence is the basis of belief. This is what makes it rational. And to help our students understand that science is rational, we need to help them understand (a) what the evidence is and (b) how evidence justifies the belief. Moreover, we have to help them think like scientists, by practicing the skill of using evidence to justify a belief. This is why arguing from evidence is one of the eight scientific practices found in the Next Generation Science Standards (NGSS).

After all, science brings into being a whole host of new entities—atoms, molecules, cells, elements, nuclei, germs, mass, acceleration, joules, newtons, light rays, circulatory systems, electric current, energy, power, and many more. Why should the student believe in this strange plethora of objects—most of which cannot be seen, let alone touched or felt?

The idea that students need to be *convinced* of such scientific entities is not a view of science found in most classrooms. Rather, we suspect that much science is presented as a statement of fact—this is the way the world *is*—with a justification that is reliant on trust in the authority of the teacher. After all, teachers of science are there because they are an authority and, standing at the front, their words carry an implicit message of "believe me, I do know what I am talking about." But many students find their faith tested. So many of the ideas of science are strange that our students learn them but don't really believe them. After all, it took years for most societies to accept the idea that the Earth orbits the Sun, that the continents were once one, and that diseases spread through microorganisms, let alone to accept evolution! So, why should your students accept these ideas any more rapidly? In short, argument matters for two reasons:

1. If teachers provide students an opportunity to look at the evidence, it both makes the case for what we want students to believe and helps to show why what they think might be wrong. When it comes to believing a new idea, knowing why you are wrong matters as much as knowing why you are right. Ideas always exist in competition. For example, making the case that the weight of an object makes no difference to the rate at which it falls (in the absence of air friction) means *also* making the case as to why the idea that heavier things always *do* move faster is *flawed*. Evidence shows that teachers who explicitly address the common misconceptions that students hold are more effective teachers of science (Hattie, 2008; Sadler, Sonnert, Coyle, Cook-Smith, & Miller, 2013). Providing students with opportunities to work through this dichotomy—while more time-consuming—makes them much more likely to see how scientific evidence justifies a belief.

2. Constructing and criticizing arguments is a much more engaging and challenging activity than simply being asked to remember lots of factual information that is poorly understood. The opportunity to hone this skill will deepen students' understanding and knowledge of science itself.

"But what," we hear you say, "if they convince themselves of the wrong idea?" That is a reasonable concern. However, this concern demonstrates a lack of conviction in the scientific idea, the evidence for it, and the arguments against common student misconceptions. Our job, as teachers of science, is to put forward the scientific case, to question the weaker arguments that students may offer, and to challenge flawed thinking—not so much a case of playing devil's advocate but being science's advocate.

This book aims to help you to get your students going with scientific argumentation.

Chapter 1 begins by making an extended case for why argumentation is central to science and how it is a key practice in learning how to reason and think. In this chapter, we also look at why there has been an increasing emphasis on argumentation in education, not just in science but also in mathematics and language arts. In addition, the chapter outlines what the elements of an argument are, as we need a language for talking about argument. To help here, we provide a few exercises that ask you to use the language of argument to think about some simple scientific arguments that might be made in the classroom. Finally, we also explore the difference between argument and explanation as this can be confusing. The goal here is to give you a conceptual overview of what scientific arguments are and to start thinking of what we teach as needing an argument to justify what we are asking students to believe.

Chapter 2 aims to give you an overview of the many instructional strategies that you can use to support students to engage in argumentation. As well as ones that are familiar, such as think-pair-share, we introduce ones that might be less familiar, such as argument lines, four corners, and listening triads. It is these strategies that we draw on for the 24 activities that come later in the book, so it is a good idea to read this chapter to get a sense of what we are talking about in those activities. Most of these strategies are for supporting students to discuss opposing scientific ideas, but we finish the chapter by looking at ways of supporting written arguments as well.

Chapter 3 looks at how you can support argument in the classroom so that it is productive—in that it helps students to learn and understand science. If students are going to engage in argumentation, certain social norms have to be adhered to. This chapter explores what these are and why they are needed. As the teacher, you will need to make these norms explicit. In addition, good discourse does not happen on its own so, as the teacher, you need certain types of questions to use that press students to elaborate their thinking, help to clarify what they have said, and challenge their ideas. The chapter describes these and how you might use them.

The 24 Activities are the main substance of the book. These are arranged by Earth and Space Sciences (Activities 1–8), Life Sciences (Activities 9–16), and Physical Sciences (Activities 17–24). Each of these activities focuses on a specific question, starting with a brief introduction of its main purpose and goal. Outlined for you are the specific learning goals and an NGSS performance expectation that the activity is addressing. We also discuss the science content as it is important that, as the teacher, you are familiar with the ideas that the activity is addressing. Engaging students in scientific argumentation means that you as the teacher need to be familiar with both the arguments for the science and the arguments why common everyday ideas might be flawed. Thus, we also discuss what knowledge you might need for teaching this topic and the likely prior knowledge that the students may have on which you will have to build.

Each activity has a set of teacher instructions for running the activity and students' sheets, which can be photocopied or downloaded as pdfs from https://resources.corwin.com/OsborneArgumentation. Suggested timings are also included, and most of these activities should take no more than one lesson. To give you some idea of the outcomes of the activity, we offer exemplars of good student responses. These are only meant to be indicative of what students might say and should not be regarded as the "right answer." The points that students might make are many and varied. The only judgment that you have to make as the teacher is whether their discussion is getting them closer to a scientific understanding. Finally, many of the activities finish with additional resources and extension activities.

If you have not used activities of this form before, we recognize that you are taking a leap. It helps to know that whenever we try something new, it threatens our feelings of confidence, competence, control, and comfort (the 4 "Cs" of learning). However, we believe that these activities and this manner of teaching will help you give students a window into what science is really about. It is this kind of approach and work that makes science exciting—the creative struggle to find answers to questions that are both challenging and engaging. After all, what matters in learning science is not only what we know but *how* we know what we know—and *how* that knowledge came to be. Anything less offers only a partial view of the achievements of science.

Acknowledgments

This book is a product of 20 years work on the topic of argumentation and a belief in its value for learning, teaching, and understanding science. The people who have helped along the way and who I would like to acknowledge are Rosalind Driver, Rick Duschl, Sibel Erduran, Shirley Simon, Mark Wilson, Helen Quinn, Evan Szu, and all my co-authors. I have learnt much from each individual.

—Jonathan Osborne

Publisher's Acknowledgments

Corwin wishes to acknowledge the following peer reviewers for their editorial insight and guidance.

Amanda Dykes
Instructional Technology Coach, Former Middle School Science Teacher
Jefferson County Schools
Birmingham, Alabama

Bryan Flaig
Science Curriculum Specialist
University of California, Berkeley
Berkeley, California

Phil Keck
Seventh/Eighth-Grade Science Teacher
Live Oak School
San Francisco, California

Susan Leeds
Gifted Specialist (former middle school gifted science teacher)
Winter Park High School
Winter Park, Florida

Maria Mesires
3–5 Science Coach
Indian River School District
Watertown, New York

Melissa Miller
Science Educator
Randall G. Lynch Middle School
Farmington, Arkansas

Dana Sanner
Middle School Science Teacher
Sanibel School
Sanibel, Florida

PART 1

Understanding and Teaching for Argumentation

CHAPTER 1

What Is Argumentation and Why Does It Matter in the Teaching of Science?

Why Argumentation Is Central to Science

Many people think that most scientific ideas are common sense. This is a mistake. A moment's thought makes you realize that many of the concepts we teach in science sound crazy or unbelievable. Take, for instance, the idea that day and night are caused by a spinning Earth. Why should anyone believe this when it seems patently obvious that it is the *Sun* that moves, rising in the East and setting in the West? Moreover, if you think about it, it is approximately 25,000 miles around the Equator and, if the Earth rotates once every 24 hours, this means that the speed at the Equator is over 1,000 miles per hour. Surely, we would be flung off? Finally, if the Earth were spinning that fast, then surely, when we jumped up, we would not land in the same spot. Looked at this way, the canonical explanation for day and night—something that is taught in elementary schools—seems crazy. Surely, then, to convince anybody that the standard scientific explanation is correct, we have to produce the evidence to justify such claims. In short, we have to put forward an evidence-based *argument*. Somewhat surprisingly, most people are hard pushed to identify the two pieces of empirical evidence that do support the scientific explanation—Foucault's pendulum[1] and a photograph of the night sky taken by a camera with the shutter left open and pointed at the pole star.[2]

Lest you think that this is one special example, there are many more. Take the idea that the continents once were one. Why should you believe that? What force is capable of moving mountains, let alone continents? Indeed, this idea was summarily dismissed when first put forward by Alfred Wegener in 1915 for this reason. Or the idea that you look like your parents because every cell in your body carries a chemically coded message about how to reproduce you, or the idea that diseases are caused by tiny living microorganisms that are invisible to the naked eye, or the idea that we live at the bottom of a sea of air whose pressure is equivalent to 10 m of seawater, or the idea that most of the atom is empty space—that is, if you think of the nucleus as being about the size of a tennis ball, the nearest electron will be three quarters of a mile away. We have only come to believe all of these ideas because scientists have made arguments from evidence that ultimately have proven to be better than other ideas. It is this idea that is captured in Figure 1.1, which comes from the *Framework for K–12 Science Education* (National Research Council, 2012b).

What this figure says is that, in any science, three spheres of activity interact. On the left, there is an investigation space. Here scientists do things like make observations, collect data, and build instruments to test their ideas. On the right, there is space where they invent ideas and hypotheses

---

1 Foucault's pendulum is a long pendulum with a large heavy mass at the bottom supported on a frictionless pivot. During the course of the day, the plane of the swing appears to move by anywhere up to 360 degrees when there is no force acting on it. Foucault realized that it was not the pendulum that was moving but the earth beneath it.

2 Such photographs show a set of circular trails with all the stars appearing to be going round the pole star. There are two explanations: (a) all the stars are going around the pole star, or (b) the ground on which the camera is placed is turning. In science, we apply Occam's razor—commonly known as the KISS principle—and go for the simplest explanation that it is the Earth that is moving.

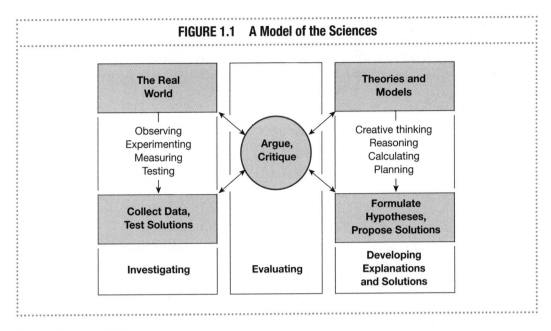

FIGURE 1.1   A Model of the Sciences

Source: Osborne (2011).

about the way the material world behaves. These ideas depend on creative and imaginative thinking and often use models. These models enable predictions. It is these ideas that are the real achievement of science. For instance, think of a famous scientist. Our guess would be that the overwhelming majority of you would think of somebody who is famous for a new idea—Einstein, Darwin, Hawking, Wegener, Maxwell, Copernicus, or Bohr—rather than somebody who is famous for an experiment. What this shows is that you get your name in lights in science for devising a new idea or theory or that it is theories that are "the crowning glory of science" (Harré, 1984).

Fundamentally, science is about building new ideas. Experiments are simply the means of testing the ideas. Deciding on which ideas are best, however, requires argument—arguments about whether the ideas are supported by the evidence, arguments about the nature of the experimental tests and their validity, or arguments about the interpretation of the data. Arguments are thus central to what it means to do science. For this reason, the history of science can be seen as history of vision, argument, and error (Allchin, 2012; Crombie, 1994). And, just like any other group, science and scientists learn from their mistakes.

What is the difference then between argument and *argumentation,* you might ask? Argumentation is a process of considering arguments and counterarguments. We can give you an argument for why day and night are caused by a spinning Earth and you could give us a counterargument as to why they are not. If we were to do this, we would be arguing, as you would be criticizing our idea using counterarguments and engaging in the process of argumentation that could also be called *critique.*

Learning to Argue Is Learning to Think?

Argumentation is necessary in science as there are always multiple explanations that compete. In particular, in teaching science, the scientific explanation often has to compete with students' preexisting but flawed ideas. Deciding on the best explanation is a matter of argument and a choice that is justified by how well any given explanation fits with the data—in essence, how coherent the explanation is with observations. This means that argument is a core feature of science. Whether it is new theories, novel ways of collecting data, or fresh interpretations of old data, argumentation is the means that scientists use to make their case for new ideas (Latour & Woolgar, 1986), and in response, other scientists attempt to identify weaknesses and limitations (Popper, 1963). Peer review is the formal mechanism for conducting this process within the scientific community. Over time, ideas that survive critical examination are accepted. In this way—through argumentation and critique—science maintains its objectivity (Longino, 1990). It is not a case of anything goes—any idea has to fit with the evidence, and everybody has to be convinced that it does.

Thus, critique is not some peripheral feature of science, but rather, it is core to its practice. Without critique, the construction of reliable knowledge would be impossible. Likewise, in learning science, developing an understanding of scientific ideas requires both construction and critique (Ford, 2008). Or, to put it another way, when you are learning science, knowing why the wrong idea is wrong matters as much as knowing why the right idea is right. However, students will only begin to see how central argument is to science, and to developing the critical disposition that is the hallmark of the scientist, if they are provided with regular opportunities to engage in constructing arguments from evidence. Moreover, if students are not occasionally offered some windows into how the knowledge that we are asking them to believe came to be, then school science cannot defend itself against the accusation that it is simply a "miscellany of facts" to be learnt dogmatically. And, a set of facts in science is no more of substance than a pile of stones is a house. Indeed, without any attempt to explain how we know what we know, school science education finds it hard to defend itself against the accusation that what it offers is no better than the religious dogma the masses were expected to believe before the Enlightenment. Some would go further, arguing that to ask students to believe ideas without justifying why they should be believed is morally questionable (Norris, 1997).

These are the reasons why arguing from evidence is one of the eight practices in the Next Generation Science Standards (NGSS). As argued in the *Framework for K–12 Science Education* (National Research Council, 2012b), the basis of the NGSS standards, the science is not "not just a body of knowledge that reflects current understanding of the world; it is also a set of practices used to establish, extend, and refine that knowledge" (p. 26). Teaching students to be scientifically literate requires us to give them the opportunity to experience what these practices are and how scientists think.

The traditional approach to science education does not commonly do this (Newton, Driver, & Osborne, 1999; Weiss, Pasley, Sean Smith, Banilower, & Heck, 2003), and very little material in textbooks approaches ideas in this manner (Penney, Norris, Phillips, & Clark, 2003). This book is an attempt to remedy that deficiency. What you will find in this book are 24 activities spread across the science topics that are taught in middle schools. Each of these is designed take 30 to 60 minutes of classroom time. You will find concrete guidance about how to use these activities, and to start with, it is probably best to follow the activity as suggested. At the end of the book, we summarize the standard strategies that can be used to support argument in the classroom.

The major point to be made at the moment is that "argument" often carries a negative connotation for many young people. For that reason, it is important to start with strategies that *separate the idea from the person,* such as discussion of instances, a concept cartoon, an argument line, or four corners. It might also be better to say that you are asking your students to "discuss" or "debate" ideas. However, fundamentally, what you are asking your students to do is to think critically and to learn that reason and understanding are the product of difference, not fond consensus. Or, to put it another way, that learning to think is learning to argue.

Why So Much Emphasis on Argument?

You may have noticed that the word *argument* seems to feature in the talk not just about science but also about mathematics and language arts. For instance, in the Common Core Mathematics Standards, one of the mathematical practices is that students are expected to "construct viable arguments and critique the reasoning of others" (Common Core State Standards Initiative, 2010) while in the Common Core Standards for Language Arts—notably not just for English language but also history, social studies, *and science*—students are expected at Grade 6 to be able to "trace and evaluate the argument and specific claims in a text." By Grade 9/10, the Common Core in

Language Arts requires the ability to evaluate arguments as well (i.e., "Delineate and evaluate the argument and specific claims in a text"). Why, then, so much emphasis on argument?

First, it does not take much to realize that people have ever-increasing expectations of education. As well as students who know a lot, society wants education to develop higher order competencies—often called 21st-century skills—of critique, evaluation, and synthesis ("Coming to an Office," 2014; Gilbert, 2005; National Research Council, 2012a). Clearly, students are not going to develop this kind of competence if they are not given the opportunity to practice these kinds of cognitive processes. Increasingly, we are living in world where jobs requiring low-level skills are being replaced by machines. As information is so readily accessible, this is no longer a prized individual attribute. Rather, in a world where there is an oversupply of information, it is now the ability to make sense of information that is the scarce resource. Making sense of information requires the ability to distinguish good information from the bad both at the personal level and in work. At the personal level, we are confronted by issues of environmental degradation, whether to vaccinate our children, or whether to exercise. At work, there is a plethora of information competing for our attention about how to be more productive and effective. Distinguishing the good from the bad, the wheat from the chaff, so to speak, requires us to engage in argumentation and critique.

What Are the Elements of an Argument?

There is a language for talking about the elements of an argument. This language comes from the conception of an argument first put forward by Stephen Toulmin in 1958 (Toulmin, 1958). Toulmin suggested that everyday arguments or informal arguments (as opposed to logical deductive arguments) consisted of

- a **claim** about the world,
- some **evidence** to support that claim, and
- a **reason** that explained why or how the data supported the claim.

This concept of an argument is shown diagrammatically in Figure 1.2.

Argumentation happens when people decide to criticize either the evidence or the reason. They can do this by advancing a rebuttal. This is essentially a counterargument explaining why either the reason or the evidence is flawed. Alternatively, they might choose to suggest that the argument has a qualifier—that is, that it is only true for certain instances. This is represented by Figure 1.3.

An example of an actual argument using these terms is shown in Figure 1.4.

In talking about argument with students, though, we have learnt that the word *claim* can be confusing as students think of claims in English or history class as a right or entitlement. In contrast to literary and historical claims, scientific claims are statements or assertions about the *natural world*. Scientific claims include what happens in nature and what causes natural phenomena to occur. Hence, in this book, we tend to talk about a claim as what somebody might be "arguing for" or is trying to "justify."

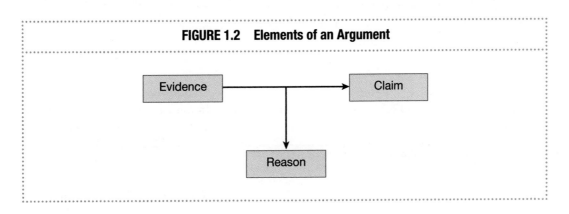

FIGURE 1.2   Elements of an Argument

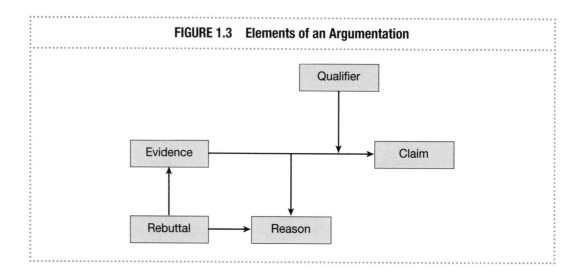

FIGURE 1.3   Elements of an Argumentation

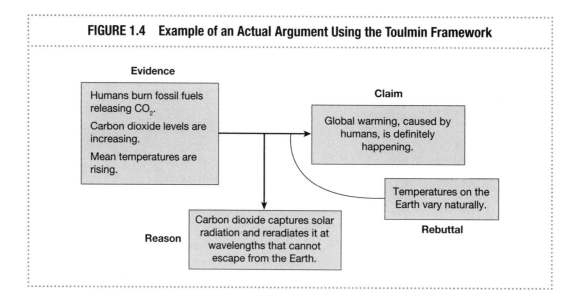

FIGURE 1.4   Example of an Actual Argument Using the Toulmin Framework

At this point, you might ask what the difference is between "data" and "evidence." In short, "data" become "evidence" when they are used in an argument. More or less anything can be data, but they are only evidence when we choose to use them in an argument. So while all evidence consists of data, not all data are evidence. In the examples above, specific data have been selected and are being used as evidence.

Figure 1.5 presents an example of another scientific argument. See if you can identify the separate elements of the argument.

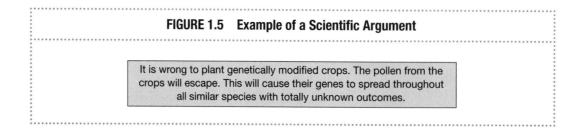

FIGURE 1.5   Example of a Scientific Argument

It is wrong to plant genetically modified crops. The pollen from the crops will escape. This will cause their genes to spread throughout all similar species with totally unknown outcomes.

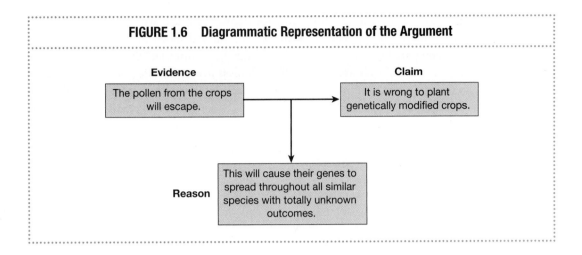

FIGURE 1.6　Diagrammatic Representation of the Argument

Our answer would be that "it is wrong to plant genetically modified crops" would be the claim. "The pollen from the crops will escape" is the evidence as that is essentially a fact. In that sense, data are not just restricted to numbers but can also be facts. Finally, the last sentence, "This will cause their genes to spread throughout all similar species with totally unknown outcomes," is the reason (see Figure 1.6).

Figure 1.7 presents another example. See what you think are the elements of an argument in this example.

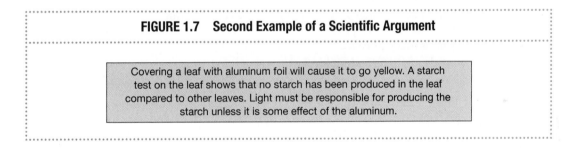

FIGURE 1.7　Second Example of a Scientific Argument

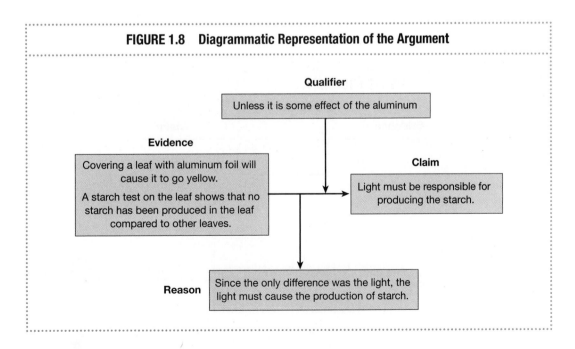

FIGURE 1.8　Diagrammatic Representation of the Argument

In this example, the evidence is the first sentence ("covering a leaf with aluminum foil will cause it to go yellow") and second sentence ("a starch test on the leaf shows that no starch has been produced in the leaf compared to other leaves"). There is then a claim that "light must be responsible for producing the starch," followed by a qualifier "unless it is some effect of the aluminum." There is really no reason in this example other than the tacit inference that because the only difference was the light, the light must cause the production of starch (see Figure 1.8). Sometimes arguments are incomplete (see Figure 1.9).

FIGURE 1.9   Third Example of a Scientific Argument

We see objects because light enters the eye; as we cannot see in the dark, vision must be caused by light entering the eye rather than rays leaving the eye.

In this third example, the claim is that "we see objects because light enters the eye" and later that "vision must be caused by light entering the eye rather than rays leaving the eye." Many students have a concept that vision is an active process and something that is directed by the eye. The evidence is that "we cannot see in the dark." What this argument lacks is a good reason relating the claim to the evidence of the form that, if vision were a process where something came out of the eye, then we would be able to see in the dark. As we cannot, it must occur because light enters the eye. If there is no light, therefore, we cannot see. Try sketching a diagrammatic representation of this argument for yourself.

Now try and apply this mode of thinking to some of the things that we commonly teach in science. For instance, what arguments would you give to convince a dubious student that

- Living matter is made of cells.
- Matter is made of atoms and molecules.
- Plants take in carbon dioxide and give out oxygen during photosynthesis.
- Matter is conserved in a chemical reaction.
- Energy is conserved.
- Lithium, sodium, and potassium are similar elements.
- We live at the bottom of a sea of air.
- Seasons are caused by the tilt of the Earth's axis.

Try mapping out the argument for any one of these claims about the world using Figure 1.10.

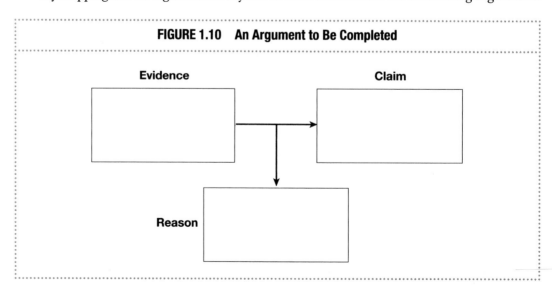

FIGURE 1.10   An Argument to Be Completed

Evidence

Claim

Reason

Part of the skill of being an effective teacher is to know the arguments not only for the scientific worldview but also for why students' commonsense conceptions are flawed (Sadler et al., 2013). What, for instance, would you say to a student who argued the following:

- Gases do not weigh anything.
- Sugar disappears forever when dissolved in water.
- Heavier things fall faster.
- There is no gravity in space.
- The matter in a plant comes from the soil.
- Humans are not animals.

Again, try mapping out the substance of your response using Figure 1.10.

What we are trying to show with all of these examples is that science is a body of ideas that we have had to argue for. The history of science is a litany of mistakes of what might be seen as flawed arguments—just think of phlogiston, Ptolemy's epicycles, the ether, the Church's defense of a geocentric worldview, Lamarkianism and the claim that species could adapt within their lifetime, Weber and his claim to detect gravity waves, and more recently cold fusion. In the end, a scientific idea succeeds because the arguments for it are more coherent with the data and the ideas have greater predictive power. Thus, Torricelli's arguments that the space at the top of the barometer tube is a vacuum wins in the end as it better explains why the height of the column of mercury drops when you go up a mountain. Einstein's theory of special relativity explains why measurements of the speed of light do not vary depending on which direction the Earth is moving and, moreover, it predicts a relationship between matter and energy that is later confirmed by experiment.

What Is the Difference Between an Explanation and an Argument?

The Next Generation Science Standards have two practices that seem related—constructing explanations and engaging in argument from evidence. Inevitably, you might ask, what is the difference? The issue is especially confusing as there is a view that explanations consist of claims, evidence, and reasoning. This is unfortunately wrong. Arguments consist of claims, evidence, and reasoning. Explanations consist of the thing to be explained (e.g., why it rained yesterday, how humans reproduce, why earthquakes happen). All of these explanations have sets of descriptive or factual statements, which are causally related and that describe how the thing to be explained came to be. Thus, the dinosaurs became extinct because an enormous meteorite threw a large amount of dust and ash into the atmosphere (a descriptive statement) that caused (defining the link) a sudden temperature drop on the Earth's surface (a descriptive statement). Explanations need to be consistent with the evidence, and arguments are needed to show that they are consistent, but it is not correct to say that argument and explanation are the same thing.

Explanations work because they generate a feeling of increased understanding. As a consequence, there are various levels of explanation, and this is well illustrated by Richard Feynman's response to a reporter asking for an explanation of why magnets attract each other (https://www.youtube.com/watch?v=MO0r930Sn_8). Basically, he responds by asking, what level of explanation do you want and what would you be satisfied with?

By contrast, arguments in science are claims about the world. Such claims draw on evidence and theories to produce the justification or reason that relates the evidence to the claim. Such claims often include an explanatory hypothesis and so look very similar to explanations, but the language is couched in conditional language. So *if* carbon dioxide levels rise above 400 parts per million, the argument is made that the global temperature *may* then rise by more than 2°C because of the way in which carbon dioxide traps solar radiation and re-radiates it at wavelengths that cannot escape the atmosphere (which is an explanation). However, fundamentally, this is an argument that exists in competition with another explanation that such warming is a product of natural variation. Thus, another vital feature of any situation where argumentation might occur is that there exist different or competing views.

Moreover, another big distinction between explanations and arguments is that an explanation—the thing to be explained—is often something that is well established. Clearly, day and night do happen, the dinosaurs did die out, and sugar does dissolve. Why these happen, or happened, requires an explanation. There may be more than one explanation. Deciding which is best requires an argument. So Galileo makes an argument that the heliocentric theory is a better explanation than the geocentric explanation of the motion of the Sun and stars. While there are many arguments for Galileo's position, at the time, there were many arguments against it. Thus, in science, what happens is that there are arguments about which of the competing explanations is best.

In school science, for instance, students may argue that most of the mass in a plant comes from the soil. After all, why does the plant have roots and why do we water it? As the teacher of science, you are putting forward a competing explanation that most of the mass comes from the synthesis of carbon dioxide and water in the plant to make sugar. To convince students that your explanation (an explanatory hypothesis) is better, you will have to point to the evidence that supports your view, as well as point to the evidence for why their argument is flawed.

What Is Argumentation and How Does It Contribute to Learning?

Argumentation is a process of deliberative discussion of competing claims. Commonly, it is done orally, but it can also be done in writing. Its purpose is to allow students to contest competing claims and come to an agreement about "how they might know something," "in turn, building more secure conceptual models" or "inspiring new questions or models" (Manz, 2015). Over the past two decades, research has explored the contribution of collaborative discourse and argumentation to learning. Drawing on the notion that language is core to learning and thought and language are inseparable, the implications of these ideas for education have been developed by a number of people (Alexander, 2005; Halliday, 1993; Mercer & Littleton, 2007; Mercier & Sperber, 2011; Wertsch, 1991). A critical feature of this work is a view that learning is the product of the difference between the intuitive or old models we hold and the new ideas we encounter (Bachelard, 1968). Through a process of comparison and contrast, supported by discussion, the individual then develops a new understanding. Consequently, learning requires opportunities for students to advance claims, to justify the ideas they hold, and then to be challenged. Although this may happen internally, it is debate and discussion with others that are most likely to enable new meanings to be tested through argument and counterargument.

In this sense, learning to argue is seen as a core process in learning to think and construct new understandings (Billig, 1996; Kuhn, 1992). Comprehending why ideas are wrong then matters as much as understanding why other ideas might be right. For example, students who read texts that explained why common misconceptions were flawed (as well as explaining why the right idea was right) had a more secure knowledge than those who had only read texts that explained the correct idea (Hynd & Alvermann, 1986). Likewise, researchers have found that groups holding differing ideas learn more than those who hold similar preconceptions, many of whom make no progress whatsoever (Howe, Tolmie, & Rodgers, 1992; Schwarz, Neuman, & Biezuner, 2000). Indeed, one study found that even if the difference between individuals was based for both on incorrect premises, significant learning gains can occur—a case of two wrongs making a right—and with learning effects that were still significant on delayed posttests (Ames & Murray, 1982).

These findings are also supported by a number of classroom-based studies, all of which show improvements in conceptual learning when students engage in argumentation (Asterhan & Schwarz, 2007; Mercer, Dawes, Wegerif, & Sams, 2004; Sampson & Clark, 2009; Zohar & Nemet,

2002). For instance, students who were asked to engage in small-group discussions significantly outperformed a group of control students in their use of extended utterances and verbal reasoning, something that is rare in formal science education (Lemke, 1990). Significant improvements were also produced in their nonverbal reasoning and understanding of science concepts (Mercer et al., 2004). Another study with two classes of 16- to 17-year-old students studying genetics required students to engage in argumentative discourse about the appropriate answer to specific problems. Compared to a control group, the frequency of students who used biological knowledge appropriately (53.2% vs. 8.9%) was significantly higher (Zohar & Nemet, 2002).

Finally, a meta-analysis of 18 studies grouped learning activities into three major categories: those that are interactive and require collaborative discourse and argumentation (either with a peer or an expert tutor), those that are constructive and require individuals to produce a product such as an essay or lab report, or those that are active, such as conducting an experiment (Chi, 2009). Research shows conclusively that a hierarchy of learning activities exists from interactive (the most effective), to constructive, to active (the least effective). That is, students are more likely to learn when they have the opportunity to discuss and argue about the ideas than when they simply write essays or do experiments.

Studies show, however, that group discourse that contributes to effective learning depends on a number of factors. Most important, students need to be taught the norms of social interaction and to understand that the function of their discussion is to persuade others of the validity of their arguments. In addition, exemplary arguments need to be modeled, and teachers need to define a clear and specific outcome while groups need materials to support them in asking the appropriate questions and help in identifying relevant and irrelevant evidence (Barron, 2003; Berland & Reiser, 2008; Blatchford, Kutnick, Baines, & Galton, 2003; Mercer, Wegerif, & Dawes, 1999).

So in Summary . . .

Argumentation is not something that is peripheral to science but lies at its very core. It is also tremendously important in learning science, as science is a set of rather strange ideas about the world. Students are only going to start believing these ideas if (a) they hear what the evidence is for the scientific case, and (b) time is spent convincing them that the commonsense view of science (e.g., that plants get their food from the ground, that air has no weight, or that heavier things fall faster) is challenged through a process of discussion and argumentation.

Argumentation is the process of engaging in constructing both arguments and counterarguments. A sound scientific argument has three essential features—a claim that it is seeking to advance about the material or living world, evidence to support that claim, and a reason that shows how that evidence justifies the claim.

How, though, do we engage students in this process? In Chapter 2, we will look at ways of supporting argumentation in the classroom, some of the challenges that it poses, and how to address them.

How Can I Support Scientific Argumentation in My Classroom?

There are various structures for supporting argumentation. The fundamental concern is to separate the idea from the individual so that what is being discussed is an idea and so that that idea is not associated with any one individual. Why? Put simply, there is a growing body of evidence that young people find it difficult to engage in argument for fear of offending their peers (Kuhn, Wang, & Li, 2011). In addition, it is challenging for some cultures—particularly students from an Asian background, where there is a tendency to defer to authority and to find a "middle way" between competing ideas (Becker, 1986; Nisbett, 2003).

These structures are necessary because the most common format of classroom discussion—one where the teacher leads the whole class in a discussion—is the most difficult one to undertake and the least likely to succeed. Its fundamental problem is that any idea is associated with an individual, and too few individuals are willing or able to put forward their thinking and have it criticized—albeit constructively.

And why is such discussion such a powerful learning tool? Put simply, most of us are sloppy or lazy thinkers. Individually, we are often convinced by the first simplistic reason that comes to mind. However, when it comes to other people's ideas, we are much more vigilant and much more willing to point out their flaws (Mercier & Sperber, 2011). Consequently, engaging students in discussion uses their mutual knowledge and resources to identify the weaknesses in their arguments. Because knowing why something is wrong matters as much as knowing why something is right, this process helps students build a deeper understanding.

Throughout this book, we refer to or use the following structures that support students to engage in argumentation. Hence, we describe here in more detail each of the structures, their use, and advantages and disadvantages.

THINK-PAIR-SHARE

This is probably the most familiar structure to most teachers. The idea is that a question is posed to the class such as, "What is the difference between photosynthesis and respiration?" or "What is the evidence that the Earth is a sphere and not flat?" and students are then asked to write down their thoughts and possible answers. Then they come together to discuss the question in pairs. The time for this activity can vary depending on the nature of the question but rarely should be longer than 5 minutes. After their paired discussion, the teacher can then call on the pairs (note not the individual) for their thoughts and arguments. After any contribution, you as the teacher can ask if others wish to "add on," "elaborate," or if they have an alternative or better point to make. In each case, your role is to press students for the evidence and reasoning that supports their position.

One way to improve this activity is to make it a written activity using Figure 2.1.

FIGURE 2.1 Think-Pair-Share

An electronic copy of this form is available on the companion website at https://resources.corwin.com/OsborneArgumentation.

My Name _____

Partner's Name _____

THINK—my thoughts or understanding at this time	PAIR—what I understand my partner is telling me

SHARE—our common understanding after talking, what we can share with others, and what was most important from our discussion

ARGUMENT LINE

FIGURE 2.2   Argument Line

PLUTO: TOTALLY LEGIT PLANET

PLUTO: SORRY LITTLE ROCK

Source: Reprinted with permission of the SERP Institute from http://serpmedia.org/rtl, David Dudley, Illustrator.

Another strategy to promote discussion is to use an argument line (see Figure 2.2). The question for debate is put up on the board with two opposing alternatives posted. Students are then given up to 2 minutes to think about which position they believe to be true and the evidence for why they believe it to be true. Once again, this strategy separates the idea under discussion from the individual.

After this time, students are asked to go to the side of the room that represents the view that they hold. Students who think there are reasons for both being right can go to the middle.

Once with others who hold the same view, they should be asked to discuss two things:

1.   What are the arguments that justify where they have chosen to go?

2.   What are the arguments for why the others are mistaken?

Typically, students can be given up to 5 minutes to discuss their views and work out their arguments.

After this, you as the teacher can call on students on one side to explain why they are there. Then, likewise, you can call on students from the other side to explain why they have chosen that side.

Then, you can ask each side to explain why they think the other is wrong. If you have students in the middle, you may wish to call on them. Productive talk moves (see Chapter 3) may again be very helpful here in helping to advance the discussion.

Ultimately, your job is to steer the discussion so that the evidence for the scientific case is seen to be stronger. If students are not able to do this on their own, you may have to play devil's advocate for the scientific case.

Notes

_____

_____

_____

FOUR CORNERS

This is a variant on an argument line. Instead of there being two sides of the room, you use all four corners of the room, as shown in Figure 2.3.

FIGURE 2.3 Four Corners

Source: Reprinted with permission of the SERP Institute from http://serpmedia.org/rtl, David Dudley, Illustrator.

This strategy is useful for issues where there might be a range of opinions. For instance, imagine you were studying ecosystems or food chains and wanted students to apply these concepts to a topical question, such as the following:

Should wolves be reintroduced into California?

Would becoming a vegetarian be better for the planet?

Will genetically modified plants help to feed the world's ever growing population?

Is there is no such thing as an invasive species of plant?

All that is needed is to provide a claim that answers the question and draw a diagram of this nature on the board or a PowerPoint slide (see Figure 2.4).

Once with others who hold the same view, they should be asked to discuss two things:

1. What are the arguments that justify where they have chosen to go?

2. What are the arguments for why the students in other corners are mistaken?

Typically, students can be given up to 5 minutes to discuss their views and work out their arguments.

After this, you as the teacher can call on one corner to explain why they are there. Then, likewise, you can call on the other corners to explain why they have chosen that side.

Then, you can ask each corner to explain why they think the other is wrong. Productive talk moves may again be very helpful here in helping to advance the discussion.

Ultimately, your job is to steer the discussion so that the evidence for the scientific case is seen to be stronger if the issue has a clearly agreed on answer. In many cases, such as the examples above, there is no agreed on answer, and the focus of the discussion should be on identifying what the science is and the competing arguments. Students can then be asked to write a summary of the arguments afterward and include points about why they think the counterarguments are flawed.

FIGURE 2.4   An Example of a Four Corners Issue

 An electronic copy of this form is available on the companion website at https://resources.corwin.com/ OsborneArgumentation.

Strongly Agree	Agree

Becoming a vegetarian would be better for the planet.

Disagree	Strongly Disagree

Notes

_____

_____

_____

_____

_____

_____

_____

LISTENING TRIADS

FIGURE 2.5   Listening Triad

Source: Reprinted with permission of the SERP Institute from http://serpmedia.org/rtl, David Dudley, Illustrator.

The listening triad (Figure 2.5), as its name suggests, is an alternative discussion structure designed to encourage students to listen to the point being made by another student. In this structure, one student takes on the role of the talker, one student takes on the role of the questioner who questions what the talker is saying, and another student takes on the role of the note taker, noting the major points of the discussion. Every 3 minutes, the roles can be rotated so that students all get a chance to take on the different roles. Notably, to ask a question or take notes, students have to listen!

This structure is useful when discussing the points made in a text, a concept cartoon, or the answers to a question, such as the ones in Figure 2.6.

FIGURE 2.6   An Example of a Science Topic to Use for a Listening Triad Discussion

Student experiments on battery-powered buggy

Alice is investigating the speed of a battery-powered buggy.

- She can make a buggy with **small** wheels or **large** wheels.
- She can make a **light** buggy or a **heavy** buggy (with a 500-g load).
- She can use **ordinary batteries** or **long-life batteries.**

She wants to find out if these make any difference to the speed of the buggy. She makes many measurements and these are her means.

(Continued)

(Continued)

	Wheel Size	Load	Type of Batteries	Time (in sec) for 5 m
Experiment 1	Small	Heavy	Ordinary	8.6
Experiment 2	Large	Light	Ordinary	7.5
Experiment 3	Large	Heavy	Long-life	8.3
Experiment 4	Small	Light	Ordinary	7.5

1. **What do these results tell you about the effect of wheel size on the time for 5 m?** (Choose one)

    A. Large wheels make the buggy use less time for 5 m.

    B. Large wheels make the buggy use more time for 5 m.

    C. Wheel size makes no difference to the time for 5 m.

2. **Which two experiments are needed to work this out?**

    Experiments _____

3. **What do these results tell you about the effect of weight on the time for 5 m?** (Choose one)

    A. A heavy load makes the buggy use less time for 5 m.

    B. A heavy load makes the buggy use more time for 5 m.

    C. A load makes no difference to the time for 5 m.

4. **Which two experiments are needed to work this out?**

    Experiments _____

An electronic copy of these prompts is available on the companion website at https://resources.corwin .com/OsborneArgumentation.

The following prompts can be given to students to help scaffold each of their roles.

Questioner

- What do you think?
- Why do you think that?
- Let's think again.
- Can you say a bit more?
- What else do we know?
- I can tell you about. . . .
- Can you explain?
- I hadn't thought of that until you said it.
- I disagree because. . . .
- But. . . .
- I agree but. . . .
- I believe that. . . .
- I think. . . .
- A different point of view is . . .
- I can't see how your point fits in with. . . .

Talker

- My reason for saying that is. . . .
- Because. . . .
- I have noticed that. . . .
- I have found out that. . . .
- I see it differently. . . .
- If. . . .
- What if. . . .
- Why?
- Maybe we could. . . . ?
- I have a suggestion. . . .

Listener

Record only what you think are the MAIN or GOOD points that are made.

RECORDING IN NOTE FORM IS ACCEPTABLE AT PRESENT.

Giving students 3 minutes in each role will provide a total of 9 minutes for discussion.

After this, you as the teacher can run a whole-group discussion calling on each group for the main points that came up in the discussion. You can ask groups if they agree or if they have a different view. Where there is difference, try to get them to justify what their arguments and evidence are.

Ultimately, your job is to steer the discussion so that the evidence for the scientific case is seen to be stronger. If students are not able to do this on their own, you may have to play devil's advocate for the scientific case and raise points that they have not considered.

USING TECHNOLOGY TOOLS: POLL EVERYWHERE, SOCRATIVE, KAHOOT, AND BRAINCANDY

Another way to involve students in argument and discussion is to use one of the many websites that make some form of electronic polling or quizzing available. These are all free. As the teacher, you have to join them, and you can place the question that can then be seen by all students when they log on. Students then have to submit a response that you can display using your computer. The great thing is that all the responses can be anonymous, so it separates the individual from his or her contribution. From a teaching point of view, what it means is that you are being provided with instant feedback from the students so you can see what concepts and ideas the students are struggling with.

Quizzes can be either true/false quizzes or multiple-choice items (see Figure 2.7).

The second approach, though, exposes which students have got it wrong. Nevertheless, such methods are a very good way of engaging students in scientific reasoning and argumentation.

FIGURE 2.7   An Example of Questions That Can Be Presented for Discussion in an Online Poll

The two bulbs in this circuit are identical.

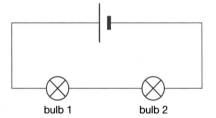

1. How bright will the bulbs be?

    A. Bulb 1 is lit; Bulb 2 is off.

    B. Bulb 2 is lit; Bulb 1 is off.

    C. Both bulbs are lit; Bulb 1 is brighter than Bulb 2.

    D. Both bulbs are lit; Bulb 2 is brighter than Bulb 1.

    E. Both bulbs are lit with the same brightness.

This can then be followed by the question that asks for the justification.

2. How would you explain this?

    A. The first bulb uses up **all** of the electric current, so there is none left for the other one.

    B. The first bulb uses up **some** of the electric current, so there is less left for the other one.

    C. The electric current is shared equally between the two bulbs.

    D. The electric current is the same all around the circuit.

When you get the responses, you can ask students who have chosen one to explain why they think students who have chosen another response are wrong. This can be done by posing the question electronically and asking students to type in the responses to Question 3 or by asking students to give their reasoning in class.

3. Explain why you think one of the other choices is wrong and justify your idea.

Notes

_____

_____

CONCEPT CARTOONS/FORMATIVE ASSESSMENT PROBES

Concept cartoons were an idea developed and promoted by Brenda Keogh and Stuart Naylor (Naylor & Keogh, 2000) from the United Kingdom. They all present a phenomenon with different explanations for why it happens or what is going to happen such as the example in Figure 2.8. Students are then asked to discuss the suggestions made by the cartoon characters and argue for which one they think is correct and which ones are flawed. The American version of these are Page Keeley's Formative Assessment Probes (Keeley et al., 2005) published by the National Science Teachers Association (NSTA) and Corwin, which can be used in a similar way.

FIGURE 2.8   A Concept Cartoon

Source: Reprinted with permission of the SERP Institute from http://serpmedia.org/rtl, David Dudley, Illustrator.

The important thing about concept cartoons is that they separate the idea from the individual again because students are not talking about their ideas but about the ideas of the cartoon characters.

Concept cartoons can be discussed using think-pair-share, listening triads, or three corners (if there are three ideas) or four corners (if there are four ideas). Such cartoons can be used formatively to elicit what students' understanding is before or after teaching a topic as a way of applying what students have learned and to see how well the concept has been understood.

TOWN HALL MEETING

The following procedure has been adapted from Facing History and Ourselves.[1]

In this format, different perspectives are often shared as people from different backgrounds and experiences take the floor. This teaching strategy mimics the process of a town hall meeting by providing a structure for different positions to be argued for.

Begin by dividing the class into four to six groups (depending on the number of readings/data sets/interest groups). Give students the opportunity to read and annotate any background information. Then, students discuss the reading among themselves, answering questions such as the following: What does this text say? What do these data show? How do the data support my position?

Now begin the discussion by arranging chairs in a circle, providing one chair per group. The person assigned to summarize for each group sits in the chair. The other students then form a larger standing circle around the chairs. Make it clear that each student in the class will have an opportunity to be heard. Students can only speak when they have entered the circle and are seated. Then, each representative summarizes the group's argument.

After all readings have been summarized, invite students seated in the circle to comment on what they have heard or to ask one of their peers a question. Students in the outer circle are then allowed to enter the conversation by "tapping" the shoulder of someone in their own group and taking their seat. If desired, students can vote by secret ballot on the decision to be made.

Finally, after the discussion, students can reflect on the following in their notebook:

How did your ideas about the topic change during this activity, if at all? Explain what caused your ideas to change or why you think your ideas did not change at all.

Notes

_____

_____

_____

_____

_____

_____

_____

_____

_____

_____

_____

1 See https://www.facinghistory.org/for-educators/educator-resources/teaching-strategy/town-hall-circle.

SUPPORTING WRITTEN ARGUMENTS

There are several ways of supporting written arguments. The two discussed here are anticipation guides and writing frames.

Anticipation Guides

Anticipation guides are designed to be used with texts to help students extract evidence to support a particular argument. Figure 2.9 shows a guide that is to be used with a text that explains the seasons. They are useful for activating students' prior knowledge about science concepts and focusing students' attention on key content in a text.

To use one, select an appropriate grade-level text, and pick four to eight salient concepts in it. Formulate statements about each of these concepts, some true and some false, and list the statements down the left side of a table. Before students read the text, have them discuss whether they think each statement is true or false. Then after students read the text, have them reassess which statements in the anticipation guide are true and false, and note the evidence from the text.

Once they have extracted the information from the text, the students can be asked to write an argument that is relevant to the text—in this case, what they would say to convince somebody that it does not get hotter in summer because the Earth is tilted and so is closer to the Sun.

FIGURE 2.9 An Example of an Anticipation Guide

Statements	What I think		What the text says		Evidence from the text
The earth travels around the sun once per year.	*True*	False	*True*	False	Text says that's the definition of a year.
The amount of energy the earth receives from the sun varies significantly at different points in the earth's orbit.	*True*	False	True	*False*	Text says earth gets the same energy from sun year round.
When it is summer in the northern hemisphere, it is winter in the southern hemisphere.	*True*	False	*True*	False	Say seasons north and south are opposite.
The axis of the earth's rotation is perpendicular to the plane of the earth's orbit around the sun.	True	*False* ?	True	*False*	Yes – text says earth is tilted 23.5 degrees.

Source: Reprinted with permission of the SERP Institute from http://serpmedia.org/rtl, David Dudley, Illustrator.

Writing Frames

Most science textbooks deal with the unequivocal, the unquestioned, and the uncontested—in short, the canon of consensually accepted science. However, argument is a very important part of the writing of scientists themselves, even in its popular forms. For instance, the works of Richard Dawkins (1976), such as *The Selfish Gene,* are carefully constructed arguments for his interpretation of evolution. Opportunities to examine scientific argument focus on the important question of "how we know what we know." Such writing foregrounds the practices of science rather than its "facts" and develop confidence, faith, and trust in the means by which science derives its knowledge—something that is important for the future public understanding of science.

Some appreciation of the genre can be developed by asking students to discuss the arguments for and against issues such as the following:

- The Earth is flat versus the Earth is round.
- Day and night are caused by a spinning Earth versus a Sun that moves round the Earth.
- We live at the bottom of a "sea of air."
- Most of the matter in a plant comes from the air and not the soil.
- Acquired characteristics cannot be inherited.
- Mixtures are not the same as chemical compounds.

Constructing an argument for any piece of scientific knowledge requires the use of evidence and the consideration of counterarguments. Consequently, any frame to support the process of such writing should encourage a focus on the reasons for one position and its opposing view. Figure 2.10 is an example of a student response to a frame used to discuss the first statement in the previous list.

Essentially, the frame acts as a scaffold. After the students have worked on the main points, they can be asked to turn them into a logical and coherent piece of text using appropriate logical connectives that relate claims to the warrants and reasons for belief. Students should be encouraged to draw from a range of words such as *because, consequently, therefore,* and others when they translate the notes from the frame into a second, fuller draft. We encourage you to use sentence frames less over time so students gradually become more independent in writing arguments.

Another way to support written argument is to use the frame in Figure 2.11, which is shown in many of our activities. This asks students to identify the claim, think about the evidence that would support it, and, most important, determine the reason that connects or "bridges" the evidence to the claim.

FIGURE 2.10   A Frame to Support Argument

There is a lot of discussion about whether . . .

The Earth is flat.

The people who agree with this idea claim that . . .

It looks flat.

If it was round, people would fall off, ships would drop off the edge.

They also argue that . . .

Photographs could be faked.

A further point they make is . . .

It looks flat in photographs taken from the air.

However, there are also strong arguments or evidence against this view. These are . . .

Pictures of the Earth from space show that it is round.

The shadow of the Earth on the Moon is round.

It explains why shadows of the Sun vary from nothing at the Equator to much longer lengths toward the North Pole.

Furthermore, they claim that . . .

People are held onto a round Earth by the force of gravity.

After looking at different points of view and the evidence, I think that . . .

Although it looks flat, the evidence says that it is round.

FIGURE 2.11   Claim, Reasoning, Evidence

 An electronic copy of this form is available on the companion website at https://resources.corwin.com/ OsborneArgumentation.

CLAIM	REASONING	EVIDENCE

Taken together, the claim, evidence, and reasons make up the argument.

Argument in science is an important feature of doing science, and providing such opportunities helps foster students' ability to think scientifically and their ability to reason from evidence to conclusions. As Siegel (1988) points out, "To understand the role of reasons in judgment is to open the door to the possibility of understanding conclusions and knowledge-claims generally and to develop a respect for reasons" (p. 44). More generally, we would hope that developing an inclination to seek reasons, based in good evidence, would help to develop a general commitment to the ideal of rationality as a guide to life and that "the critical spirit characteristic of science" developed by such exercises is "the critical spirit we seek to impart to students as we help them to become critical thinkers" (p. 110).

Evaluating Student Arguments

Rubrics are one potentially powerful tool to support the evaluation of student arguments. Figure 2.12 can be used to evaluate students' ability to construct and critique arguments. We encourage you to share the rubric with students and provide models of arguments that exemplify different performance levels (emerging, developing, proficient). In addition, students would benefit from opportunities to self-assess and evaluate the arguments of their peers (Sadler & Good, 2006). Finally, it would be of value for students to revise their arguments based on their self-assessments and the feedback from you and their peers. Effective use of rubrics entails gathering information about student learning and using it to inform teaching. That is to say, rubrics have the most impact on student learning when they are used as tools for formative assessment (Black & William, 2006; Hattie & Timperley, 2007). In contrast, simply grading student work with a rubric will have little effect.

And So in Summary . . .

In this chapter, we have presented a number of strategies that can support argumentation in the classroom—both oral and written. This is not an exhaustive list, but the ones we have provided make a good place to start with. Remember, using an instructional strategy for the first time is like trying out a recipe for the first time. It may not go quite to plan and you should at least give it a second go. We hope that you will find, as we have, that these kinds of activities are engaging for students as they get to the heart of what science is about.

In the next chapter, we turn to look at some of the specific challenges that engaging students in argumentation in the classroom raises and how these can be addressed.

FIGURE 2.12   Example Argumentation Rubric

	Emerging	Developing	Proficient
Argument Construction	Makes a claim and supports it with evidence OR partial reasoning	Makes a claim and supports it with evidence AND **partial reasoning**	Supports a claim with multiple pieces of evidence and **clear reasoning**
Argument Critique	Identifies a problem in someone else's argument	Identifies at least one problem in someone else's argument and provides a **partial justification** for why there is a problem	Identifies at least one problem in someone else's argument and provides a **complete justification** for why there is a problem

Note: We do not intend for the levels to translate to particular grades or scores. Students' ability to engage in argumentation depends on a number of factors: content knowledge, prior experience engaging in argumentation, reading ability, and so on. Thus, you might expect your students to reach "developing" at a particular time of the year or for a particular topic. Over time, you might expect students to support their claims with clearer reasoning, in which case, you might expect students to reach the "proficient" level. We encourage you to adapt the rubric to the needs of your students.

CHAPTER 3

How Can I Make Argumentation in the Classroom Productive and Support Deeper Learning?

Establishing Classroom Norms

(The following section has been taken from the work of Catherine O'Connor, Erin Ruegg, and Sara Michaels and their work on academically productive talk. We are grateful for their permission to reproduce what is some of the best advice on establishing a dialogic classroom where talk is taken seriously.)

Most teachers set behavioral norms for their students at the beginning of the year. Often these are posted: "Be respectful," "Show effort," "Come prepared to work," and so on. We have learned from many teachers that productive academic talk actually requires an additional set of norms: norms that are designed to support you and your students in using discussion and debate.

What is required to have an academically productive discussion? For all students to benefit from a discussion you need to ensure that *all students participate*. This is not easy. Several big factors have to be in place to get all students to participate.

First, the classroom context needs to be *respectful*. If discussions descend into people talking over one another, personal attacks, or hostility, you will not succeed in getting students to participate. They won't feel safe, and many of them will just keep silent, rather than invite ridicule or disrespect. This is why we strongly advise starting with some of the strategies that separate the person from the idea and help students to feel safe.

Second, discussion must be *equitable*—that is, all students should be encouraged and given opportunities to participate. Discussion is not just for the few students who always want to talk or for the few academically strongest students. It must also include those who are shy, those who feel unsure of their abilities, those who have more difficulty with the content, and English language learners.

Finally, it is really important that all students *can hear and see one another*. This may sound totally obvious, but in many classrooms, this is not a trivial problem. The acoustic conditions in many older school buildings are not good. In elementary grades, there is usually a carpet or rug area where students can sit in a circle, and this guarantees that even quiet students can be heard. But in middle schools, there may be problems. If every student is seated facing the teacher, it will be difficult to hold a really productive discussion, even if everyone can hear fairly well. This means that you should think of altering the classroom configuration so that people are at least turning inward and to face each other.

How to Start and What to Include

The capacity for good discussions in classrooms is developed over time. Establishing and developing a shared understanding of expectations for discussion is the first step. Just as sports teams depend on shared expectations for interactions on the field, students must understand and adhere to the expectations you have of them to interact productively in a discussion.

Establish Your Norms

Introduce and develop *discussion norms* with your students. Consider how you have introduced more general behavioral norms in your classroom. If these methods were successful, you should certainly try adapting them for introducing discussion norms. However, at first discussion norms may be more complex than other norms, because discussion itself will be new to some students. Some students are not used to talking about their ideas. They may find it difficult to feel safe in expressing their views. They may not feel entitled to respond to others' views.

On the other hand, you may have students (even if there's only a few) who feel perfectly comfortable talking about their own views and critiquing the views of others. This may have a negative effect on the participation of those students who are not used to sharing their ideas.

Therefore, setting up norms and allowing students time to practice and develop productive discussion *are really important steps* in a process. We strongly encourage you not to have a full-blown discussion or debate until you and your students feel confident with classroom discussion norms. Rather, try out one of the other participation activities we have suggested in Chapter 2 where students can discuss ideas in smaller groups and where the idea is separated from the person.

What Should the Norms Include?

You might start the discussion by talking about something fairly straightforward. If we're going to have *discussions* about our work, we need to make sure of several things:

- Everyone has a chance to participate.
- Everyone feels that they will be respected.
- Everyone can hear what is said and see who is talking.

You can ask students questions about these principles to get their ideas:

- What might get in the way of your participating? How can we make sure that everyone gets a turn?
- What might make someone feel disrespected? How should we deal with that if it happens?
- How can we make sure everyone can hear, when some people have very quiet voices?
- Create a chart of norms with your class. Let students participate in describing what a good discussion will look like, sound like, and feel like. This will help them to visualize an ideal setting with themselves contributing with successful talk. The following are three examples created by teachers who have succeeded in creating conditions for consistently productive discussion.

Examples

Here are three different ways norms can be developed and displayed as wall charts or printed out on sheets for student binders, or both.

The "Green Sheet"

This is a set of norms agreed upon by a fifth-grade class. The teacher printed these out on green paper, and had students put them in a binder. The green sheet was a tool for developing discussion and a reference once students and teachers became confident with using argumentation and discussion in their classroom (see Figure 3.1). Yours may be similar or may differ.

FIGURE 3.1   Green Sheet

An electronic copy of this figure is available on the companion website at https://resources.corwin .com/OsborneArgumentation.

Students' Rights

1. You have the right to ask questions.

2. You have the right to be treated respectfully.

3. You have the right to have your ideas discussed, not you personally.

4. You have the right to be listened to carefully, and to be taken seriously by your classmates.

Students' Obligations

1. You have a responsibility to speak loud enough for others to hear.

2. You have an obligation to answer questions seriously.

3. If you cannot hear or understand what someone says, you have a responsibility to ask them to repeat or explain.

4. You have an obligation to treat others with respect.

5. You will be called on to discuss other people's ideas, to agree or disagree, and to explain your reasoning.

Student and Teacher Wall Chart

In the next example, students and teacher work together to create a wall chart about norms that reflect their own guidelines for a productive discussion (see Figure 3.2).

The teacher holds a discussion to generate answers to the questions in the poster:

- What does discussion in our class look like?
- What does discussion in our class sound like?
- What does discussion in our class feel like?

As a whole-class activity, the group then develops consensus statements, and these are written on the poster to use as norms going forward. As discussion skills are developed in the classroom, the chart is used as a reflection tool that can be added to throughout the year.

FIGURE 3.2   Student and Teacher Wall Chart

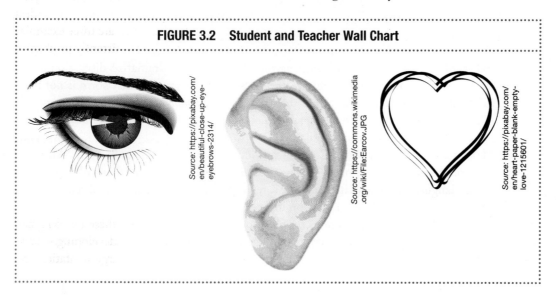

Source: https://pixabay.com/ en/beautiful-close-up-eye- eyebrows-2314/

Source: https://commons.wikimedia .org/wiki/File:Earcov.JPG

Source: https://pixabay.com/ en/heart-paper-blank-empty- love-1215601/

Norms in Progress

In the third example, from an eighth-grade class (special thanks to Liz Berges), yet another approach is taken. These norms are developed over time, not all at the beginning of the year. Every few weeks, the teacher holds a discussion and the group decides on a new norm, based on their experience with discussion up to that point. In this group, we see many of the issues mentioned earlier, but in addition, there is a concern with *authentic* discussion and an emphasis on responsibility for one's own learning. This is appropriate for eighth graders and shows that this teacher is in tune with her students' developmental stage and growing intellectual capacity.

Discussion Norms

1. We come *prepared* for discussion with examples, stories, notes, and text.

2. We are active participants responsible for our *own learning*. This means we

   speak,

   request clarification,

   show agreement or confusion,

   verify, and

   ask others to repeat.

3. We strive to have *authentic* conversations that are *academically rich*. This means we

   use target vocabulary,

   stay on topic, and

   ask what we really want to know.

4. We push ourselves *and each other* to think beyond the obvious, popular, or easy answers. This means we

   request proof or reasoning,

   point out misinformation,

   disagree with parts,

   draw others out, and

   are open to changing our minds.

Practice and Develop

As you develop these norms with your students, you may want to provide opportunities for students to develop a shared meaning of these norms. Some ways to get used to these discussion norms outside of an actual discussion include the following strategies:

- **Act it out.** In small groups or with partners, students can dramatize discussion scenes where norms are being compromised. The class can try to guess which norm is not being followed, and the team can correct themselves. *For example, students can "interrupt," not listen, forget to use evidence from the text, attack a person instead of the person's idea, or let their talk wander into an unrelated tangent.*
- **Make a class-created rubric.** Create a rubric with your class for each norm. Make the descriptions of acceptable participation clear and concise, letting students offer and contribute language as you write them. Ask regularly about the success of discussions and debates using the rubric as a reflection tool.
- **Create a class book.** Let student teams illustrate and describe a norm on paper. Use student work to compile a book. Use a plastic binding and keep the book in your classroom library.

Just as practicing a sport is essential to becoming a great player, as your students *practice* these norms and goals, they will become great participants in discussion. As you hold your first discussions, students will need help in practicing the norms. These are some of the rules that you will need to follow.

Be consistent. As soon as the rules are established, as the teacher and leader of the classroom, you are responsible for making sure they are understood and used well. Practicing norms and referring to them before, during, and after discussions will elevate their significance and improve student ownership of the discussion goals.

Don't tolerate disrespect. If you have a successful behavioral system in place, with sanctions and/or incentives, use this to enforce the norms. Many teachers have found that it's important not to tolerate disrespect in discussions. If students are afraid they will be ridiculed or put down, even in a subtle way, they will just stop contributing—*sometimes for the entire school year!* So make it clear from the beginning that you won't tolerate even minimal signs of disrespect: a "tsk" or an eye-roll can really undermine your success. Make it known what the consequences will be and then be consistent in your enforcement.

Note, however, that *you* are the final arbiter of what is acceptable behavior. Some classes have a greater tolerance for humor, intense conversation, and other things that might be unhelpful at a lower grade level or in a situation with other conflicts going on. Use your judgment and continue to monitor.

Stop everything. When students are interrupting one another, straying off on tangents, not listening to one another, or not being respectful, it is time to stop the discussion. By letting it continue, you are actually sending a message that these behaviors are okay. Stop, gather students, and ask them what they were doing well and what needed to be better. Ask them to refer to the written version of the norms, whether it is a wall chart or a "green sheet" in their binder. This may seem disappointing and time-consuming at first, but in the long run, it will be a huge time saver and skill builder.

Reflect on your norms. Provide time to reflect about students' use of the norms. Just as sports team members reflect and review game highlights, it will help you to build in time to *reflect* with your class on how your discussions are going.

- Take time! As simple as this sounds, time in a classroom can slip away very easily. Leaving time at the end of a discussion or debate to reflect on the class adherence to norms and development as a team is never time wasted! In fact, this kind of reflection is essential to keeping your posted list of norms a dynamic and significant document in your classroom.
- A useful reflection can be done in 1 to 5 minutes. You can reflect with a short discussion, voting by holding up one to four fingers or using high, medium, or low thumbs. Encourage students to reflect on their own behaviors as well as those of others and to consider their own strengths and weaknesses in the discussion.

Productive Talk Moves

Discourse in the classroom is notoriously dominated by a sequence that is called initiation, response, evaluation (IRE). This is where the teacher asks a question—something that in itself is strange since, in normal discourse, it is the person who does *not* know the answer who asks the question. Overwhelmingly, this question is a closed question in that it is looking for one very specific answer. This elicits a short, phrase-like response from a student. Generally, this is a small subset of students who are confident enough to believe they have the right answer. This is then followed by an evaluative comment about whether the response is correct. This form of discourse is so familiar to students that it is reduced to a game of guessing what is in the teacher's mind. Moreover, it tells you, the teacher, little about how much the idea has really been understood.

The primary function of what is really a rather perverse form of discourse is to make the correct idea public—all the students get to hear what they are supposed to know. However, there are many criticisms of it as a form of dialogue that will support learning. First, research shows that teachers rarely wait longer than a second for an answer. Moreover, if they can train themselves to wait more than 3 seconds, the length of student responses increases considerably (Rowe, 1974). These findings, while old, have been replicated so often that you wonder why this is not firmly embedded in teachers' practice. Perhaps it is rather like the educational equivalent of washing your hands in hospitals—everybody knows that you should do it but laziness lets them down?

Second, the discourse is rarely equitable in that it is a small subset of students who commonly answer the questions. In particular, girls often lose out. Finally, what counts as an acceptable response is often a short phrase or one-word answer. However, if we want students to appropriate the language of science, there has to be a practice that encourages longer answers and more extended use of scientific language. In short, the goal is to move from Model A, shown in Figure 3.3, to Model B.

FIGURE 3.3 Two Types of Classroom Discussion	
MODEL A	**MODEL B**
TYPE OF TALK	
Brief answers	Longer, more elaborate answers
• in teacher's language	• in student's language
DISCUSSION DYNAMICS	
Student responses are characterized by unrelated bits of information	Student responses are part of ongoing, connected discussion
Little student engagement	High student engagement
Product orientated	Process orientated
All questions teacher initiated	Some questions student initiated

How, though, is the question you might ask? One obvious way of changing the structure of your classroom discourse is to use any of the group participation structures that we introduced in Chapter 2. Here students have to talk to each other. However, if you are going to use whole-class discussion, then we strongly encourage the following types of questions—called productive talk moves (Resnick, Michaels, & O'Connor, 2010). The feature of all these questions is that they are open-ended. There is no one right answer. Because of that, they enable a range of possible answers and avoid putting you the teacher into the position of having to make an evaluative comment. These questions fall into four categories, described in the sections that follow.

Questions That Encourage Individual Students to Share, Expand, and Clarify Their Own Thinking

1. *Say more:* "Can you say more about that?" "What do you mean by that?" "Can you give an example?"

2. *Verifying and clarifying by revoicing:* "So, let me see if I've got what you're saying. Are you saying. . . ?" (always leaving space for the original student to agree or disagree and say more)

3. *Wait time:* "Take your time; we'll wait."

Questions That Encourage Students to Listen Carefully to One Another

4. *Who can repeat?* "Who can repeat what Javon just said or put it into their own words?"

5. *Explaining what someone else means:* "Who can explain what Aisha means when she says that?"

Questions That Press for Deeper Reasoning

6. *Asking for evidence or reasoning:* "Why do you think that?" "What's your evidence?" "How did you arrive at that conclusion?" "How does your evidence relate to your claim?"

7. *Challenge or counterexample:* "Does it always work that way?" "How does that idea square with Sonia's example?" "That's a good question. What do you think?"

Questions That Press Students to Apply Their Own Reasoning to That of Others

8. *Add on:* "Who can add onto the idea that Jamal is building?"

9. *Agree/disagree and why?* "Do you agree/disagree? (And why?)" "Are you saying the same thing as Javed or something different, and if different, how is it different?"

If you want to see examples of teachers using these approaches, then we recommend looking at the resources that are available on the TERC Talking Science website (http://inquiryproject.terc.edu/).

What if My Students Convince Themselves of the Wrong Answer?

One of the major concerns you may have is a view that your job is to get students to understand the correct scientific idea. Getting them to discuss ideas that are flawed or incorrect is, you may think, first a waste of time, and second, students may convince themselves of the arguments for the incorrect scientific idea! Both of these are legitimate concerns.

First, we would admit that teaching in which you talked students through the standard scientific explanations one after another would be faster. However, the overwhelming body of evidence would suggest that *as a learning activity,* it is largely a waste of time. Just presenting information, however clearly, is as one commentator once remarked, "a practice by which the notes of the lecturer become the notes of the student without going through the minds of either." Research shows that if you want students to understand the ideas they are being taught, there is a hierarchy of learning activities, with activities that require students to be "interactive" being more effective than those that are "constructive," which, in turn, are more effective than those that just require the student to be "active" (Chi, 2009). What are the features of such activities?

Interactive (most effective activities). Being interactive is when a learner interacts with a peer through discussion and debate and when both students make substantive contributions to the topic or concept under discussion, by building on each other's contribution, defending and arguing a position, challenging and criticizing each other on the same concept or point, and asking and answering each other's questions. Generally, a feature of this kind of learning is that the learners are generating knowledge that goes beyond the information given in the learning materials.

Constructive (less effective than interactive activities). Constructive activities require the student to produce some sort of overt outputs, such as explanations from self-explaining, notes from note taking, hypotheses from inducing, questions from question asking, predictions from theories, concept maps from drawing, and self-report assertions such as "I don't understand" from formative assessment. A second characteristic of constructive activities is that they tend to ask learners to produce some outputs that are not contained or presented in the learning materials. That is, they do not require them just to summarize ideas from a text.

Active (less effective than constructive activities). Being active is the requirement that the student is doing something physically. This could be manipulating laboratory equipment, underlining or copying and pasting some parts of a text, filling in the blanks in a piece of text, copying problem solution steps, summarizing paragraphs by annotating the text, selecting from a menu of choices, and so forth.

Essentially, learning requires a student to engage in the cognitive acts of defining, describing, explaining, explicating, arguing, and predicting. Listening to a teacher or just watching him or her demonstrate a phenomenon makes very few of these demands, which is why rushing students across the scientific landscape results in very little learning.

So to the next question: What if students emerge from their discussion more strongly convinced of the nonscientific answer? Isn't this running the risk of failure to achieve the goal I am charged with? The honest answer is "yes" only if you yourself are not convinced that you can ultimately argue the scientific case. After all, if the canonical scientific explanation is accepted by all and sundry, then as a teacher of science, we ought to be able to make the case for it. This means that you may well be called on to make the argument as devil's advocate and to counter fallacious arguments that seem superficially convincing. How, for instance, would you argue with a student who said the following:

- Day and night must be caused by a moving Sun as the Sun moves from east to west during the day.
- Plants must get their "food" from the ground as why else do they have roots and why else do you water them?
- Clearly gases do not weigh anything. There is nothing there and we don't feel anything when we walk through it.

Research shows that knowing the counterarguments to these types of arguments makes you a more effective teacher (Sadler et al., 2013). Moreover, what it means is that you are saying to students that the reason I am asking you to believe these ideas is not just because I, the authority on these matters, am telling you they are true, but because there is evidence for my ideas and evidence that your ideas are flawed. Asking students to hold ideas that they cannot justify to others is ultimately poor currency for them, and students deserve, from time to time, some insights into how and why science has come to know what it knows.

Clearly, we do not have time to go through all the evidence for the many ideas we present. It took years to build such ideas and some of the brightest minds in the first place. But we can do it from time to time. After all, the statement that somebody "knows some science" is a statement not only about what a phenomenon is and why it happens but a statement about how it relates to other events, why it is important, and how this particular view of the world came to be.

Finally, if we do really believe that learning science develops the ability to reason like a scientist, then this is only going to happen if we give students the opportunity to do just that—argue from evidence. Not only does it do justice to science, but it also does justice to students—asking them to think, which they too find more engaging.

Where to Go From Here?

This book can only be a start to the process of building your expertise as somebody who makes greater use of argumentation and dialogue for learning. We would be the first to acknowledge that good teaching is a highly complex activity. As a teacher, you are forced to respond to a context that is constantly challenging and changing, and this requires expert professional judgment.

Such expertise emerges through many hours of practice and learning from others. What this book offers is a set of activities around which you can start to develop your expertise with argumentation in the science classroom. Developing your competency further means attending professional development, working with other teachers, and exploring other resources. A good starter is the TERC Talking Science website (http://inquiryproject.terc.edu/prof_dev/pathway/). The reward for improving your capability is the satisfaction that comes from teaching science in a manner that students begin to understand and find engaging and where they enjoy learning. We hope that this book offers you a way of beginning or adding to your expertise and would, of course, welcome any feedback that might improve our suggestions and ideas!

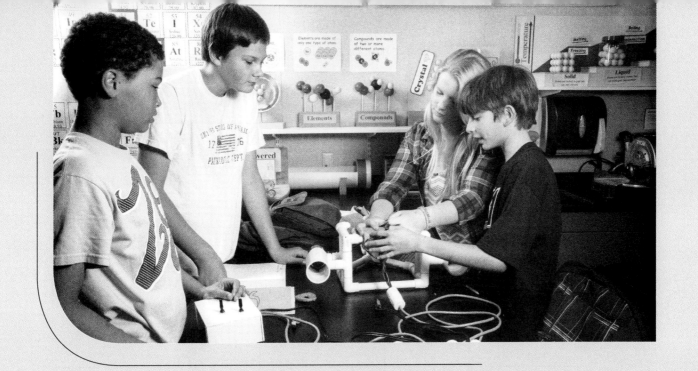

PART 2

Classroom Activities for Scientific Argumentation

Topic Guide: Earth and Space Sciences

Activity	Topic	NGSS Performance Expectation
1. What's the Difference Between One Rock and Another?	Rock Classification	MS-ESS2-3
2. Were the Continents Once One?	Continental Drift	MS-ESS2-3
3. What Has Caused Global Warming?	Climate Change	MS-ESS3-5 MS-ESS3-4
4. Why Does the Moon Appear to Change Shape?	Phases of the Moon	MS-ESS1-1
5. Can the Sun or Moon Disappear?	Eclipses of the Sun and Moon	MS-ESS1-1
6. Why Is It Warmer in Summer and Cooler in Winter?	The Seasons	MS-ESS1-1
7. How Big and Far Away Are the Planets?	Scale of the Solar System	MS-ESS1-3
8. Why Do Planets Orbit the Sun?	The Role of Gravity in the Solar System	MS-ESS1-2

Topic Guide: Life Sciences

Activity	Topic	NGSS Performance Expectation
9. Why Do Leaves Have Different Shapes?	Adaptation to the Environment	MS-LS1-5
10. What Is Happening to Pteropods?	Effects of Changes in the Environment on Ecosystems	MS-LS2-4
11. What Factors Affect the Number of Moose on Isle Royale?	Population Dynamics and the Impact of Resources	MS-LS2-1
12. Should We Reintroduce the Wolf to Isle Royale?	The Importance of Biodiversity to Ecosystems	MS-LS2-5
13. Is Rotifer Reproduction Sexual or Asexual?	The Role of Sexual and Asexual Reproduction and Its Effects on Genetic Variation	MS-LS3-2
14. Why Don't Lions Have Stripes?	Evolution of Traits	MS-LS4-2

Activity	Topic	NGSS Performance Expectation
15. How Do You Design a Test of Evolutionary Theory?	Adaptation by Species to the Local Environment and Designing an Experiment to Test a Hypothesis	**MS-LS4-4**
16. What Is Killing the Cats in Warner County?	Evolution and Adaptation	**MS-LS4-6**

Topic Guide: Physical Sciences

Activity	Topic	NGSS Performance Expectation
17. How Do Forces Affect the Way an Object Moves?	The Effects of Gravity	**MS-PS2-4**
18. Is There Gravity Beyond the Earth?	Gravity in Space	**MS-PS2-4**
19. What Has Energy Got to Do With Movement?	Kinetic Energy and Energy Transfer	**MS-PS3-5**
20. If You Fall From a Plane, Will You Go Faster and Faster?	Free Fall and Terminal Motion	**MS-PS3-1**
21. Two Models to Explain the Behavior of Matter— Which Is the Best?	The Particle Model of Matter	**MS-PS1-4**
22. What Particle Model for Boiling Water Fits Best With the Evidence?	The Particle Model of Matter	**MS-PS1-4**
23. Is Matter Always Conserved?	Conservation of Matter in a Chemical Reaction	**MS-PS1-5**
24. Where Oh Where Have the Atoms Gone?	Conservation of Matter in a Chemical Reaction	**MS-PS1-5**

Introduction

In the sections that follow, there are 24 activities for supporting students to engage in scientific argumentation. Eight are from the Earth and Space Sciences, eight from the Life Sciences, and eight from the Physical Sciences. In each section, the activities are ordered by level of demand—what we think the easiest coming first and the hardest last.

For each of these activities, we provide the following sections:

- **Learning Goals:** This explains the kind of knowledge and understanding of science the activity aims to develop.
- **NGSS Reference:** These activities have been selected to address specific NGSS performance expectations in middle school science. The performance expectation each activity

is addressing is stated along with the clarification statement that is provided in NGSS. Clarification statements, which are drawn verbatim from the NGSS document, are intended to help clarify the meaning of the performance expectation and set the boundaries of what it is reasonable to expect students to be able to do.

- **Science Background:** This provides some of the essential science concepts that you need to know before asking your students to engage in the activity. We do not claim it is totally comprehensive—there is always more to the science, but we hope it gives you some pointers.
- **Knowledge for Teaching:** This section provides a brief overview of key things that a teacher might need to know before teaching this topic other than the science. Its major focus is on the common preconceptions (often called misconceptions) that students might have and should be addressed by the activity.
- **Prior Knowledge for Students:** This section describes what level of understanding and knowledge the activity assumes the students will have.
- **Teaching Sequence:** This section contains details of any materials needed, the instructions for how to organize the activity, and the student materials.
- **Suggested Responses:** These are offered as indications of what a "good" student answer might look like. The intention is to provide some kind of indicator of what the outcome of the activity might look like.
- **Additional Resources:** This points to other materials and websites that might help supplement the activity or your knowledge.
- **Extension Activities:** These are suggestions for further student activities that you might like to undertake.

For each of the activities, you will need to make copies of the student materials. These are also available as pdfs from https://resources.corwin.com/OsborneArgumentation. We urge you to read the preliminary notes. Most important, you need to be clear about the scientific idea addressed by the topic and the possible ideas that the students might bring to the table, which, although understandable, are typically not the consensual scientific ideas.

We imagine that most of these activities would take approximately one lesson, depending on the students and your familiarity with the activity. In the notes for the teachers, we set out suggested timings for each activity. However, it is best to regard these activities as being like a set of recipes and scripts. The first time around, it helps to follow it carefully—after that, it will improve if you make it your own and modify it to suit the needs of your students.

CHAPTER 4

Earth and Space Sciences

What's the Difference Between One Rock and Another?

Learning Goals

The goals of this activity are for students to learn to

- use evidence to justify claims that a rock sample is either sedimentary, igneous, or metamorphic;
- develop a set of criteria for matching the evidence to the rock type;
- discuss how rock characteristics can provide evidence for the past movement of tectonic plates;
- recognize that a good argument that uses evidence to justify claims and oppose counter-claims requires the use of evidence, not assertion;
- learn and consolidate the geological concepts that are central to the study of rock types.

NGSS Reference

MS-ESS2-3

Analyze and interpret data on the distribution of fossils and rocks, continental shapes, and sea-floor structures to provide evidence of the past plate motions.

Clarification Statement: Examples of data include similarities of rock and fossil types on different continents, the shapes of the continents (including continental shelves), and the locations of ocean structures (such as ridges, fracture zones, and trenches).

Assessment Boundary: Paleomagnetic anomalies in the oceanic and continental crust are not assessed.

This activity encourages the use of argument to evaluate evidence presented on cards to classify different types of rocks. The students are asked to work in groups and also to conduct presentations of their conclusions following the group work.

Science Background

Content Knowledge

This activity is an example of a classification activity. Classification is an essential and important activity in science necessary to define what exists in the world. Biologists classify species, insects, plants, and the parts of living structures; chemists classify substances such as molecules and atoms; physicists rely on differentiating concepts such as current, charge and voltage, and more. Classification is always done by defining the criteria for categories. In the case of this exercise, there are three categories defined in terms of physical attributes of each rock:

- *Sedimentary:* Rock that is physically unchanged from the time when it was deposited. Hence, the particles will rub off relatively easily and the rock may appear to be "soft" compared to other rocks so it can easily be scratched. Such rock tends to be less dense than metamorphic and igneous rock.

- *Igneous:* Molten lava cooling produced this rock. The rock is very hard to scratch, often is quite dense, and can appear to have crystals.
- *Metamorphic:* Rock that has been physically changed by heat and/or pressure. As a result, the rock tends to be harder and less easy to scratch. There are no obvious layers in the rock.

Because metamorphic rocks need to be exposed to high temperature and pressure to undergo metamorphism in the first place, and this exposure to temperature and pressure occurs *beneath the surface* of the Earth, places on Earth with lots of metamorphic rocks *at the surface* suggest that there was tectonic plate movement—namely, tectonic uplift.

Knowledge for Teaching

There may be a tendency for students to classify attractive specimens as crystals, while considering dull or unattractive specimens to be rocks. The size of the specimen—as opposed to the composition—is also a feature that may stand out to students, leading them to classify in terms of size as opposed to in terms of composition.

Prior Knowledge for Students

For this activity, students will need to have been introduced to the three main rock types—sedimentary, igneous, and metamorphic—and the features that distinguish them.

Teaching Sequence

Materials

Make sure that you have rock samples such as slate and granite. The evidence cards for this activity are based on the assumption that Rock 1 is limestone, Rock 2 is granite, Rock 3 is slate, Rock 4 is basalt, Rock 5 is sandstone, and Rock 6 is marble. If you change the rocks, you will have to modify the evidence cards. Rock kits for less than $10 can be found for purchase online, such as the following: http://www.amazon.com/Toysmith-7921-Rock-Science-Kit/dp/B002IF7NZU.

Instructions for Activity

- **(2 min)** Introduce the activity. Tell the students that they are going to work as teams of geologists who have to work out what type of rock they will have. For each one, they will have the rock and an evidence card. The goal of this lesson is for them to identify each rock as sedimentary, igneous, or metamorphic and justify why. At the end of the lesson, each group will present their results to the whole class.
- **(3 min)** Put the students into groups of two to four and distribute the rocks and their accompanying evidence card to each group.
- **(20 min)** Ask the groups to complete the activity sheet for that sample in about 2 to 3 minutes. Emphasize that they need to justify their reasons why they think the sample is igneous, sedimentary, or metamorphic. After 2 to 3 minutes, ask each group to move to another rock. Alternatively, tell them to pass on the rock and the evidence card. Spend about 2 to 3 minutes on each rock so that at the end of the lesson, each group has been able to view the six rocks and complete the activity sheet.
- **(10 min)** Begin with one group and ask them what they think Rock 1 is and why. Ask if there is any group that disagrees and let them explain why. Then ask the original group what their response would be or open it up to contributions from other groups. Tell them to think of evidence that they would use to counter the other group's idea. In this fashion, promote discussion between groups. Throughout this discussion, encourage students to refer to evidence cards to support their points of view.

- **(5 min)** Next, ask the students to complete the following table.

 An electronic copy of this form is available on the companion website at https://resources.corwin.com/ OsborneArgumentation.

Rock Type	Features
Sedimentary	
Igneous	
Metamorphic	

- **(10 min)** To this point, students will have focused on rock features as they classify them. To link this activity to the NGSS performance expectation that the features of rocks can provide evidence of past motions of tectonic plates, finish this activity with a think-pair-share discussion where you pose the following prompts and driving question:

- Scientists have found places on Earth with lots of METAMORPHIC rocks. In this activity, you identified features of metamorphic rocks that were the result of changes caused by heat and pressure BENEATH the surface of the Earth.
- If metamorphic rocks are formed beneath the surface of the Earth, why are scientists finding lots of them at the surface? Have students first think about this question independently. Then ask each student to pair with a peer to discuss their thinking. Finally, ask students to share with the class what they and their partner discussed.

- ○ If you have difficulty getting students to share their thinking, a free student response system such as Braincandy (www.braincandy.org) allows students to submit anonymous written responses that are instantly displayed on the instructor's computer. The responses can be displayed in the form of a word cloud in which words from student responses are displayed with a size that is proportional to the frequency in which students used the words. This word cloud can be used as a conversation starter; for example, why does this word [point to one of the larger words] tend to show up in a lot of your responses?
- ○ During the classroom sharing portion of the think-pair-share, each time a student shares, ask the class if there are others who disagree. Another possible talk move, after someone has shared his or her thinking with the class, is to ask if anyone in the class would like to add on to what was just shared.

Sedimentary, Igneous, or Metamorphic?

 An electronic copy of this form is available on the companion website at https://resources.corwin.com/ OsborneArgumentation.

Rock	Type of Rock?	Defend Your Group's Decision by Using Evidence You Have Gathered
1		
2		
3		
4		
5		
6		

Evidence Cards

 Electronic copies of these cards are available on the companion website at https://resources.corwin.com/OsborneArgumentation.

Evidence for Rock 1

It is possible to carve a groove in the rock's surface using a fingernail.

It is not as heavy as the other samples.

It is light in color.

It was found at the top of a mountain.

It wears off on your clothes easily.

It contains fossils.

Evidence for Rock 2

It is multicolored.

It is heavier than the other samples.

It is very hard.

It contains crystals.

It is difficult to scratch.

It reflects light.

Evidence for Rock 3

It is very brittle and will snap fairly easily.

It has some layers.

It is almost black in color.

It is quite hard to scratch.

It can be used on tables.

It doesn't smell.

Evidence for Rock 4

It is not particularly heavy.

It is impossible to scratch with a fingernail.

It is a dark color.

It was found buried in the bottom of a stream.

It has no crystals.

Evidence for Rock 5

The rock contains grains.

It crumbles.

It wears off on your clothes.

It is easy to scratch.

It was found at the base of a mountain.

Evidence for Rock 6

It is light in color.

It is very hard.

It is quite difficult to scratch.

It reflects light.

It was found at a high altitude.

It is regularly used by people in its natural form.

Suggested Responses

Beneath is an indication of the possible responses to this activity that would demonstrate a good understanding of the science.

The following table offers plausible responses to the task.

Rock	Type of Rock? (Claim)	Defend Your Group's Decision by Using Evidence You Have Gathered (Evidence, Reasoning, and Justification)
1	Sedimentary	This rock has many of the characteristics of <u>sedimentary</u> rock: It is easy to scratch, crumbles easily, and is light-colored. Sedimentary rock often has fossils in it because dead plants and animals would get caught in the pieces of dirt and rock (sediments) and then more layers of sediment would pile on top of them. This rock can't be igneous because it crumbles and igneous rock is hard and not crumbly. This rock can't be metamorphic because it is crumbly and metamorphic rock is usually hard (the hardest of the three).
2	Igneous	This rock has characteristics of metamorphic rock and igneous rock (for example, it is harder than the sedimentary rock). But it is also very difficult to scratch and contains crystals. This makes this type of rock <u>igneous</u>. Igneous rock has crystals embedded inside because as the lava cools, sometimes crystals form. The rock cannot be a metamorphic rock and sedimentary rock does not contain crystals, so the presence of crystals is strong evidence that this sample is igneous. This rock is unlikely to be sedimentary as it does not scratch easily.
3	Igneous	Like Rock 2, this rock has some characteristics of metamorphic and igneous rock (brittle, hard to scratch). However, the evidence card says that the rock is black in color, which sounds like basalt (a type of igneous rock). It also says that it has some layers and metamorphic rock generally does not have layers. Therefore, this rock can be classified as <u>igneous</u>. It cannot be sedimentary because it is hard and does not scratch easily, and sedimentary rock is soft and easy to scratch.
4	Metamorphic	This rock is most likely <u>metamorphic</u> rock because it is harder than sedimentary rock (the evidence card says it cannot be scratched), but it does not contain crystals, which are sometimes characteristic of igneous rock.
5	Sedimentary	This rock must be <u>sedimentary</u> because it is soft, is crumbly, and scratches easily. It also has visible grains. Neither igneous rock nor metamorphic rock crumbles easily—they are both hard and very difficult to crumble or scratch.

(Continued)

(Continued)

Rock	Type of Rock? (Claim)	Defend Your Group's Decision by Using Evidence You Have Gathered (Evidence, Reasoning, and Justification)
6	Metamorphic	This rock is probably igneous or metamorphic because it is hard and difficult to scratch (unlike crumbly sedimentary rock). Also, it says that this rock type is found at a high altitude, which means probably at the top of a high mountain. Both metamorphic and sedimentary rock can get pushed up to the surface when plates come together and then end up at the tops of mountains; however, sedimentary rock would be soft, so this suggests that the rock could be metamorphic. Furthermore, it reflects light and is used by humans—this sounds like marble, which is a type of metamorphic rock.

Extension Activities

- Instead of using evidence cards above, allow students access to instrumentation and rock samples that would allow them to make these observations themselves.
- For each rock, ask them to list "points of evidence" that lead them to conclude what type of rock it is.

Suggestions for Improving the Quality of the Argumentation

- If the discussion seems to be stalling, try asking, "How do you explain [this piece of information on the evidence card that does not completely fit within the description]?"
- For example, the evidence card for Rock 4 has less information, and the piece of evidence that seems to distinguish it as metamorphic rather than igneous is the *lack of crystals*. However, certain types of igneous rock may also lack crystals. And the information that it is dark in color also does not truly distinguish igneous from metamorphic.
- Sometimes, rocks do not fit neatly into a category: For example, pumice is a type of igneous rock because it is formed directly from the cooling of hot lava. However, it cools so quickly that air pockets form, which makes this type of rock relatively easy to grind up. If students use "crumbly" as a piece of evidence for sedimentary rock, offer pumice as a counterexample, and see if the students can still justify the sedimentary rock type.

Other ways to "press" students' arguments:

- Press for students' critique of evidence: "How helpful is the description 'heavy' on the evidence card? Does that tell you very much about the type of rock?"
  - (In theory, a big rock could be heavy but not dense. So, it is more helpful to talk about density as a characteristic.)
- Press for rebuttal: "What would you say to a student who disagreed with you and said, 'No, this rock is metamorphic'?"

Were the Continents Once One?

Learning Goals

The goals of this activity are for students to learn to

- justify why we believe that the continents were once one and have drifted apart
- argue why other theories may be incorrect.

NGSS Reference

MS-ESS2-3

Analyze and interpret data on the distribution of fossils and rocks, continental shapes, and sea-floor structures to provide evidence of the past plate motions.
 Note: This activity focuses more on the interpretation of data than their analysis.

This activity provides an opportunity to explore the relationship between evidence and theory by looking at the evidence for continental drift. Students have to examine evidence statements and see if they support or do not support two theories for the origins of the continents. The activity helps to build an understanding of the concept of continental drift and plate tectonics as well as showing that not all evidence is unequivocal. Sometimes there are good reasons for believing the wrong idea. Moreover, error in science is actually a very common event. Or, to put it another way, hindsight is a wonderful thing!

Science Background

Content Knowledge

Our modern understanding of how the Earth has been shaped is really only less than 60 years old. With the emergence of the science of geology in the early 1800s and the recognition that the Earth was much older than the biblical account, ideas about how the Earth was shaped emerged. A mere glance at rock strata shows that they have been put down in layers that have then been folded. Geologists asked what kinds of forces could have caused this to happen. In the 19th century, the predominant theory was the idea that the surface of the Earth would have been like the skin of a drying apple, which becomes wrinkled as it dries. The mountains would have been the wrinkles. There are two consequences to this idea, though. First, most mountains would be about the same age, and second, the mountains would still be increasing in height as the Earth is still "drying out." Neither of these is true.

   Alfred Wegener's idea emerged from the work he did looking at the fossil and rock structure of South America and Africa. The first clue that they might have been joined is that the east coast of South America looks like it fits the west coast of southern Africa. Then there are parts where the fossil record and the rock structure match. This suggests that the two were once joined. However, when Wegener first put forward the theory in 1915, nobody could imagine a mechanism that would move whole continents, and people found the idea beyond belief and many were highly dismissive. It is only with the discovery of seafloor spreading in the late 1950s where magma was found to be welling up and pushing the seafloor sideways did people realize that this offered a mechanism for pushing the continents apart.

Knowledge for Teaching

Continental drift and plate tectonics do not form part of students' daily experience, so it is unlikely that they will have prior conceptions that need to be challenged. The main difficulty most students will have is imagining that there is a force that can move continents, let alone mountains.

Prior Knowledge for Students

This activity assumes that students

- understand what fossils are and that they may be millions of years old,
- realize that rocks exist in strata and that the layers can be bent, and
- have some sense of the shapes of the major continents on Earth.

Teaching Sequence

Instructions for Activity

Introduce the activity for the students as one where together you are going to explore the evidence for two theories about how the Earth came to have its current form. Arrange the students in groups of two or four students.

Hand out the student activity sheet and tell them that their task is to discuss each statement and decide which theory it supports, whether it supports both or neither.

For each of their choices, they must try and provide, at least in note form, a reason for their choice. Give them 10 to 15 minutes to work through the sheet discussing their choices.

Next run a whole-classroom discussion where you ask each group to tell the class what their choice is and their argument for that choice. Each time, ask if there is another group that disagrees. Other talk moves here that would be productive are "Can anyone add on?" "Can you elaborate?" You may also have to use "revoicing" for students who do not put their points terribly well—that is, "Let me see, this is what I think you are saying. . . ."

Finally, you may want to show them the evidence for seafloor spreading, which finally countered the argument that there was no force capable of moving continents. There are many examples on YouTube (e.g., https://www.youtube.com/watch?v=ZzvDlP6xd9o).

Student Activity

 An electronic copy of this activity is available on the companion website at https://resources.corwin.com/OsborneArgumentation.

Continental Drift Sheet

There have been many theories about why the Earth has a wrinkled surface that is covered with mountains and deep ocean trenches. In the 1800s, the major theory was the "shrinking Earth" theory. According to theory, the Earth started off as a molten ball of rock material, orbiting the Sun. As this ball cooled, a skin was formed, much like skin forms on cooling custard. The cooled outer skin is referred to as the crust.

When things cool down, they shrink. As the crust cooled, it would shrink and wrinkle, in the same way that the skin of an apple wrinkles when it has been left for too long without being eaten. Likewise, the mountain ranges of the Earth were thought to be the wrinkles formed when the crust cooled.

The shrinking Earth theory predicted that mountain ranges would appear randomly all over the Earth's surface. It also predicted that mountains would constantly grow higher. Another part of the theory stated that volcanoes and earthquakes would occur at random, all over the surface of the Earth. As with all scientific ideas, eventually someone challenged it when new information could not be made to fit in with the theory.

In 1915, Alfred Wegener put forward an alternative theory: that the continents were once one but had broken into several separate "plates." These rigid plates "floated" on a layer beneath, called the mantle, and had moved apart—a process that is shown in Figure A.2.1. The problem for Wegner was simply what force could possibly move a whole continent. It is hard enough to imagine a force that would move a building, let alone a continent.

In this activity, you are asked to discuss the following pieces of evidence and decide whether they support Wegner's theory or the shrinking Earth theory.

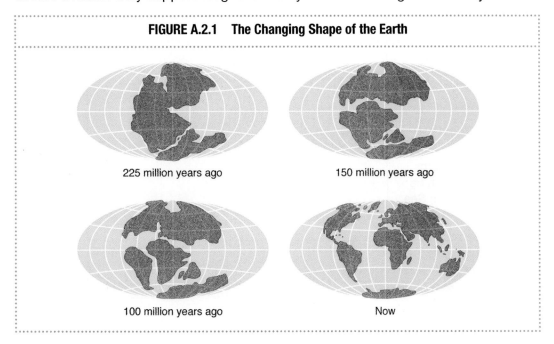

FIGURE A.2.1 The Changing Shape of the Earth

225 million years ago

150 million years ago

100 million years ago

Now

Source: © David R. Dudley, Illustrator.

	Supports Wegner's Theory	Supports Shrinking Earth Theory	Supports Neither	Supports Both	Reasons
The shape of the west coast of Africa matches the east coast of South America.					
Similar fossils, plants, and types of rock are found in South America and Africa.					
There is no known force that can move a whole continent.					
Not all of the Earth is wrinkled—there are mountains in some places, and in other places it is very flat.					
Even hard layers of rock can be seen to have been folded or bent.					
Volcanoes show that the interior of the Earth is molten.					
The Earth bulges at the Equator.					
Bones of mammoths and dinosaurs can be found in the North Sea.					
Some plant fossils found in the Arctic are from plants that only exist in temperate climates.					

Suggested Responses

The following shows an indication of the possible responses to this activity that would demonstrate a good understanding of the science.

	Supports Wegner's Theory	Supports Shrinking Earth Theory	Supports Neither	Supports Both	Reasons
The shape of the west coast of Africa matches the west Coast of South America.	X				The argument here is that the continents would have matching shapes if they had been together and then split apart.
Similar fossils, plants, and types of rock are found in South America and Africa.	X				If the continents had been together, the rock strata would match as would two halves of a pie and its contents.
There is no known force that can move a whole continent.		X			Wegener has no explanation for what could possibly move a continent. The wrinkling Earth theory has the forces generated by an elastic skin drying out and shriveling.
Not all of the Earth is wrinkled— there are mountains in some places, and in other places it is very flat.			X		This piece of evidence does not support Wegener, but it does call into question the wrinkling Earth theory. Why are there not wrinkles (mountains) spread uniformly across the Earth?
Even hard layers of rock can be seen to have been folded or bent.			X		All this shows is that rocks are not rigid. They can either be bent after they have solidified or as they are solidifying.

(Continued)

(Continued)

	Supports Wegner's Theory	Supports Shrinking Earth Theory	Supports Neither	Supports Both	Reasons
Volcanoes show that the interior of the Earth is molten.	X				If anything, this supports Wegener. If the Earth was drying out and wrinkling, how come there are still spots where it is still very molten and liquid? And if it is molten, that suggests that there is a liquid layer on which the crust can float and slide.
The Earth bulges at the Equator.			X		While this is true, it really supports neither. All it says is that what appears solid can behave like a fluid that would be flung out from the center if it was spinning.
Bones of mammoths and dinosaurs can be found in the North Sea.		X			The shrinking Earth theory predicts that while some wrinkles will be mountains, others will become valleys. Those valleys could be so deep that they ultimately are filled in by the sea, which would explain this evidence.
Some plant fossils found in the Arctic are from plants that only exist in temperate climates.	X				This finding tends to support Wegener. Either the whole Earth was once much warmer, which would explain this finding, or alternatively, the continent has moved from the tropics to the Arctic because it drifted there from another region of Earth.

Extension Activities

The United States Geological Service (USGS) offers another version of this activity as a puzzle with printed sheets showing rock strata and fossils embedded in the continents. Students cut them out and see how they could have once fit together and then justify the choices by drawing on the evidence that is provided in an additional sheet. See http://volcanoes.usgs.gov/about/edu/dynamicplanet/wegener/.

What Has Caused Global Warming?

Learning Goals

The goals of this activity are for students to learn to

- ask questions to determine whether humans or natural factors are the main cause of increases in global temperatures over the past century
- identify whether evidence supports claims about the causes of increases in global temperatures over the past century
- construct an argument for whether humans or nature are the main cause of global increases in global temperatures over the past century

NGSS References

MS-ESS3-5

Ask questions to clarify evidence of the factors that have caused the rise in global temperatures over the past century.

Clarification Statement: Examples of factors include human activities (such as fossil fuel combustion, cement production, and agricultural activity) and natural processes (such as changes in incoming solar radiation or volcanic activity). Examples of evidence can include tables, graphs, and maps of global and regional temperatures; atmospheric levels of gases such as carbon dioxide and methane; and the rates of human activities. Emphasis is on the major role that human activities play in causing the rise in global temperatures.

MS-ESS3-4

Construct an argument supported by evidence for how increases in human population and per-capita consumption of natural resources affect Earth's systems.

Clarification Statement: Examples of evidence include grade-appropriate databases on human populations and the rates of consumption of food and natural resources (such as freshwater, mineral, and energy). Examples of impacts can include changes to the appearance, composition, and structure of Earth's systems as well as the rates at which they change. The consequences of increases in human populations and consumption of natural resources are described by science, but science does not make the decisions for the actions society takes.

The goal of this activity is to build a deeper understanding of the evidence for the causes of the average increase in global temperatures over the past century. The activity provides two claims about the causes of global warming, and students will write a scientific question to clarify which claim is better. Then, students will examine eight pieces of evidence and identify which claim is supported. Finally, students will construct an argument for one of the claims and critique the alternative claim.

Science Background

Content Knowledge

There is scientific consensus that human activities are the main cause of the increase in average global temperature in the past century. There have been natural variations in the temperature of the Earth, but the increase in global temperature over the past century far exceeds natural patterns. Human have caused the increase in average global temperature by emitting large amounts of greenhouse gases. To understand how greenhouse gases have caused the temperature of the Earth to increase, consider all of the electromagnetic radiation from the Sun (i.e., solar radiation) that arrives at Earth's atmosphere. Clouds, atmospheric particles, or bright ground surfaces such as sea ice and snow reflect about 29% of solar radiation. The Earth absorbs about 48% of the solar radiation. The Earth also emits energy, some of which is in the form of infrared radiation that is then absorbed by greenhouse gases in the atmosphere. When greenhouse gases absorb infrared radiation, the molecules vibrate faster and transfer energy to other molecules through collisions, thereby increasing temperature.[1] Greenhouse gases in the atmosphere absorb the remaining 23%[2] of solar radiation and re-radiate long-wavelength radiation that cannot pass through the atmosphere to space without being reabsorbed. "Without the natural greenhouse effect, the average temperature at Earth's surface would be below the freezing point of water. Thus, Earth's natural greenhouse effect makes life as we know it possible. However, human activities, primarily the burning of fossil fuels and clearing of forests, have greatly intensified the natural greenhouse effect, causing global warming."[3]

Greenhouse gases include, but are not limited to, carbon dioxide, methane, and nitrous oxide. The mass of carbon dioxide that has been emitted by humans is substantially greater than that of other greenhouse gases. However, nitrogen dioxide and methane are more potent greenhouse gases, as measured by their global warming potential (GWP), which is "how much energy the emissions of one ton of a gas will absorb over a given period of time, relative to the emissions of one ton of carbon dioxide. The larger the GWP, the more that a given gas warms the Earth compared to carbon dioxide over that time period."[4] Humans have primarily emitted greenhouse gases through the burning of fossil (i.e., petroleum-based) fuels for energy and transportation. Agriculture is the primary source of nitrous oxide emissions and a substantial source of methane emissions. "Methane's lifetime in the atmosphere is much shorter than carbon dioxide (CO_2), but CH_4 is more efficient at trapping radiation than CO_2. Pound for pound, the comparative impact of CH_4 on climate change is more than 25 times greater than CO_2 over a 100-year period."[5]

Knowledge for Teaching

Consistent with the language of the NGSS, the activity uses the phrase "increases in global temperature" rather than "global warming" because many changes to the climate are occurring, in addition to increases in global temperatures. Despite the scientific consensus on climate change, 13% of Americans "are uncertain whether global warming is occurring or not, but believe that if it is happening, it is attributable to natural causes, not human activities."[6] The media have contributed to the public's perception because the media exaggerate the notion that there is a scientific debate about the causes of climate change.[7] Thus, it is likely that some students will think that nature or natural variation is the primary cause of the increase in average global temperature.

---

1   http://www.acs.org/content/acs/en/climatescience/greenhousegases/properties.html

2   http://earthobservatory.nasa.gov/Features/EnergyBalance/page4.php

3   https://www.ipcc.ch/publications_and_data/ar4/wg1/en/faq-1-3.html

4   http://www3.epa.gov/climatechange/ghgemissions/gwps.html

5   http://www3.epa.gov/climatechange/ghgemissions/gases/ch4.html

6   http://environment.yale.edu/climate-communication/article/climate-stability-as-understood-by-global-warmings-six-americas

7   http://www.sciencedirect.com/science/article/pii/S0016718507000188

Prior Knowledge for Students

Students should understand that greenhouse gases such as methane, water, and carbon dioxide absorb and re-radiate infrared radiation (IR). When greenhouse gases absorb IR, the molecules vibrate faster and transfer energy to other molecules, thereby increasing temperature. The natural greenhouse effect makes life as we know it possible because without greenhouse gases, the Earth would be so cold, all the water would be frozen. In addition, it would be helpful for students to understand the difference between weather and climate. "Weather is the combination of sunlight, wind, snow or rain, and temperature in a particular region at a particular time" (NGSS ESS2.D), and "climate describes a range of an area's typical weather conditions and the extent to which those conditions vary over years" (NGSS 3-ESS2-2).

Teaching Sequence

- **(10 min) Introduction:** Elicit prior knowledge of the greenhouse effect by having students label and interpret the diagram of the greenhouse effect. An example of a labeled diagram is provided in Figure A.3.1. Frame the lesson: "The goal of this lesson is for you to use evidence and your knowledge of the greenhouse effect to make an argument about the cause of the increase in the temperature of the Earth over the last 100 years."

FIGURE A.3.1   What Happens to the Sun's Rays When They Hit the Earth

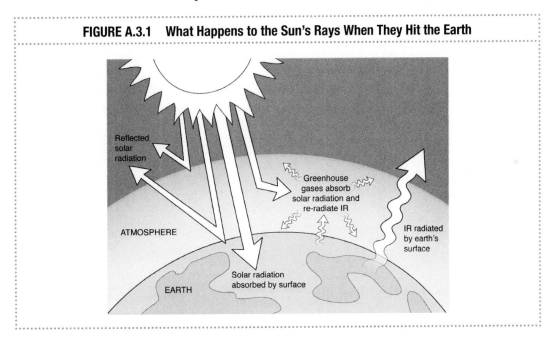

Source: © David R. Dudley, Illustrator

- **Part 1: Question (10 min)** Instruct students to write questions that correspond to each of the topics shown on the student activity sheet. Suggestion: Elicit possible questions for the first topic to provide models for students. Then, have students work individually and/or in pairs to write questions for the other topics.
- **Part 2: (25 min)** Students are provided with evidence of the human and natural causes to the increase in global temperatures in the past century. Each student should complete the graphic organizer and construct their argument. Next, facilitate an Argument Line activity, where one line corresponds to Ethan's claim and another line corresponds to Mia's claim. Here are some suggested questions:
  - "What is the evidence that supports your claim that (Ethan's/Mia's) idea is better?"
  - "What is a problem with (Ethan's/Mia's) idea?"

○ Prompt students to respond to each other's claims using talk moves such as, "Could someone restate what [student name] just said?" and "Do you agree/disagree with [student name's] idea? Explain your thinking." "What has someone else said that has changed your thinking?"

Note: If students don't converge on the idea that Ethan's claim is better, make sure to play devil's advocate for the "right" (i.e., scientifically accepted idea) answer. Also, we recommend emphasizing to students that the more humans reduce their contributions to climate change now, the more they reduce the potential negative impacts of climate change to humans and the environment. Making this point is intended to reduce the hopelessness that students may feel after recognizing that greenhouse gas emissions by humans are the main cause of the increase in average global temperature in the past century. After the argument line activity, students should revise their arguments.

Student Activity: What Has Caused Global Warming?

 An electronic copy of this activity is available on the companion website at https://resources.corwin.com/OsborneArgumentation.

Introduction

Review your understanding of the greenhouse effect by labeling Figure A.3.2. Then, below the diagram, summarize what the diagram is showing in a few sentences.

FIGURE A.3.2   What Happens to the Sun's Rays When They Hit the Earth (Without Labels)

Source: © David R. Dudley, Illustrator

PART 1: Data and Two Claims

The Earth has warmed about .85°C (1.5°F) over the past century (100 years). Two students are discussing what has caused this change.

> **Ethan says:** I think greenhouse gas emissions from human activities are the main cause of the increase in temperature in the past century.

> **Mia says:** I think nature is the main cause of the increase in temperature in the past century.

Help Ethan and Mia by completing the following table. What questions could you ask to determine if Ethan or Mia is correct? The following table has topics related to Ethan's and Mia's claims. Next to each topic, write a scientific question that is relevant to that topic.

Greenhouse gases emitted by humans	
Greenhouse gases emitted naturally	
Temperatures on Earth over the past 10,000 years	

PART 2: The Evidence

Ethan says: I think greenhouse gas emissions by humans are the main cause of the increase in temperature in the past century.

Mia says: I think nature is the main cause of the increase in temperature in the past century.

Evidence	Whom Does the Evidence Support?		
	Ethan	**Mia**	**Neither**
Humans emit over 10 times the amount of greenhouse gases than they did a century ago.[8]			
Earth's hottest periods occurred before humans existed.[9]			
The temperature of the Earth in the past century has increased more than any other time in the past 10,000 years.[10]			
Volcanoes release greenhouse gases.[11]			
In 2010, humans released over 100 times the amount of greenhouse gases than all the volcanoes in the world.[12]			

8   http://www3.epa.gov/climatechange/ghgemissions/global.html

9   https://www.climate.gov/news-features/climate-qa/whats-hottest-earths-ever-been

10   http://www.ces.fau.edu/nasa/module-3/temperature-changes/exploration-2.php

11   https://volcanoes.usgs.gov/hazards/gas/climate.php

12   http://www3.epa.gov/climatechange/ghgemissions/gwps.html

Evidence	Whom Does the Evidence Support?		
	Ethan	**Mia**	**Neither**
Ninety-seven percent of papers in scientific journals support the idea that changes in the climate are caused by humans.[13]			
Methane and nitrogen dioxide are stronger greenhouse gases than carbon dioxide.[14]			
In the United States, since 1990 there has been a 54% increase in the emissions of methane and nitrogen dioxide emissions from livestock.[15]			

Now that you have examined the evidence, do you think Ethan or Mia's claim is better? Explain why you think one claim is better and the other is not as good. Use evidence and reasoning to support your claims.

---

13   http://iopscience.iop.org/article/10.1088/1748-9326/8/3/031003

14   http://www3.epa.gov/climatechange/ghgemissions/gwps.html

15   http://www3.epa.gov/climatechange/ghgemissions/sources/agriculture.html

Suggested Responses

PART 1: Data and Two Claims

Greenhouse gases emitted by humans	How much greenhouse gases have humans emitted over the past century?
Greenhouse gases emitted naturally	What greenhouse gases are emitted naturally? What are some ways that nature emits greenhouse gases?
Temperatures on Earth over the past 10,000 years	How much has the temperature of the Earth changed over the past 10,000 years?

PART 2: The Evidence

Ethan says: I think greenhouse gas emissions by humans are the main cause of the increase in temperature in the past century.

Mia says: I think nature is the main cause of the increase in temperature in the past century.

Evidence	Whom Does the Evidence Support?		
	Ethan	Mia	Neither
Humans emit over 10 times the amount of greenhouse gases than they did a century ago.[16]	X		
Earth's hottest periods occurred before humans existed.[17]		X	
The temperature of the Earth in the past century has increased more than any other time in the past 10,000 years.[18]	X		
Volcanoes release greenhouse gases.[19]		X	
In 2010, humans released over 100 times the amount of greenhouse gases than all the volcanoes in the world.[20]	X		

---

16   http://www3.epa.gov/climatechange/ghgemissions/global.html

17   https://www.climate.gov/news-features/climate-qa/whats-hottest-earths-ever-been

18   http://www.ces.fau.edu/nasa/module-3/temperature-changes/exploration-2.php

19   https://volcanoes.usgs.gov/hazards/gas/climate.php

20   http://www3.epa.gov/climatechange/ghgemissions/gwps.html

Evidence	Whom Does the Evidence Support?		
	Ethan	Mia	Neither
Ninety-seven percent of papers in scientific journals support the idea that changes in the climate are caused by humans.[21]	X		
Methane and nitrogen dioxide are stronger greenhouse gases than carbon dioxide.[22]			X
In the United States, since 1990 there has been a 54% increase in the emissions of methane and nitrogen dioxide emissions from livestock.[23]	X		

Now that you have examined the evidence, do you think Ethan or Mia's claim is better? Explain why you think one claim is better and the other is not as good. Use evidence and reasoning to support your claims.

Ethan's idea is better than Mia's because the evidence better supports his idea. First, "humans emit over 10 times the amount of greenhouse gases than they did a century ago" and greenhouse gases absorb infrared radiation, which causes temperature to increase. Second, volcanoes release greenhouse gases, but it is a small amount compared to the amount of greenhouse gases emitted by humans. Third, "the temperature of the earth in the past century has increased more than any other time in the past 10,000 years," which suggests that the current temperatures cannot be explained by natural causes. Finally, the evidence that "97% of papers in scientific journals support the idea that changes in the climate are caused by humans" supports the claim that humans are the primary cause of the increase in global temperature since temperature over time is an example of climate.

Additional Resources

This website provides a concise evidence-based argument for how humans have caused the increase in global temperatures in the past century: http://www.esrl.noaa.gov/gmd/aggi/.

National Ice Core Laboratory—this website includes videos that show how scientists estimate historical temperatures: http://www.icecores.org/icecores/videos.shtml.

Extension Activities

- Facilitate students' analysis of the data provided in the footnoted websites in the Background Knowledge section by asking them to describe patterns in the data and exceptions to the patterns.
- Ask students whether they think individuals should reduce their emissions and identify the political, economic, and social issues that arise, in addition to the science.

---

21   http://iopscience.iop.org/article/10.1088/1748-9326/8/3/031003

22   http://www3.epa.gov/climatechange/ghgemissions/gwps.html

23   http://www3.epa.gov/climatechange/ghgemissions/sources/agriculture.html

As NGSS performance expectation MS-ESS3-4 notes, "The consequences of increases in human populations and consumption of natural resources are described by science, but science does not make the decisions for the actions society takes."

- Show the students the infographic http://www.cowspiracy.com/infographic and have them discuss it in small groups and as a full class. Suggested questions:

  o What changes in our habits/behaviors might reverse some of the data trends presented in the infographic? Why would these changes change the data?
  o What argument would you make using these data for becoming a vegetarian?
  o If you were a dairy farmer, what counterargument might you make in response?

Acknowledgments

This activity has been adapted with permission from the Stanford Center for Assessment, Learning and Equity.

The greenhouse effect image was modified from http://houseland.site/greenhouse-effect-diagram-for-kids/.

Notes

_____

_____

_____

_____

_____

_____

_____

_____

_____

_____

_____

Why Does the Moon Appear to Change Shape?

Learning Goals

The goals of this activity are for students to learn to

- record observational data from a simple investigation,
- draw evidence from recorded data to construct a claim as to what causes the phases of the Moon
- recognize that a good argument uses evidence to justify claims through reasoning

NGSS Reference

MS-ESS1-1

Develop and use a model of the Earth-Sun-Moon system to describe the cyclic patterns of lunar phases, eclipses of the Sun and Moon, and seasons.
    Clarification Statement: Examples of models can be physical, graphical, or conceptual.

This activity encourages the use of argument to think about what causes the various phases of the Moon. Students are asked to gather evidence from a simple investigation and learn how to construct a scientific argument based on that evidence.

Science Background

Content Knowledge

The Earth orbits the Sun in a plane called the *ecliptic*. The Moon orbits the Earth in a plane that lies at a 5-degree angle to the ecliptic (Figures A.4.1 and A.4.2). It is the changing orientation of the Earth-Sun-Moon system that results in the different phases of the Moon. A full Moon occurs when the Sun, Earth, and Moon are in line and the Earth is between the Sun and the Moon. In this orientation, the full face of the Moon is lit up by the Sun. People on the side of the Earth in darkness, away from the Sun, can look up and will see whole disc lit up by the Sun. In contrast, when the Moon is between the Earth and the Sun, the Moon cannot be seen because we are in daylight and the sunlight is lighting up the side of the Moon we cannot see, so the side of the Moon facing the Earth is not visible from the vantage point of the Earth. When the Moon is elsewhere—to the side of the Earth—a fraction of the Moon will be illuminated from the vantage point of the Earth. It is also important to understand that the orbital plane of the Moon about the Earth is at an angle to the orbital plane of the Earth about the Sun (i.e., what we call the *ecliptic*). This is shown in Figure A.4.2. Were it not, we would always observe a full lunar eclipse when the Moon was on the side of the Earth where it is furthest from the Sun (i.e., the configuration typically associated with a full Moon) because the Earth would block any light from the Sun reaching the Moon.

FIGURE A.4.1   Orbital Plane of Moon About the Earth

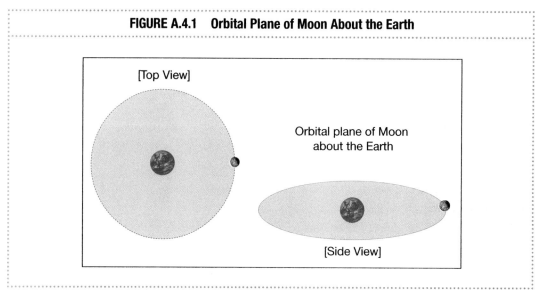

Earth: Image https://commons.wikimedia.org/w/index.php?title=Category:Lunar_phases&filefrom=East-Side-Phase-181.jpg#/media/File:East-Side-Phase-181.jpg; NASA Media Usage Guidelines http://www.nasa.gov/multimedia/guidelines/index.html

Moon: Jay Tanner. License http://creativecommons.org/licenses/by-sa/3.0/; Image https://commons.wikimedia.org/w/index.php?title=Category:Lunar_phases&filefrom=East-Side-Phase-181.jpg#/media/File:East-Side-Phase-181.jpg

FIGURE A.4.2   Orbital Plane of Moon About the Earth Relative to the Ecliptic

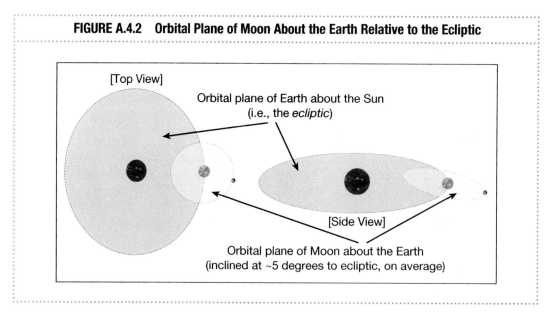

Earth: Image https://commons.wikimedia.org/w/index.php?title=Category:Lunar_phases&filefrom=East-Side-Phase-181.jpg#/media/File:East-Side-Phase-181.jpg; NASA Media Usage Guidelines http://www.nasa.gov/multimedia/guidelines/index.html

Moon: Jay Tanner. License http://creativecommons.org/licenses/by-sa/3.0/; Image https://commons.wikimedia.org/w/index.php?title=Category:Lunar_phases&filefrom=East-Side-Phase-181.jpg#/media/File:East-Side-Phase-181.jpg

Sun: Image http://photojournal.jpl.nasa.gov/catalog/PIA03149; NASA Media Usage Guidelines http://www.nasa.gov/multimedia/guidelines/index.html

If you are not clear about why the Moon has phases, you should watch a video as it helps to have a visual explanation as well. A good one can be found at https://www.youtube.com/watch?v=wz01pTvuMa0.

Knowledge for Teaching

A common student preconception (also known as misconception) is that the phases of the Moon are caused by the shadow of the Earth on the Moon. Another common preconception is that the orbital plane of the Moon about the Earth is parallel to the orbital plane of the Earth about the Sun, which would mean that there would be a full lunar eclipse once per month—when the Moon is at the full Moon position. An additional preconception about the phases of the Moon is that the different phases are due to clouds in the atmosphere obstructing part of the Moon.

Prior Knowledge for Students

Students need to know that the Moon orbits the Earth, while the Earth orbits the Sun. Students also need to be aware that solar and lunar eclipses do not happen every month. For example, if students believe that lunar eclipses happen every month, then it may be difficult for them to distinguish a lunar eclipse from a new Moon.

Teaching Sequence

Materials

- No. 2 pencils
- Small Styrofoam balls (these will represent the "Moon")
- Table lamps (these will represent the "Sun")
- Paper or notebook for data collection

Instructions for Activity

This activity can be done individually or in groups (if the latter, put students into groups of two to four). By recording data on the appearance of the "Moon" at different orientations with the "Earth" and "Sun," students have ownership in the data that they will be asked to make sense of through evidence-based argumentation.

- **(2 min)** Explain to your students that this activity will build on their knowledge of the Earth, Moon, and Sun. Tell students that the goal of this activity is to explain what causes the different shapes of the bright part of the Moon at different times of the year (perhaps show students images of the lunar phases). The different shapes of the bright part of the Moon are called *phases* (write the definition on the board and have students restate the meaning of phases of the Moon and/or the purpose of the activity).
- **(3 min)** Elicit students' ideas about what causes the phases of the Moon. Note these ideas on the board.
- **(40 min)** Tell students that in this activity, we will use a lamp, a Styrofoam ball, and our heads to represent the Sun-Moon-Earth system. Commence the student activity by asking students to follow the steps detailed below. Try and keep the hands-on investigation to no more than 20 minutes to provide ample time for the main focus of the activity, which is evidence-based argumentation. For this, you will need to get the students to work in teams of at least two, preferably three. Ask them to complete the claim, evidence, and reasoning template, drawing on the evidence provided by the use of the model. The goal of the activity is to get them to show how the model explains the phases of the Moon—that is, what evidence from the model supports their explanation? If there is time, you may want to call on one or two groups to present their thinking and then discuss with the class which group made the better argument.
- **(5 min)** In the remaining time, return to the student ideas about the phases of the Moon that were noted prior to the investigation. Particularly focus on initial ideas that were not scientifically accurate and prompt students to explain why these incorrect ideas are flawed.

Student Activity: Why Does the Moon Appear to Change Shape?

 An electronic copy of this activity is available on the companion website at https://resources.corwin.com/OsborneArgumentation.

Follow these steps:

1. Turn out classroom lights and turn on a lamp. Let the lamp represent the Sun.

2. Attach a Styrofoam ball to a pencil. Let the ball represent the Moon.

3. Face the lamp (the Sun). Your head represents the Earth.

4. Per Figure A.4.3, stretch out your arm and hold the pencil/ball slightly out in front of you at a level slightly above your head with the ball pointed upward as in the picture. Make a note how the "Moon" appears. For example, can you see a fully illuminated/bright surface on the ball, a fully shaded/dark surface on the ball, or somewhere in between "completely lit up" or "completely dark"?

FIGURE A.4.3   Cartoon Sketch of Student Activity

Source: © David R. Dudley, Illustrator

5. Holding your arm in the same position, rotate your entire body clockwise 45 degrees. Note how the "Moon" appears again.

6. Rotate another 45 degrees. Note how the "Moon" appears again.

7. Continue noting how the "Moon" appears at each 45-degree increment until you have made one full circle.

The notes you have made are your data.

We're going to use your data to try and answer the following question: *Why do there appear to be different phases of the Moon?*

Look at your data and provide an answer to the following question: *Why do there appear to be different phases of the Moon?*

Your answer to this question is your *claim*. The data that helped you arrive at this claim are your *evidence.* Write down both your claim and your evidence in the following corresponding boxes.

CLAIM	REASONING	EVIDENCE

You will note that sandwiched between claim and evidence is *reasoning.* Reasoning serves as a "bridge" between your answer to a question (i.e., the claim) and the data that led you to that answer (i.e., the evidence). In your own words, write down in the reasoning box above why your evidence led you to your claim.

Together, your claim, evidence, and reasoning form your evidence-based argument for why the Moon appears to have different phases.

Suggested Responses

The following provides an indication of the possible responses to this activity that would demonstrate a good understanding of the science.

CLAIM	REASONING	EVIDENCE
There are different phases of the Moon because the Moon is in different positions relative to the Earth and the Sun.	When the Moon is at different positions relative to the Earth and the Sun, different amounts of Sunlight get reflected off the Moon. This means that at different times, different amounts of the Moon appear to be bright.	When my head (representing the "Earth") was in between the "Moon" and the lamp (representing the "Sun"), the entire side of the "Moon" I was looking at appeared completely bright. When the "Moon" was in between my head (representing the "Earth") and the lamp (representing the "Sun"), the entire side of the "Moon" I was looking at appeared completely dark. At all other positions, only a fraction of the side of the "Moon" I was looking at appeared bright.

Additional Resources

Lunar Phase Simulator: http://astro.unl.edu/naap/lps/animations/lps.swf.

For an excellent demonstration of the investigation involved in this activity, watch the first 3 minutes of the following video: https://www.youtube.com/watch?v=wz01pTvuMa0.

Extension Activities

1. Have students provide feedback to each other either verbally or by exchanging papers. If you choose to have students share their arguments verbally, have one student be the "talker" and the other the "expert scientist," the person who provides feedback. Here are some suggested prompts to use for feedback:
   - The claim/evidence/reasoning is clear because. . . .
   - The claim/evidence/reasoning is not clear because. . . .
   - The claim/evidence/reasoning is accurate because. . . .
   - The claim/evidence/reasoning is inaccurate because. . . .

As a class, ask if they can see any flaws with the Earth-Sun-Moon model. For example, the scales are inaccurate. About 1.3 million Earths would fit within the volume of the Sun. Thus, the ratio of the volume of the Styrofoam ball to the lamp is substantially greater than the actual volume of the Earth compared to the Sun. In addition, the Earth is about 93 million miles from the Sun while the distance from the Earth to the Moon is relatively much shorter—only a quarter of a million miles. If the distances between the Earth and the Sun and Moon were accurately proportioned, the lamp would need to be about 400 times further away from the Styrofoam ball than the Styrofoam ball is to the head of the student performing the activity. Other flaws include the lack of movement of the "Earth," both in terms of its orbit and rotation (having students rotate their heads represents the Moon's orbit about the Earth, not the Earth's orbit about the Sun).

It is important to remind students that there are also flaws in scientists' models, but we use them nonetheless. While some models may not be perfect, they can still be useful in helping to explain and make predictions about the natural world.

Students can be provided an opportunity to construct a model of the phases of the Moon with matching between two sets of cards. The first set of cards has pictures of different Moon phases. The second set of cards has different Earth-Sun-Moon configurations (from a side view) corresponding to the different Moon phases depicted in the first set of cards. Note: These configurations are from a side view—the planes are roughly circular if viewed from above. Students are to match each Moon phase card in the first set with a single Earth-Sun-Moon configuration card they think corresponds to the best match. Both sets of cards are provided in Figure A.4.4 and Figure A.4.5. Mix up the cards before you distribute them to your students.

An electronic copy of this sheet is available on the companion website at https://resources.corwin.com/ OsborneArgumentation.

| **FIGURE A.4.4 Moon Phase Cards:
Position of the Moon** | **FIGURE A.4.5 Moon Phase Cards:
Pictures of the Appearance of the Moon** |

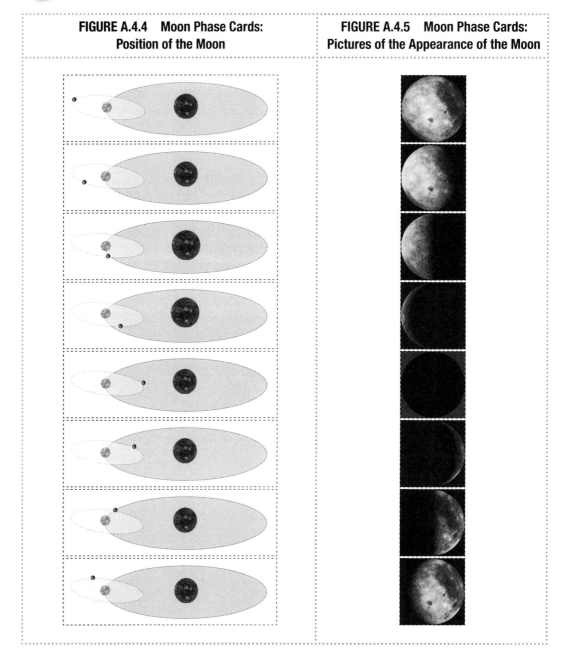

Earth: Image https://commons.wikimedia.org/w/index.php?title=Category:Lunar_phases&filefrom=East-Side-Phase-181.jpg#/media/File:East-Side-Phase-181.jpg; NASA Media Usage Guidelines http://www.nasa.gov/multimedia/guidelines/index.html

Moon: Jay Tanner. License http://creativecommons.org/licenses/by-sa/3.0/; Images https://commons.wikimedia.org/w/index.php?title=Category:Lunar_phases&filefrom=East-Side-Phase-181.jpg#/media/File:East-Side-Phase-181.jpg; https://commons.wikimedia.org/w/index.php?title=Category:Lunar_phases&filefrom=EastSidePhase-181.jpg#/media/File:East-Side-Phase-227.jpg; https://commons.wikimedia.org/w/index.php?title=Category:Lunar_phases&filefrom=East-Side-Phase-181.jpg#/media/File:East-Side-Phase-268.jpg; https://commons.wikimedia.org/w/index.php?title=Category:Lunar_phases&filefrom=East-Side-Phase-181.jpg#/media/File:East-Side-Phase-319.jpg; https://commons.wikimedia.org/w/index.php?title=Category:Lunar_phases&filefrom=East-Side-Phase-181.jpg#/media/File:Far-Side-Phase-001.jpg; https://commons.wikimedia.org/w/index.php?title=Category:Lunar_phases&filefrom=Far-Side-Phase-024.jpg#/media/File:Far-Side-Phase-039.jpg; https://commons.wikimedia.org/w/index.php?title=Category:Lunar_phases&filefrom=Far-Side-Phase-024.jpg#/media/File:Far-Side-Phase-090.jpg; https://commons.wikimedia.org/w/index.php?title=Category:Lunar_phases&filefrom=Far-Side-Phase-024.jpg#/media/File:Far-Side-Phase-127.jpg

Sun: Image http://photojournal.jpl.nasa.gov/catalog/PIA03149; NASA Media Usage Guidelines http://www.nasa.gov/multimedia/guidelines/index.html

Can the Sun or Moon Disappear?

Learning Goals

The goals of this activity are for students to learn to

- compare and contrast two competing models of the Earth-Sun-Moon system
- critically evaluate both models by constructing a possible critique of each
- use an empirical data table to identify evidence in support of the model they deem superior

NGSS Reference

MS-ESS1-1

Develop and use a model of the Earth-Sun-Moon system to describe the cyclic patterns of lunar phases, eclipses of the Sun and Moon, and seasons.
   Clarification Statement: Examples of models can be physical, graphical, or conceptual.

This exercise builds on the Phases of the Moon activity—namely, by using evidence-based argumentation to develop a model of the Earth-Sun-Moon system in which the orbital plane of the Moon about the Earth is not parallel to the orbital plane of the Earth about the Sun.

FIGURE A.5.1   Orbital Plane of Moon About the Earth Relative to the Ecliptic

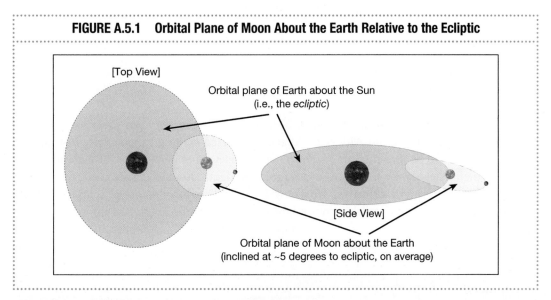

Earth: Image https://commons.wikimedia.org/w/index.php?title=Category:Lunar_phases&filefrom=East-Side-Phase-181.jpg#/media/File:East-Side-Phase-181.jpg; NASA Media Usage Guidelines http://www.nasa.gov/multimedia/guidelines/index.html

Moon: Jay Tanner. License http://creativecommons.org/licenses/by-sa/3.0/; Image https://commons.wikimedia.org/w/index.php?title=Category:Lunar_phases&filefrom=East-Side-Phase-181.jpg#/media/File:East-Side-Phase-181.jpg

Sun: Image http://photojournal.jpl.nasa.gov/catalog/PIA03149; NASA Media Usage Guidelines http://www.nasa.gov/multimedia/guidelines/index.html

Science Background

Content Knowledge

The Earth orbits the Sun in a plane called the *ecliptic*. The Moon orbits the Earth in a plane that lies at a 5-degree angle to the ecliptic (Figure A.5.1). It is the changing orientations of the Earth-Sun-Moon system that result in lunar and solar eclipses. These vary in both frequency and the amount that the Earth or the Sun is eclipsed. Solar eclipses occur when the Moon casts a shadow upon the Earth. This is during a new Moon when the Moon moves between the Earth and the Sun and the orbit of the Moon about the Earth lies in the plane of the orbit of the Earth about the Sun (i.e., the *ecliptic*). This does NOT happen every new Moon, as the orbit of the Moon about the Earth is, on average, at about a 5-degree angle to the plane of the ecliptic. The closer a new Moon gets to a perfect intersection with the ecliptic, the greater the percentage of the Sun that is eclipsed.

In contrast, lunar eclipses occur when the Earth casts a shadow on the Moon. This is during a full Moon when the Earth comes between the Moon and the Sun and the orbit of the Moon about the Earth is in the plane of the ecliptic. As is the case with solar eclipses, this does not happen every month, as the Moon's orbit is not in the same place as the ecliptic lying at about a 5-degree angle. The closer a full Moon gets to a being in the plane of the ecliptic, the greater the percentage of the Moon that is eclipsed.

Knowledge for Teaching

A common student preconception (also known as misconception) about eclipses is that during solar/lunar eclipses, the Sun/Moon always disappear entirely. Another preconception is that solar/lunar eclipses look the same no matter where you are on Earth.

Prior Knowledge for Students

Students need to know that the Moon orbits about the Earth, while the Earth orbits about the Sun, and that the plane of each of these orbits is not the same. Students also need to be aware that solar and lunar eclipses do not happen every month. For example, if students believe that lunar eclipses happen every month, then it may be difficult for them to reconcile a lunar eclipse from a new Moon.

Teaching Sequence

Materials

- **Student handout and/or digital projector.** Students need to see the two competing models—Model A and Model B—that are depicted below in the activity instructions. Students can be presented these models, either via a paper handout or through projection of the models to the front of the classroom. Students also need to see the claims of two fictitious students, Jackson and Mia, as well as a table of lunar and solar eclipse data from 2014 to 2015. A printed handout might be optimal to distribute this information, as it allows students to make their own annotations, which may prove particularly helpful for making sense of the eclipse data.

Instructions for Activity

- **(2 min)** Introduce the activity. Tell students that they will be presented with two plausible models of the Earth-Sun-Moon configuration when an eclipse occurs. Their job will then be to examine real eclipse data to determine which of the two models is superior. Now present Model A and Model B to the students (found in student activity detailed below).

- **(2 min)** Question for class discussion: What is Jackson's claim and what is Mia's claim? [Jackson's claim is that Model A is correct, while Mia's claim is that Model B is correct.]
- **(2 min)** Question for class discussion: What might be a critique Jackson can make about Mia's claim? [e.g., because the Moon's orbital plane about the Earth is at an incline, you would never see a full solar or full lunar eclipse]
- **(2 min)** Question for class discussion: What might be a critique Mia can make about Jackson's claim? [e.g., under Jackson's model, there would be a full lunar eclipse once per month]
- **(40 min)** Which claim—Jackson's or Mia's—is right? To decide, we need to look at some data. At this point, put students into groups of two to four and commence the student activity detailed subsequently.

Student Activity: Can the Sun or Moon Disappear?

 An electronic copy of this activity is available on the companion website at https://resources.corwin.com/OsborneArgumentation.

Jackson and Mia have different models of why lunar and solar eclipses occur. Jackson thinks that the plane of the orbit of the Moon around the Earth is *parallel* to the plane of the orbit of the Earth around the Sun. For example, Jackson would agree with Model A of a lunar eclipse (Figure A.5.2).

FIGURE A.5.2   Model A of a Lunar Eclipse

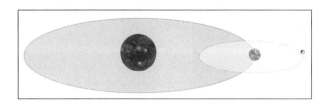

(The darker-shaded ellipse represents the orbital plane of the Earth about the Sun. The lighter-shaded ellipse represents the orbital plane of the Moon about the Earth. Note: This is from a side view—the planes are roughly circular if viewed from above.)

Earth: Image https://commons.wikimedia.org/w/index.php?title=Category:Lunar_phases&filefrom=East-Side-Phase-181.jpg#/media/File:East-Side-Phase-181.jpg; NASA Media Usage Guidelines http://www.nasa.gov/multimedia/guidelines/index.html

Moon: Jay Tanner. License http://creativecommons.org/licenses/by-sa/3.0/; Image https://commons.wikimedia.org/w/index.php?title=Category:Lunar_phases&filefrom=East-Side-Phase-181.jpg#/media/File:East-Side-Phase-181.jpg

Sun: Image http://photojournal.jpl.nasa.gov/catalog/PIA03149; NASA Media Usage Guidelines http://www.nasa.gov/multimedia/guidelines/index.html

Mia thinks that the plane of the orbit of the Moon around the Earth is not parallel to the plane of the orbit of the Earth around the Sun. For example, Mia would agree with Model B of a lunar eclipse (Figure A.5.3).

FIGURE A.5.3   Model B of a Lunar Eclipse

(The darker-shaded ellipse represents the orbital plane of the Earth about the Sun. The lighter-shaded ellipse represents the orbital plane of the Moon about the Earth. Note: This is from a side view—the planes are roughly circular if viewed from above.)

Earth: Image https://commons.wikimedia.org/w/index.php?title=Category:Lunar_phases&filefrom=East-Side-Phase-181.jpg#/media/File:East-Side-Phase-181.jpg; NASA Media Usage Guidelines http://www.nasa.gov/multimedia/guidelines/index.html

Moon: Jay Tanner. License http://creativecommons.org/licenses/by-sa/3.0/; Image https://commons.wikimedia.org/w/index.php?title=Category:Lunar_phases&filefrom=East-Side-Phase-181.jpg#/media/File:East-Side-Phase-181.jpg

Sun: Image http://photojournal.jpl.nasa.gov/catalog/PIA03149; NASA Media Usage Guidelines http://www.nasa.gov/multimedia/guidelines/index.html

The following is a table of both lunar and solar eclipses between 2014 and 2015. Included in the table is information about the year the eclipse occurred, whether the eclipse was lunar or solar, whether the eclipse was full or only partial, and where on Earth the eclipse was visible.

Lunar and Solar Eclipses: 2014–2015

Year	Type of Eclipse	Portion Eclipsed	Where Visible?
2015	Lunar	Total	Europe, Southwest Asia, Africa, North America, South America, Pacific, Atlantic, Indian Ocean, Arctic, Antarctica
2015	Solar	Partial	South Africa, Antarctica, and locations in the Indian and Atlantic Oceans
2015	Lunar	Total	North America, South America, Asia, and parts of Australia
2015	Solar	Partial	Europe, Northern and Eastern Asia, and Northern and Western Africa
2014	Solar	Partial	United States and Canada
2014	Lunar	Partial	Eastern Europe, much of Asia, Australia, North America, South America, Pacific, Atlantic, Indian Ocean, Arctic, Antarctica
2014	Solar	Partial	Southern Asia, Australia, Pacific, Indian Ocean, and Antarctica
2014	Lunar	Partial	Western Europe, South and East Asia, much of Australia, much of Africa, North America, South America, Pacific, Atlantic, Indian Ocean, and Antarctica

Carefully look over the data table to provide an argument that answers the following question: *Which claim is right, Jackson's or Mia's?*

Your answer to this question is your claim. The data that helped you arrive at this claim are your evidence. Write down both your claim and your evidence in the corresponding boxes below.

CLAIM	REASONING	EVIDENCE

You will note that sandwiched between claim and evidence is reasoning. Reasoning serves as a "bridge" between your answer to a question (i.e., the claim) and the data that led you to that answer (i.e., the evidence). In your own words, write down in the Reasoning box above why your evidence led you to your claim.

Together, your claim, evidence, and reasoning form your evidence-based argument for why the Moon appears to have different phases.

Now, answer the following question: *Which claim is wrong, Jackson's or Mia's?*
Write down your claim, evidence, and reasoning in the corresponding boxes below.

CLAIM	REASONING	EVIDENCE

Suggested Responses

Beneath are an indication of the possible responses to this activity that would demonstrate a good understanding of the science.

CLAIM	REASONING	EVIDENCE
Mia's claim (Model B) is correct. Jackson's claim (Model A) is incorrect.	Model A would predict 12 solar and 12 lunar eclipses each year. This is not consistent with the evidence. Model A would predict that all eclipses would be visible from the same locations on Earth. This is evidence against Jackson's claim that Model A is correct.	In both 2014 and 2015, there were only two lunar and two solar eclipses each year. Based on the eclipse table, locations where the eclipses were visible tend to vary.

Extension Activities

This activity can be linked with the Phases of the Moon activity in this book. Following the hands-on investigation in the Phases of the Moon activity, ask students to hold the Styrofoam "Moon" at the location they determined to correspond to a full Moon. Ask students why they held the "Moon" slightly above their head. (After completing this Eclipses of the Sun and Moon activity, students should realize that holding the "Moon" slightly above their head is meant to represent the inclination of the Moon's orbital plane relative to the ecliptic.)

Now instruct the students to bring the "Moon" down to eye level. Ask students to write down any changes they see in the "Moon's" appearance when they bring it down to eye level from the full Moon position. (What students should observe is that the full "Moon" becomes eclipsed.)

Have students contrast a lunar eclipse with a full Moon, in particular noting that in both cases, the Moon is on the opposite side of the Earth from the Sun, but that only in the case of the lunar eclipse is the shadow of the Earth relevant. Key points to emphasize here are that without accounting for the inclination of the Moon's orbit relative to the ecliptic, we would have one full lunar eclipse per month, and correspondingly, that we would never see a full Moon.

For simplicity, the Models A and B that students were asked to critique with evidence both depicted lunar eclipses. As this activity is intended to allow students to come to the realization that Model B is superior to Model A, perhaps ask students to—assuming Model B is scientifically correct—sketch a possible Earth-Sun-Moon configuration during a solar eclipse. Figure A.5.4 and Figure A.5.5 present a couple of examples (Note: This is from a side view—the planes are roughly circular if viewed from above).

FIGURE A.5.4   Possible Solar Eclipse Configuration 1

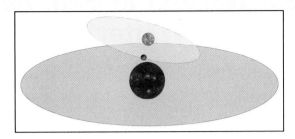

Earth: Image https://commons.wikimedia.org/w/index.php?title=Category:Lunar_phases&filefrom=East-Side-Phase-181.jpg#/media/File:East-Side-Phase-181.jpg; NASA Media Usage Guidelines http://www.nasa.gov/multimedia/guidelines/index.html

Moon: Jay Tanner. License http://creativecommons.org/licenses/by-sa/3.0/; Image https://commons.wikimedia.org/w/index.php?title=Category:Lunar_phases&filefrom=East-Side-Phase-181.jpg#/media/File:East-Side-Phase-181.jpg

Sun: Image http://photojournal.jpl.nasa.gov/catalog/PIA03149; NASA Media Usage Guidelines http://www.nasa.gov/multimedia/guidelines/index.html

FIGURE A.5.5   Possible Solar Eclipse Configuration 2

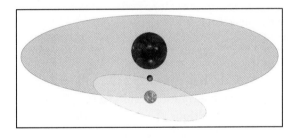

Earth: Image https://commons.wikimedia.org/w/index.php?title=Category:Lunar_phases&filefrom=East-Side-Phase-181.jpg#/media/File:East-Side-Phase-181.jpg; NASA Media Usage Guidelines http://www.nasa.gov/multimedia/guidelines/index.html

Moon: Jay Tanner. License http://creativecommons.org/licenses/by-sa/3.0/; Image https://commons.wikimedia.org/w/index.php?title=Category:Lunar_phases&filefrom=East-Side-Phase-181.jpg#/media/File:East-Side-Phase-181.jpg

Sun: Image http://photojournal.jpl.nasa.gov/catalog/PIA03149; NASA Media Usage Guidelines http://www.nasa.gov/multimedia/guidelines/index.html

Why Is It Warmer in Summer and Cooler in Winter?

Learning Goals

The goals of this activity are for students to learn to

- interpret data statements to critically evaluate a flawed model based on common preconceptions
- form an evidence-based critique of the flawed model
- revise a flawed model to construct a more scientifically accurate model that is consistent with the data statements they are asked to interpret

NGSS Reference

MS-ESS1-1

Develop and use a model of the Earth-Sun-Moon system to describe the cyclic patterns of lunar phases, eclipses of the Sun and Moon, and seasons.
    Clarification Statement: Examples of models can be physical, graphical, or conceptual.

This activity aims to develop students' understanding of how the changing orientation of the Earth to the Sun over the course of a 1-year revolution results in the changing seasons. In doing so, students will develop an evidence-based critique of a flawed model of the seasons and then construct a more scientifically sound model that improves upon the flawed model.

Science Background

FIGURE A.6.1   Orbital Plane of Earth About the Sun

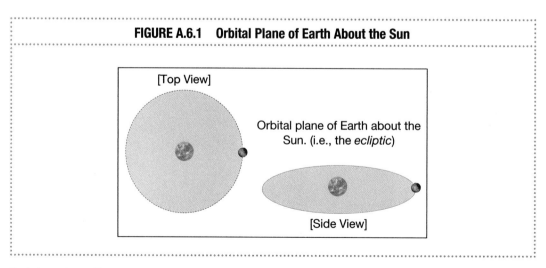

Earth: Image https://commons.wikimedia.org/w/index.php?title=Category:Lunar_phases&filefrom=East-Side-Phase-181.jpg#/media/File:East-Side-Phase-181.jpg; NASA Media Usage Guidelines http://www.nasa.gov/multimedia/guidelines/index.html

Sun: Image http://photojournal.jpl.nasa.gov/catalog/PIA03149; NASA Media Usage Guidelines http://www.nasa.gov/multimedia/guidelines/index.html

Content Knowledge

The Earth orbits the Sun in a plane called the *ecliptic* (Figure A.6.1). One complete cycle about the Sun is what we call a year on Earth. Earth's orbit about the Sun is nearly circular, meaning that at all points along Earth's orbit, the distance between Earth and the Sun is approximately the same. This means that Earth's distance to the Sun cannot explain the changing average temperatures that come with the different seasons. Indeed, in the Northern Hemisphere, we are actually 2 million miles further away from the Sun in summer compared to winter.

To account for the different seasons, we must recognize that Earth rotates about an axis, and if we were to draw an imaginary line that is perpendicular to the ecliptic plane, Earth's rotational axis is at approximately a 23.5-degree incline to this imaginary line. This is shown in Figure A.6.2. This means that at different points along Earth's orbit, different hemispheres receive more or less direct rays from the Sun. In winter in the Northern Hemisphere, the tilt of the Earth means that the rays from the Sun come in at a much more oblique angle. Hence, they are spread over a much larger area and warm the ground on which they fall less. The extreme example of this is the Arctic Circle, where no Sun falls in winter. In summer, in contrast, the tilt of the Earth means that the rays come in much more directly and are spread over a much smaller area, consequently warming the ground more. Note that in this explanation, the distance to the Sun is not a factor. Naturally, when one hemisphere of the Earth is experiencing summer (and tilted toward the Sun), the other hemisphere is experiencing winter (and tilted away from the Sun) and vice versa. Being tilted does not mean that you are nearer the Sun. The tilt makes no difference to the distance as the Sun is 93 million miles away.

FIGURE A.6.2 Orientation of Earth Relative to the Sun During Each Season

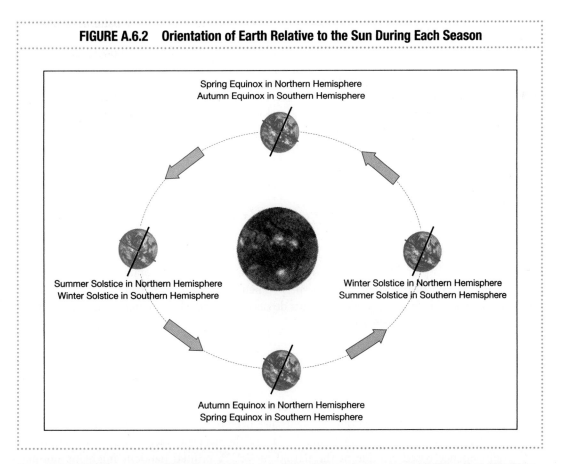

Knowledge for Teaching

Some common student preconceptions (also known as misconceptions) about seasons include the following:

- Summer is when the Earth is closest to the Sun and winter is when it is farthest from the Sun. This preconception implies that rather than a nearly circular orbit, the Earth revolves around the Sun in an *elliptical* orbit, where the distances between the Earth and the Sun noticeably differ over the course of a full orbit. There are several consequences to such a preconception:
  - If the Earth had a highly elliptical orbit, then when Earth was at its closest to the Sun, one hemisphere would experience a very hot summer, while the other hemisphere would experience a mild winter. In contrast, when Earth was at its furthest from the Sun 6 months later, the same hemisphere experiencing the very hot summer would now experience a very cold winter, while the hemisphere that experienced the mild winter would now experience a mild summer.
  - The hemisphere with the very hot summer and very cold winter would be much less conducive to growing plants than the hemisphere with the mild winter and mild summer.
  - Evidence showing summer/winter temperatures in each hemisphere and/or agriculture production in each hemisphere could help dispel the preconceptions about a highly elliptical orbit.
  - Also, the major evidence against this is measurement of the distance from the Sun. In summer, we are 93 million miles away, and in winter, we are closer, being only 91 million miles away.
- The Earth's tilt substantially changes over the course of the year, and that's what causes the different seasons.
  - Evidence against this is that while the Earth's axis does vary its tilt, it does so rather gradually over thousands of years.
  - Major changes in the Earth's tilt would result in Polaris (i.e., the "North Star") being at very different locations in the night sky over the course of a year.
  - Everywhere on Earth experiences the same seasons at the same time.
  - Evidence against this could be in the form of a data table with average temperatures in major cities in both the Northern and Southern Hemispheres.

Prior Knowledge for Students

Students need to know that the Earth orbits about the Sun in an orbital plane and that the Earth rotates about an axis. Students also need to know that the Earth can be divided into a *Northern Hemisphere* and a *Southern Hemisphere* and that the United States is located in the Northern Hemisphere. At this point, students do not need to know that Earth's rotational axis is tilted at approximately a 23.5-degree angle from the perpendicular to the ecliptic plane (i.e., the plane of Earth's orbit about the Sun). However, students do need to know what the mathematical concepts of *plane, perpendicular,* and *inclination* mean.

Teaching Sequence

Materials

- **Student handout and/or digital projector.** Students need to see the flawed model of the seasons that they are to critique. Students also need to see the data statements and accompanying organizers to help them make sense of the data statements and, ultimately, make an evidence-based critique of the flawed model. A printed handout might be optimal to distribute this information, especially as the students are asked to label on the flawed model what seasons would correspond to each of the Earth positions relative to the Sun. Scratch paper would also be helpful for students to write or draw down their ideas during periods of the activity when they are asked to make their considerations independently.

- **Poster paper and markers.** Students will be asked to form teams with the goal of creating an improved model of how different points in Earth's orbit about the Sun manifest in different seasons. For this part of the activity, some poster paper and markers would be helpful, especially as students will be sharing their models with the rest of the class.

Instructions for Activity

Instruct students to do the following:

- **(5 min)** Consider Jackson's model of how the Earth orbits about the Sun. Have students label on Jackson's model what season Jackson would claim it is in the *United States* for each of the four Earth orbital positions in his model. Have students do this individually.
- **(5 min)** Pose the following questions to the entire class: "Are the data consistent with Jackson's model? In other words, do the data fit the model? How?" After fielding student responses, project the following model response to the front of the room (tell students they will be expected to provide answers in a similar fashion later in the activity):

Data Statement	The Data Are Consistent With Jackson's Model Because . . .	The Data Are Inconsistent With Jackson's Model Because . . .
The Earth orbits about the Sun in a counterclockwise direction.	The arrows in Jackson's model indicate a counterclockwise orbit.	

- **(10 min)** Now have students consider the evidence statements. Instruct them to use the provided organizer to, *for each data statement,* explain whether or not that data statement is consistent with Jackson's model and how this is so.
- **(5 min)** Next, using the evidence-based argument organizer, have students refer to the previous organizer to form an evidence-based critique of Jackson's model. Have each student do this independently.
- **(5 min)** Following the evidence-based critique of Jackson's model, ask each student to individually consider what modifications would be necessary to construct a new model that is superior to Jackson's model. Specify to students that as they do so, they must consider how their proposed modifications are more consistent with the data statements they were presented. You may want to provide scratch paper.
- **(20 min)** Have students form teams (preferably two to four students per team), with the team goal of creating a model that is better than Jackson's model. Prior to the group work, model desired student comments and questions such as, "How do you think the model could be better?" We also recommend assigning students to roles such as the recorder and timekeeper. Tell students that they will engage in a fishbowl discussion. Make it clear that not only will students have to share their model with the rest of the class but that when they share, they will need to make explicit how their modifications of Jackson's model are more consistent with the data statements. There is an organizer for this part of the activity as well. Use a fishbowl structure for students to compare, contrast, and evaluate each other's models with the goal of developing the best class model possible. We recommend framing the discussion by saying, "The goal of the discussion is for us all to develop the best model we can together, which is similar to how scientists evaluate and build on each other's models." Either you or a student could record the class's model as it is constructed during the discussion. These are some suggested questions to ask students in the discussion:
    a. What are some similarities/differences among your models?
    b. Which model is the best? What is your reasoning for why it is the best model?
    c. What makes our model better than Jackson's model?

Student Activity: Why Is It Warmer in Summer and Cooler in Winter?

 An electronic copy of this activity is available on the companion website at https://resources.corwin.com/OsborneArgumentation.

Jackson believes that the seasons are caused by the Earth being at different distances from the Sun. Jackson claims that because average temperatures in the United States are higher during the summer than they are during the winter, the Earth must be closer to the Sun during the summer than during the winter. A depiction of Jackson's model is presented in Figure A.6.3.

Jackson's Model

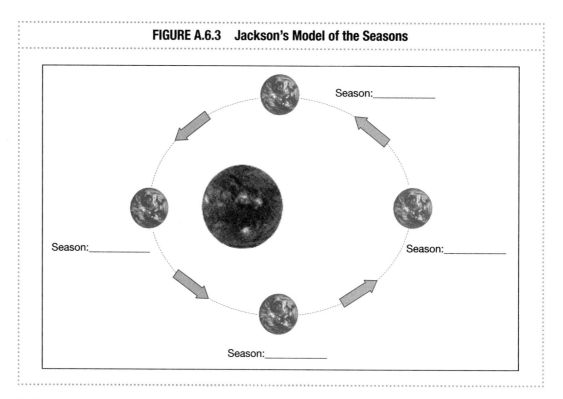

FIGURE A.6.3   Jackson's Model of the Seasons

Earth: Image https://commons.wikimedia.org/w/index.php?title=Category:Lunar_phases&filefrom=East-Side-Phase-181.jpg#/media/File:East-Side-Phase-181.jpg; NASA Media Usage Guidelines http://www.nasa.gov/multimedia/guidelines/index.html

Sun: Image http://photojournal.jpl.nasa.gov/catalog/PIA03149; NASA Media Usage Guidelines http://www.nasa.gov/multimedia/guidelines/index.html

On Jackson's model, label what season Jackson would claim it is in the United States for each of the four positions of the Earth.

In each row of the organizer provided below, consider a data statement and whether or not the data are consistent with Jackson's model. Don't just say whether or not they are consistent—say *how* the data are consistent or inconsistent with Jackson's model. Do this for all the data statements.

Data Statement	The Data Are Consistent With Jackson's Model Because . . .	The Data Are Inconsistent With Jackson's Model Because . . .
The Earth orbits about the Sun in a counterclockwise direction.		
Temperatures on Earth are higher when it is closer to the Sun than when it is further away from the Sun.		
When it is summer in the Northern Hemisphere, it is winter in the Southern Hemisphere.		
If you drew an imaginary line that was perpendicular to the plane of Earth's orbit about the Sun, the Earth's rotational axis is tilted at 23.5 degrees from this line.		
The tilt of the Earth remains nearly constant.		

Carefully look over your organizer above to provide an answer to the following question: *Is Jackson's model of the seasons completely correct?*

Your answer to this question is your claim. The data that helped you arrive at this claim are your evidence. Write down both your claim and your evidence in the following corresponding boxes.

CLAIM	REASONING	EVIDENCE

You will note that sandwiched between claim and evidence is reasoning. Reasoning serves as a "bridge" between your answer to a question (i.e., the claim) and the data that led you to that answer (i.e., the evidence). In your own words, write down in the Reasoning box above why your evidence led you to your claim.

Together, your claim, evidence, and reasoning form your evidence-based argument for why the Moon appears to have different phases.

Now, based on the evidence-based critique that you just made of Jackson's model, think about how you could make a model that is better than Jackson's. You might want to write or draw down some of your ideas.

You are now to work with a team to create a model that is better than Jackson's. Your team will need to draw out the model because you will be sharing your model with the rest of the class. When you share with the rest of the class, you will need to

1. **Explain** each of the ways your model **differs** from Jackson's model.

2. **Explain** how each of the ways in which your model is different **is more consistent with the data statements you considered earlier.**

Here is another organizer to help your team prepare your presentation for how your new and improved model is more consistent with the data statements than Jackson's model.

Ways Your Model Differs From Jackson's Model	How Is Your Modification More Consistent With the Data Statements?

Suggested Responses

Beneath are an indication of the possible responses to this activity that would demonstrate a good understanding of the science.

Data Statement	The Data Are Consistent With Jackson's Model Because . . .	The Data Are Inconsistent With Jackson's Model Because . . .
The Earth orbits about the Sun in a counterclockwise direction.	The arrows in Jackson's model indicate a counterclockwise orbit.	
Temperatures are higher closer to the Sun than they are farther away from the Sun.	Summer in Jackson's model was when the Earth was closest to the Sun. This makes sense because summer is when it is hottest.	
When it is summer in the Northern Hemisphere, it is winter in the Southern Hemisphere.		In Jackson's model, it looks like the entire Earth experiences the same season at the same time.
If you drew an imaginary line that was perpendicular to the plane of Earth's orbit about the Sun, the Earth's rotational axis is tilted at 23.5 degrees from this line.		Jackson's model does not account for the fact that the axis around which the Earth rotates is inclined.
The tilt of the Earth remains nearly constant.		Jackson's model does not mention this or explain what effect it might have.

CLAIM	REASONING	EVIDENCE
Jackson's model is *not* completely correct!	In Jackson's model, it looks like the entire Earth experiences the same season at the same time. Jackson's model does not account for Earth's rotational axis, let alone if the axis is inclined to the orbital plane.	When it is summer in the Northern Hemisphere, it is winter in the Southern Hemisphere. If you drew an imaginary line that was perpendicular to the plane of Earth's orbit about the Sun, the Earth's rotational axis is tilted at 23.5 degrees from this line. The tilt of the Earth remains nearly constant.

(clipart.com)

Ways Your Model Differs From Jackson's Model	How Is Your Modification More Consistent With the Data Statements?
Our model has a line that represents Earth's axis of rotation. We tilted our line.	Jackson's model doesn't show where Earth's axis of rotation is. Our model does and is consistent with the data statement that the axis is tilted.
The tilt of our line is the same for all the different positions of the Earth.	This is consistent with the data statement that the tilt of Earth's axis stays the same.
Because we tilt the Earth in our model, the Northern and Southern Hemispheres face the sun at different times.	This is consistent with the data statement that when it is summer in the Northern Hemisphere, it is winter in the Southern Hemisphere.

Figure A.6.4 presents an example of what an improvement over Jackson's model would look like.

FIGURE A.6.4   Improved Version of Jackson's Model

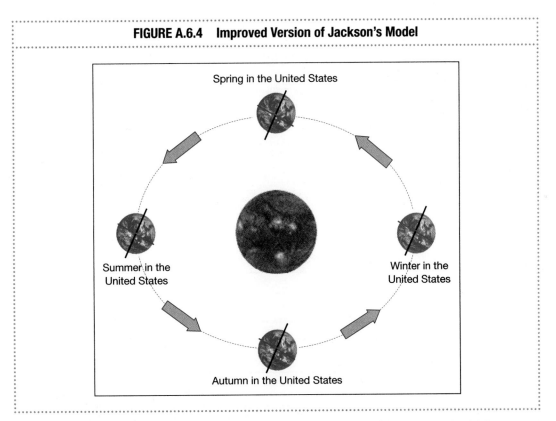

Earth: Image https://commons.wikimedia.org/w/index.php?title=Category:Lunar_phases&filefrom=East-Side-Phase-181.jpg#/media/File:East-Side-Phase-181.jpg; NASA Media Usage Guidelines http://www.nasa.gov/multimedia/guidelines/index.html

Sun: Image http://photojournal.jpl.nasa.gov/catalog/PIA03149; NASA Media Usage Guidelines http://www.nasa.gov/multimedia/guidelines/index.html

Additional Resources

The following video demonstrates how misconceptions about the seasons are prevalent, even for graduates of an elite institution like Harvard University: https://www.youtube.com/watch?v=p0wk4qG2mlg.

Extension Activities

Some of the student teams may properly account for Earth's tilted axis but may still have Earth at different distances from the Sun at different points in its orbit about the Sun. If this is so, present the following additional data statement:

- At all points along Earth's orbit, the distance between Earth and the Sun is approximately the same.

- Ask students to modify their models given this new piece of data. Then pose the following question for class discussion:

- If Earth's distance from the Sun remains nearly the same, how can you use your model to explain why it is usually a lot hotter in the United States in the summer than it is in the winter?

Notes

_____

_____

_____

_____

_____

_____

_____

_____

_____

_____

How Big and Far Away Are the Planets?

Learning Goals

The goals of this activity are for students to learn to

- interpret a data table about the solar system
- critically evaluate a flawed diagram of the solar system based on common preconceptions
- draw evidence from empirical data to construct a critique as to how the diagram under consideration is flawed
- recognize that a good argument uses evidence to justify claims through reasoning

NGSS Reference

MS-ESS1-3

Analyze and interpret data to determine scale properties of objects in the solar system.

   Clarification Statement: Emphasis is on the analysis of data from Earth-based instruments, space-based telescopes, and spacecraft to determine similarities and differences among solar system objects. Examples of scale properties include the sizes of an object's layers (such as crust and atmosphere), surface features (such as volcanoes), and orbital radius. Examples of data include statistical information, drawings and photographs, and models.

   Assessment Boundary: Assessment does not include recalling facts about properties of the planets and other solar system bodies.

This activity seeks to promote the practice of critique, by getting students to identify inconsistencies between a flawed diagram of the solar system and data obtained by scientists. Students will use the inconsistencies they identify to construct an argument for why the model is flawed.

Science Background

Content Knowledge

All of the planets of the solar system have orbital planes that do not deviate any more than approximately 6 degrees of inclination from the *invariable plane*, which, for simplicity, can be thought of as a flat plane that bisects the Sun (Figure A.7.1). The inclination of Earth's orbital plane about the Sun is only about 1 degree from the invariable plane. So, for simplicity, the motions of all the solar system planets about the Sun can be thought to orbit about roughly the same plane. While the orbital planes of each solar system planet are roughly the same, the distances between each planet are not equally spaced intervals. Nor are the sizes of the planets the same.

FIGURE A.7.1   The Invariable Plane of Planetary Orbits About the Sun

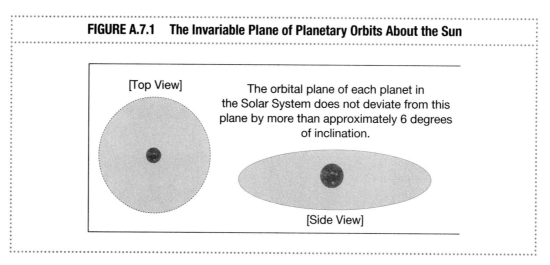

Sun: Image http://photojournal.jpl.nasa.gov/catalog/PIA03149; NASA Media Usage Guidelines http://www.nasa.gov/multimedia/guidelines/index.html

Knowledge for Teaching

Depictions of the solar system, such as those found in many textbooks, can be misleading. For example, some depictions of the solar system, such as the flawed model you will ask your students to critique, have the planets orbiting the Sun in equally spaced intervals. The planetary data table your students will be investigating includes a column about orbital periods that is not necessary to critique the proposed model. This column is included as a lesson that not all data are necessarily evidence to be incorporated into an argument.

However, keen students could use the orbital period data as additional evidence against the proposed diagram. For example, if they make the approximation that each planet orbits the Sun in a circle (in reality, most orbits are slightly elliptical, but a circular orbit is a reasonable estimate), then given that the circumference of a circle (= $2\pi r$) is proportional to the radius of the circle, they might argue that, if the proposed diagram of the solar system was correct (i.e., that the distance between each planet is the same), then the difference between orbital periods should be the same for each planet as well. This argument is not the entire picture, however, as orbital period (i.e., the time it takes for a planet to make one orbit) is actually the orbital circumference (i.e., the distance traveled in one orbit) divided by the orbital velocity (i.e., the orbital distance traveled per unit of time). The orbital velocity has a more complicated relationship to the orbital radius than the orbital circumference does, even if the distances between planets were equally spaced, so the orbital period data would not be equally spaced.

Prior Knowledge for Students

To correctly make sense of the data table, students need to know the difference in magnitude between a *million* (1,000,000 or 10^6) and a *billion* (1,000,000 or 10^9, which is 1,000 million). For example, when they see that the average distance from Uranus to the Sun is 1.79 billion miles, they need to understand this is 1,790,000,000 miles, or 1,790 million miles. Students do not need to know how orbital period relates to orbital circumference, but if they choose to pursue this line of thought, review the Content Knowledge for Teaching section.

Teaching Sequence

Materials

- **Student handout and/or digital projector.** Students need to see the solar system model and the planetary data table on page 98, either via a handout or through projection to the front of the classroom.

Instructions for Activity

- **(2 min)** Introduce the activity. Put students into groups of two. Tell students that the task for each group will be to carefully examine both a diagram of the solar system and a table with actual data for each of the eight planets in our solar system.
- **(3 min)** Either project or distribute handouts of both the solar system diagram and the planetary data table found in the student activity.
- **(45 min)** Commence the student activity by asking students to follow the steps detailed in the activity. Have students spend about 30 minutes investigating the data and about 15 minutes formulating their argument. Organizers are provided for each.

Student Activity: How Big and Far Away Are the Planets?

 An electronic copy of this activity is available on the companion website at https://resources.corwin.com/OsborneArgumentation.

Consider the diagram of the solar system presented in Figure A.7.2.

FIGURE A.7.2   Diagram of the Solar System

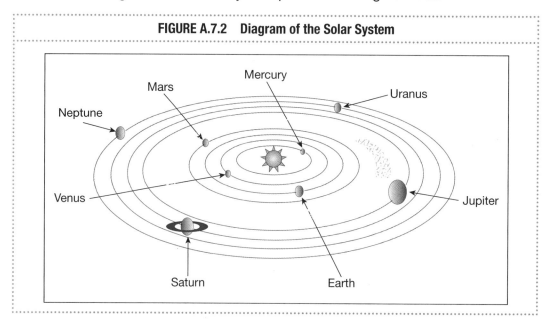

Source: Modified for this publication with permission from the copyright holder. © 2009 by The Regents of the University of California.

Now consider the following planetary data table.

Planet	Orbital Period	Diameter of Planet (at Equator)	Average Distance From Sun
Mercury	88 days	4,878 km (3,031 miles)	57 million km (35 million miles)
Venus	225 days	12,104 km (7,521 miles)	108 million km (67 million miles)
Earth	365 days (i.e., 1 year)	12,756 km (7,926 miles)	150 million km (93 million miles)
Mars	687 days	6,787 km (4,217 miles)	228 million km (142 million miles)
Jupiter	4,333 days	142,800 km (88,732 miles)	779 million km (484 million miles)
Saturn	10,756 days	120,000 km (74,565 miles)	1.43 billion km (889 million miles)
Uranus	30,687 days	51,200 km (31,814 miles)	2.88 billion km (1.79 billion miles)
Neptune	60,190 days	48,600 km (30,199 miles)	4.50 billion km (2.8 billion miles)

Your job is to list the features of the model that are consistent or inconsistent with the planetary data table.

The following organizer can help you organize your comparisons:

Data Pattern	Consistent With Model?	Not Consistent With Model?

Now, looking at your organizer and the planetary data table, provide an answer to the following question: *Is the model of the solar system that you considered a correct mod el?*

Your answer to this question is your claim. The data that helped you arrive at this claim are your evidence. Write down both your claim and your evidence in the following corresponding boxes.

CLAIM	REASONING	EVIDENCE

You will note that sandwiched between claim and evidence is reasoning. Reasoning serves as a "bridge" between your answer to a question (i.e., the claim) and the data that led you to that answer (i.e., the evidence). In your own words, write down in the Reasoning box above why your evidence led you to your claim.

Together, your claim, evidence, and reasoning form your evidence-based argument for whether or not the model of the solar system that you considered is correct.

Suggested Responses

Beneath are an indication of the possible responses to this activity that would demonstrate a good understanding of the science.

Data Pattern	Consistent With Model?	Not Consistent With Model?
Based on the planetary data table, planet diameters are different.	Many of the planets in the model appear to have different sizes, but not all, as the planetary data table suggests.	Based on the model, Uranus should be around four times the size of the Earth, but in the model, Uranus and Earth look to be roughly the same size.
Jupiter's diameter is way bigger than the Earth's diameter.	Jupiter is drawn much bigger than Earth in the model.	
The distances between planets do not appear to be the same.		The distances between the planets in the model appear to be spaced equally.
Distances from the Sun are reported as averages.		The orbits are circles in the model, meaning the distance of each planet from the Sun would always be the same—no need to average!

CLAIM	REASONING	EVIDENCE
The model of the solar system is flawed!	The distances between the planets in the model appear to be spaced equally, but this is not consistent with the evidence from the planetary data table.	The distances between planets do not appear to be the same in the planetary data table. For example, the distance between the Earth and Venus is about 42 million km, but the distance between Earth and Mars is 78 million km.

Extension Activities

Based on the organizer that students filled out, which points out both consistencies and inconsistencies between the planetary data table and the proposed model of the solar system, ask students (preferably in their same groups of two) to discuss what a better model (based on the data) of the solar system would look like. After the discussion, have each group sketch a possible better model. Then have each group share their model with the class, pointing out the features that make it an improvement upon the previous model they considered and making explicit references to the data table to highlight why their sketched model is better.

To emphasize the scale of the solar system on a deeper level, perhaps provide students an aerial map of a nearby city that students are familiar with. Ask students to, assuming the size of the city is the same size as the solar system, draw the orbits of the solar system planets over the map. You will likely have to demonstrate on the board how to scale down the average distance from the Sun values in the planetary data table. For example, you could measure the distance from the center of the city map to the periphery of the map and let this distance represent the distance from the Sun to Neptune. The scaling would then be 4.5 billion km (2.8 billion miles) divided by the number of meters or inches you measure from the center to the periphery of the map. Figure A.7.3 is an example using an aerial view of the city of Chicago, Illinois.

FIGURE A.7.3   Aerial View of Chicago

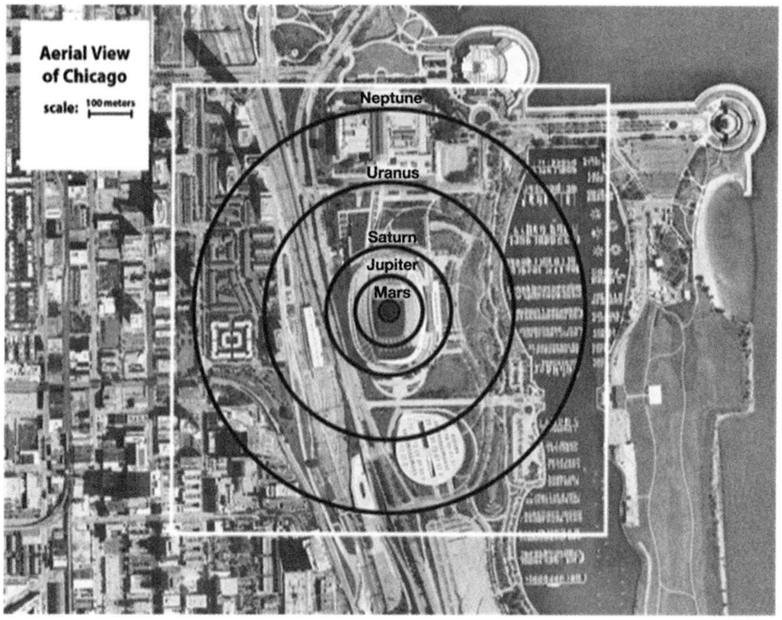

Source: *Seeds of Science/Roots of Reading: Planets and Moons.* © 2014 by The Regents of the University of California. Original image from U.S. Geological Survey and adapted by The Regents of the University of California.

Notes

_____

_____

_____

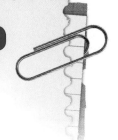

Why Do Planets Orbit the Sun?

Learning Goals

The goals of this activity are for students to learn to

- record observational data and make calculations from a simple investigation
- draw evidence from recorded data to construct an argument for the relationship between the distance between planets and their gravitational attraction
- extend this argument and make an additional argument for how the gravitational pull of the Sun affects the various orbits of the solar system

NGSS Reference

MS-ESS1-2

Develop and use a model to describe the role of gravity in the motions within galaxies and the solar system.

   Clarification Statement: Emphasis for the model is on gravity as the force that holds together the solar system and Milky Way galaxy and controls orbital motions within them. Examples of models can be physical (such as the analogy of distance along a football field or computer visualizations of elliptical orbits) or conceptual (such as mathematical proportions relative to the size of familiar objects such as students' school or state).

   Assessment Boundary: Assessment does not include Kepler's laws of orbital motion or the apparent retrograde motion of the planets as viewed from Earth.

This activity encourages students to use evidence-based argumentation to explore how gravity affects planetary orbits. Students are asked to gather evidence from a simple investigation and learn how to construct a scientific argument based on that evidence.

Science Background

Content Knowledge

Gravity plays a key role in the motions of planets about the Sun in our solar system. For simplicity, it is a reasonable approximation that planets orbit the Sun in an approximately circular motion. For objects to move in a circle, there must be a *force* that acts on the object in a direction toward the center of the circle. This is called a *centripetal* force. In the case of the solar system, think of the Sun as the center of each planetary orbit, where the gravitational tug on each planet by the Sun provides the centripetal force necessary for the planets to remain in circular orbits (note that the Sun's gravitational pull and centripetal force are not different things—**the gravitational pull of the Sun is the centripetal force** in the case of planetary orbits). (See Figure A.8.1.) If the centripetal force due to the Sun's gravitational pull was suddenly eliminated, planets would no longer orbit the Sun but rather would fly off into space in a direction that is tangential to their orbital motion at the moment the planet no longer felt the tug of the Sun's gravity.

FIGURE A.8.1   Direction of Gravitational Tug on Earth by the Sun

The gravitational tug on the Earth by the Sun, which acts toward the Sun and hence toward the center of Earth's orbit about the Sun, provides the centripetal force necessary for Earth to maintain an approximately circular orbit.

Earth: Image https://commons.wikimedia.org/w/index.php?title=Category:Lunar_phases&filefrom=East-Side-Phase-181.jpg#/media/File:East-Side-Phase-181.jpg; NASA Media Usage Guidelines http://www.nasa.gov/multimedia/guidelines/index.html

Sun: Image http://photojournal.jpl.nasa.gov/catalog/PIA03149; NASA Media Usage Guidelines http://www.nasa.gov/multimedia/guidelines/index.html

Knowledge for Teaching

Some student preconceptions (also known as misconceptions) about the relationship between gravity and orbits may include the following:

- There is no gravity in space, as evidenced by astronauts appearing to float in space.
- Gravity acts parallel to the direction of orbit (this is a consequence of the common preconception that if an object is in motion, forces must be acting on the object in the direction of its motion).
- Gravity depends on mass, but there is no mass in space, because things are weightless.
- What keeps an object in orbit is a "centrifugal" force that pulls outward to counter the inward force of gravity. We experience this on a merry-go-round, where when the merry-go-round speeds up, it feels more and more like there is a force trying to "throw us off." In reality, this sensation doesn't come from an increasing "centrifugal" force outward but rather from the *need for a larger centripetal force inward.* The consequence is that we have to exert a stronger force to hold on and provide the inward force. As it speeds up even more, the force required is even larger and we feel as if we are being pulled out because of the size of the force we have to provide to pull us in and keeping us going round.
- If objects do not touch, they do not exert forces on each other.

Prior Knowledge for Students

Students need to have at least been introduced to the concept of gravity. They need to know that gravity is an attractive force, occurs between any physical bodies that have mass, is proportional to the masses involved in the gravitational attraction, and is inversely proportional to the square of the distances between the masses (students don't necessarily need to know that it is an inverse square relationship but at least that the gravitational attraction between masses becomes weaker and weaker as those masses move farther and farther apart). There are some simple calculations required in this activity, which the students will be carefully walked through. That said, students should have a basic understanding of the concepts of measurement error, averaging, circumference, and velocity.

Teaching Sequence

Frame the activity as building on the students' background knowledge of how the masses of planets are related to their gravitational attraction (and/or elicit this background knowledge). In this activity, we will use a swinging mass to represent a planet, our hand to represent the Sun, and the rope to represent the distance between the orbiting planet and the Sun. Our goal is to determine the relationships between

- the distance between the planets and the Sun,
- the velocity the planets move around the Sun, and
- the distance the planets travel in one complete orbit around the Sun.

Materials

- One rope or heavy string
- Two small masses that can be tied to the ends of the rope/string (e.g., hanging weights, metal washers, rubber stoppers). The exact mass amount that will be tied to each end of the string isn't as important as making sure the masses won't break the rope/string when the masses are spun in a circle by the rope/string.
- One stopwatch/timer
- One tape measure/ruler that can measure in centimeters
- Simple calculators for each student
- Large pieces of paper and markers for each group of students
- Sticky notes of two different colors for each student

Instructions for Activity

This activity includes a hands-on investigation in hopes that since students obtain and record actual data, they might take more ownership when asked to analyze the data later in the activity. However, the main focus of this activity is evidence-based argumentation, so do your best to ensure that the ratio of the time spent on the investigation to the time spent on argumentation is in accordance with the suggested timings below. If you find that the hands-on investigation takes longer than estimated, you might want to forgo the investigation in future classes in favor of a premade data table that you distribute to students.

Instruct students to do the following:

- **(15 min)** Two volunteers are needed to go into the "fishbowl" and perform an investigation to obtain data that will be recorded and used by the rest of the class (using the fishbowl technique here as opposed to having many groups run the investigation will make the data consistent and free up more time for the more important part of the activity, which is to critically evaluate the data obtained by the investigation). Have one student put on eyeglasses and volunteer to swing a rope with masses tied to both ends (Figure A.8.2).
- Have the other volunteer take the role of the measurer and timekeeper.
- Have the rest of the class take the role of the data keepers—each student needs to fill out his or her own data table based on the results of the investigation in the fishbowl.
- For each of three different "orbital radii," students in the fishbowl will twirl the mass at one end of the rope *just fast enough* so that it makes a circular motion with no slack in the rope. The "orbital radius" is the measured distance from a mass at one end of the rope to where the rope swinger will place his or her hand.

FIGURE A.8.2 Cartoon Sketch of Student Activity

Source: © David R. Dudley, Illustrator.

- The "orbits" happen quickly, so for each trial (two trials per orbital radius—trials will be averaged to account for measurement error), have the rope swinger complete 10 "orbits." The timekeeper will time how long it takes to make these 10 full circles, and then the class as a whole will divide that total time by 10 and enter in the appropriate box on their data table.
- As the investigation is performed by the volunteers in the middle of the fishbowl, make sure that each student outside the fishbowl is also recording the same data in his or her own data table.
- After obtaining data for both trials for each of three different orbital radii, make sure each student averages correctly over the trials and enters these averages in his or her individual data table.
- At this point, you may want to project a filled-out data table to ensure all students proceed with the same data.
- **(35 min)** With their data recorded from the swinging mass investigation: Have students perform calculations individually and record their calculations in the appropriate section of their data table.
- For the analysis question, students may need more specific prompts such as, "What is the relationship between orbital radius and orbital period?" and "What is the relationship between orbital radius and orbital speed?"
- Put students in groups of two to four. Assign students group roles and have students write their arguments on large pieces of paper to receive feedback from their peers using a Gallery Walk structure.
- We suggest that one sticky note color be used for "warm" (positive) feedback and the other color of sticky note be used for cool (i.e., critical and constructive) feedback. Here are some suggested sentence starters:
  - Warm feedback:
    - Your claim/evidence/reasoning is clear because. . . .
    - Your claim/evidence/reasoning is accurate because. . . .
  - Cool feedback:
    - Your claim/evidence/reasoning is unclear because. . . .
    - Your claim/evidence/reasoning is inaccurate because. . . .
    - To make your claim/evidence/reasoning more clear/accurate, I suggest. . . .
  - Have students read their peers' feedback and revise their arguments.

Student Activity: Why Do Planets Orbit the Sun?

 An electronic copy of this activity is available on the companion website at https://resources.corwin.com/OsborneArgumentation.

Record the data obtained by the volunteers in the center of the fishbowl here:

Orbital Radius (Length From Hand to Orbiting Mass)	Orbital Period (Time Required to Make One Complete Orbit)			Average Orbital Speed [(2)(π)(Orbital Radius)] / [Average Orbital Period]
	Trial 1	Trial 2	Average Orbital Period [Trial 1 + Trial 2] / [2]	
15 cm				
30 cm				
60 cm				

Since there can be measurement error from one trial to the next, we averaged the orbital period times over two trials for each of the three different orbital radii. Use this average orbital period—the second to last column from the right of your table—in your calculations that will be guided below.

To calculate the average orbital period for each of the three different orbital radii, simply add the times for each of the two trials, and then divide that number by 2. In other words, the average orbital period is

[Orbital Period for Trial 1 + Orbital Period for Trial 2] / [2].

The total distance traveled in one circular orbit (i.e., the circumference of the orbit) is $2\pi r$, where r is the orbital radius.

To get the average speed at which an object travels about its orbit, we divide the distance by the time. In this case, the total distance traveled in one orbit is the orbit circumference ($2\pi r$), and the time it took to travel that distance was the average orbital period (which you recorded data for).

This means that the average orbital velocity is

[(2)(π)(Orbital Radius)] / [Average Orbital Period].

Make this calculation for each of three different orbital radii (i.e., each row of your data table) and enter your calculations into the final column on the right. Your data table for this assignment is now complete. You will need it for the remainder of this activity.

1. In your own words, explain what "orbital speed" means:

2. Analyze the data by describing any patterns that you notice:

Let's now build upon our investigation to develop a model of how gravity affects the motion of planets about the Sun in our solar system.

Now consider the following planetary data table:

Planet	Orbital Period	Average Distance From Sun	Orbital Speed Relative to Earth's Orbital Speed[a]
Mercury	88 days	57 million km (35 million miles)	1.607
Venus	225 days	108 million km (67 million miles)	1.174
Earth	365 days	150 million km (93 million miles)	1.000
Mars	687 days	228 million km (142 million miles)	0.802
Jupiter	4,333 days	779 million km (484 million miles)	0.434
Saturn	10,756 days	1.43 billion km (889 million miles)	0.323
Uranus	30,687 days	2.88 billion km (1.79 billion miles)	0.228
Neptune	60,190 days	4.50 billion km (2.8 billion miles)	0.182

[a]In the far-right column, the orbital velocities about the Sun for each planet are expressed as a fraction of the Earth's orbital velocity about the Sun. For example, Mercury has an orbital velocity that is 1.607 (i.e., 160.7%) times as fast as Earth's orbital velocity, while Neptune has an orbital velocity that is only 0.182 (i.e., 18.2%) times as fast as Earth's orbital velocity.

Thinking back to the investigation we just conducted with the swinging mass, let's pretend the swinging mass represents an orbiting planet, the student hand represents the Sun, and the length of rope between orbiting mass and hand represents the orbital radius.

Now, look at the data you recorded at the beginning of this activity and the planetary data table to provide an answer to the following question: *Are there similarities between your data and the planetary data table? If so, what are they?*

Your answer to this question is your claim. The data that helped you arrive at this claim are your evidence. Write down both your claim and your evidence in the following corresponding boxes.

CLAIM	REASONING	EVIDENCE

You will note that sandwiched between claim and evidence is reasoning. Reasoning serves as a "bridge" between your answer to a question (i.e., the claim) and the data that led you to that answer (i.e., the evidence). In your own words, write down in the Reasoning box above why your evidence led you to your claim.

Together, your claim, evidence, and reasoning form your evidence-based argument for why the Moon appears to have different phases.

Of course, rope is not what causes planets to orbit around the Sun—that's the job of gravity. Let's pretend that the tension in the rope between the orbiting mass (i.e., the "planet") and the hand (i.e., the "Sun") represents the force of gravity between the Sun and the orbiting planet.

Gravity is an attractive force between any objects that have mass, such as the Sun and the planets. Solar system planets maintain their orbit about the Sun because of the gravitational tug of the Sun on these planets, not unlike how the mass in the investigation maintained its orbit because of the tug due to the string.

In both cases—the investigation we conducted and the orbit of planets about the Sun—the tug that keeps the orbiting objects in motion acts on the object in a direction pointing toward the *center* of the orbital motion. The faster an object is orbiting, the stronger the inward force needs to be to maintain the orbit. This force that maintains the orbit and points toward the center of the orbit is called the centripetal force. The slower an object is orbiting, the weaker the centripetal force needs to be to maintain the orbit.

So, if gravity is the centripetal force for solar system planets to maintain their orbits about the Sun, draw upon both the data you recorded at the beginning of this activity and the planetary data table to provide an answer to the following question: *Is there a relationship between the strength of the gravitational pull of the Sun on an orbiting planet and the distance between that planet and the Sun?*

Once again, use the claim-reasoning-evidence framework to answer the question above.

CLAIM	REASONING	EVIDENCE

Suggested Responses

Beneath are an indication of the possible responses to this activity that would demonstrate a good understanding of the science.

CLAIM	REASONING	EVIDENCE
Yes! There are similarities!	The relationship between orbital speed and orbital radius has a similar pattern in both data tables.	When the length of the rope was increased, the average orbital speed decreased. In the planetary data table, when the planet is farther from the Sun, the orbital speed is less.
	The relationship between orbital period and orbital radius has a similar pattern in both data tables.	When the period of the orbiting mass was greater, the average orbital speed was less. In the planetary data table, when the period of orbit gets longer and longer, the orbital speed is less and less.

CLAIM	REASONING	EVIDENCE
There is a relationship. As planets are farther and farther away from the Sun, the gravitational pull they feel from the Sun is less and less.	Our evidence shows that objects orbiting at greater distances away have less orbital velocity. We were told that when the orbital velocity gets less, that means the centripetal force must be less. Since we were told that gravity provides the centripetal force, that must mean that the tug of gravity on an orbiting object is less for objects orbiting at greater distances.	In both our investigation and in the planetary data table, the greater the distance at which things orbit, the smaller their orbital velocity.

111

Extension Activities

As this activity concludes with the notion of gravity leaving its mark on how the planets of the solar system move through space, this could be a nice opportunity to throw students a possible curveball that could lead to a rich discussion. Pose the following question:

> We have just considered how gravity affects all these different planets in space. So is there gravity in space? If so, why do astronauts appear to float when they are in a ship or space station?

One way to explain this to students is that the astronaut is actually in orbit about the Earth, where the gravitational pull on the astronaut toward the Earth (yes, there is gravity in space!) actually means the astronaut is falling, but since they are moving so fast about the Earth (objects must reach velocities of at least 17,500 km/hr [28,160 km/hr] to orbit the Earth), the Earth curves away beneath them before they can get any closer to it. You can tell the same story for the ship/station the astronaut is in, so students can think of the feet of the astronaut never being able to "catch" the floor of the ship/station—both feet and floor are both falling toward Earth at the same rate.

CHAPTER 5

Life Sciences

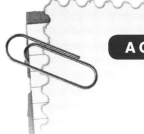

Why Do Leaves Have Different Shapes?

Learning Goals

The goals of this activity are for students to learn to

- analyze and interpret data about trees, leaves, and sunlight
- use evidence to justify claims
- recognize that a good argument uses evidence to justify claims and that to oppose counterclaims to your argument, you need to rely on evidence rather than assertions

NGSS Reference

MS-LS1-5

Construct a scientific explanation based on evidence for how environmental and genetic factors influence the growth of organisms.

Clarification Statement: Examples of local environmental conditions could include availability of food, light, space, and water. Examples of genetic factors could include large-breed cattle and species of grass affecting growth of organisms. Examples of evidence could include drought decreasing plant growth, fertilizer increasing plant growth, different varieties of plant seeds growing at different rates in different conditions, and fish growing larger in large ponds than they do in small ponds.

Assessment Boundary: Assessment does not include genetic mechanisms, gene regulation, or biochemical processes.

In this activity, students generate an argument about why leaves on different parts of an oak tree have different shapes. Then, they compare two hypothetical arguments for the differences in shape and decide which they agree with more and what the problem is with the alternative.

Science Background

Content Knowledge

Leaves of particular tree species vary in shape and size based on a number of factors. One of these factors is their position on a tree. Furthermore, there are many different mechanisms to explain *why* the leaves vary. Key to this activity is the idea that environmental and genetic factors influence the growth of leaves. Leaves are the photosynthesizing parts of plants. Only leaves contain chlorophyll, which is a molecule capable of capturing light energy and harnessing it into chemical energy (glucose) via the process of photosynthesis. Thus, natural selection acts upon genes, which affect the rate of photosynthesis in plants. Plants that maximize the photosynthetic rate are more likely to survive and pass on their genes. Larger leaves have more surface area to capture sunlight. Thus, more photosynthesis can occur in larger leaves.

But there is a trade-off, because as leaves get larger, they have the potential to lose more water to the air through the process of transpiration. Plants need water, both to maintain leaf structure and to be a reactant in photosynthesis. Plants use the process of transpiration to move water from the soil, through the roots, through the stem, and into leaves. Water evaporates and diffuses through stomates in the underside of leaves, leaving empty space behind, and water moves in to fill the space. Larger leaves have more stomates. Thus, larger leaves lose more water to transpiration, especially when the leaves are exposed to sunlight.

Scientists use the designations *sun leaves* and *shade leaves* to distinguish between leaves that differ in physiology, based on their exposure to sunlight. Sun leaves are generally smaller and narrower but have a thicker cross section. Since these leaves receive maximum sunlight (they are found at the crown of trees), a larger surface area is not necessarily more beneficial for photosynthesis, because all the surface area is being maximized. However, their smaller, narrower shape means that they lose less water via transpiration than they would if they were very broad. Shade leaves, on the other hand, are found in shadier areas on the tree (e.g., closer to the forest floor). A broader shape means that there is a greater chance that sunlight will reach the surface of the leaf. Furthermore, these leaves are in the shade; thus, loss of water due to transpiration is not significant. The mechanism by which plants achieve differential leaf morphology is that plants contain genes that "turn on" (i.e., they are expressed) when they are in the sun and "turn off" when they are in the shade and vice versa. When a gene creates a different phenotype in different environments, scientists call it an example of a gene-environment interaction.

Why is the explanation for why leaves are different shapes arguable? There are many processes at play in the growth and development of trees and leaves—it is evolutionarily favorable for plants to maximize the photosynthetic rate and minimize water loss, but the degree to which each of these processes drives gene expression is variable. Furthermore, maximizing surface area for sunlight is not the most intuitive explanation for variation in leaf size. Furthermore, there are likely lots of more intuitive (but flawed) ideas that might explain the difference. In this activity, the hypothetical student Andrew offers the idea that nutrients pool in the lower leaves, making them bigger—a simpler (and thus intuitively attractive) idea but ultimately not supported by empirical data.

Knowledge for Teaching

As with all questions that ask students to explain "why" in biology, the teacher should keep in mind that students tend to default to presenting a "just-so story" for variation in physical traits. Such "just-so" stories, also known as "teleological explanations" (Tamir & Zohar, 1991), present explanations as, "The plant 'needed' to get more sun so it made its leaves on the bottom bigger." It is a subtle distinction, but more biologically accurate, to reshape the explanation into, "Larger, broader leaves are more successful at capturing light. Thus, the leaves on the bottom of the plant, where there is less available light, tend to be larger and broader."

Prior Knowledge for Students

Plants require light, water, and nutrients to grow.

Teaching Sequence
Materials

    Group whiteboards or chart paper
    Copies of student activity
    Samples of sun and shade leaves (optional)

Instructions for Activity

- **(5 min)** Introduce the perplexing phenomenon: The leaves on the same oak tree differ in size and shape.
- Options for introducing the phenomenon include looking at the illustration on page 1 of the student activity, looking at photographs from the web (e.g., http://bioimages.vanderbilt.edu/metadata.htm?/19290/metadata/sp), or observing samples collected from nature.

- **(15 min)** Break students into groups of four. Each group receives a whiteboard. In groups, students should
    - read the introduction, observe the illustration, and brainstorm ideas together about their initial explanations;
    - use an active reading strategy to obtain information from the two background information paragraphs ("Photosynthesis" and "Transpiration"); and
    - analyze the data tables and write a summary sentence below each table.
- On the group whiteboard, construct a scientific argument about why the leaves are different shapes. The argument should have a claim, evidence from the tables, and reasoning (which should include science concepts included in the background information).
- **(20 min)** Facilitate a share-out, in which each group presents their argument and other groups are given time to ask clarifying questions and offer critiques of the claim, evidence, or reasoning.
- Project the arguments of two hypothetical students ("Andrew" and "Michael") below.

Andrew says:	Michael says:
The leaves on the bottom are larger because they get more nutrients.	The leaves on the bottom are larger because there is less sunlight there.
Leaves near the bottom of the crown are much closer to the roots, where the nutrients enter the plant.	Leaves near the bottom of the crown only get about 10% of the light that the leaves at the top get.
It is hard for nutrients to travel from the bottom of the tree to the top of the tree, so they stay in the lower leaves and make them bigger.	If there is less sunlight available at the bottom of tree, the leaves need more surface area to capture the light.

- **(5 min)** Class discussion:
    - What is the problem with Andrew's argument? Michael's argument?
    - How would you improve the two arguments?
    - Which additional data would you need to settle the argument?

Student Activity: Why Do Leaves Have Different Shapes?

 An electronic copy of this activity is available on the companion website at https://resources.corwin.com/OsborneArgumentation.

The leaves of the White Oak tree (*Quercus alba*) differ in shape depending on where on the tree they are located (Figure A.9.1). The leaves at the top and the bottom are about the same length and width, but notice how the leaves at the bottom have much more surface area. Because they have more surface area, the leaves at the bottom of the tree are larger than the leaves found at the top of the tree.

FIGURE A.9.1   Difference in Shape Between Leaves on the Top and Bottom of the White

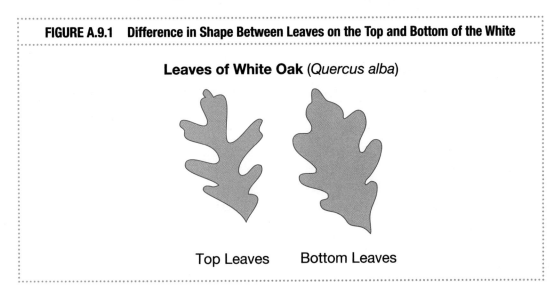

Leaves of White Oak (*Quercus alba*)

Top Leaves   Bottom Leaves

Source: 2011 Living Environment. Regents High School Examination, The University of the State of New York © 2011.

Your question to answer is: Why are the leaves different shapes?

Brainstorm about a few ideas you already have below.

Now, examine the background information and Data Tables 1, 2, and 3 to follow.

Background Information: Transpiration

Transpiration is the process that plants use to transport water throughout their structures. Water is carried through plants from the roots to small pores (holes) on the underside of leaves. Water exits plants when it evaporates and then diffuses through the pores. Transpiration is essentially evaporation of water from plant leaves. When leaves are exposed to sunlight, transpiration happens more quickly, because the water evaporates more quickly when the temperature is warmer. However, when plants transpire at a fast rate, they can become very dried out.

Background Information: Photosynthesis

Photosynthesis is the process plants use to convert light energy (from the Sun) into chemical energy that can be released later to fuel the plant's activities. During this process, carbon dioxide and water react (with the help of energy from the Sun) to form glucose and oxygen. Plants use the energy in glucose to live, so the glucose produced through photosynthesis is a form of food for the plants. Photosynthesis only happens in the *leaves* of plants. Plants need to photosynthesize to live, and the more they can photosynthesize, the more food they make for themselves.

Background Information: Nutrients

Plants need 17 different elements for normal growth. Carbon, hydrogen, and oxygen come from the air and water. Soil is the main source of other nutrients. Primary nutrients (nitrogen, phosphorus, and potassium) are used in relatively large amounts by plants. Other elements (such as molybdenum) are considered "micronutrients," and plants only need trace amounts of these nutrients.

DATA TABLE 1   Average Distance From the Ground to Each Part of White Oak Trees

Part of Tree	Distance From the Soil (Meters)
Top of crown	40.2
Middle of branches	20.1
Bottom of crown	10.6
Bottom of trunk/roots	0

DATA TABLE 2   Average Percentage of Nitrogen (a Nutrient) in Leaves at Different Heights in White Oak Trees

Part of Tree	% Nitrogen in Leaves (Grams of Nitrogen per Gram of Leaf × 100)
Top of crown	2.1
Middle of branches	2.0
Bottom of crown	1.5
Bottom of trunk/roots	No leaves present

DATA TABLE 3   Average Amount of Sunlight That Reaches Each Part of White Oak Trees

Distance From the Top of the Trees	% of Sunlight That Gets Through
0 meters (top of the trees)	100
10 meters	50
20 meters	20
30 meters	10
40 meters (forest floor)	5

On your group's whiteboard or chart paper, construct a scientific argument that answers the question, "Why are the leaves different shapes?"

CLAIM (The leaves are different shapes because. . . .)	REASONING (This evidence supports my claim because. . . .)	EVIDENCE (List data that support your claim.)

Suggested Responses

CLAIM (The leaves are different shapes because. . . .)	REASONING (This evidence supports my claim because. . . .)	EVIDENCE (List data that support your claim.)
The leaves are different shapes because they receive different amounts of sunlight (or, the variation in leaf size is related to the amount of sunlight available to the tree at different points in the crown) Other strong claims: Leaves are different shapes to prevent loss of water via transpiration. Alternate (weaker) claims: Leaves are different shapes because they are closer/further from nutrients in soil.	Plants photosynthesize to obtain energy from the sun, and photosynthesis only occurs in the leaves of plants. At the tops of trees, there is plenty of light, and so there is no advantage to having large, broad leaves to capture sunlight; furthermore, large, broad leaves lose a lot of water via transpiration when they are in direct sunlight. But there is very little light available at the bottom of the tree. Thus, leaves that are larger and broader will be able to capture necessary sunlight.	Data Table 2 shows that leaves at the top of the White Oak tree receive 100% of available sunlight. As you go down the tree, the average amount of sunlight that the leaves receive decreases. The leaves closest to the ground receive, on average, only 5% of available sunlight.

Notes

_____

_____

_____

_____

_____

_____

What Is Happening to Pteropods?

Learning Goals

The goals of this activity are for students to learn to

- observe variation in a pteropod population
- record and display data
- analyze and interpret data
- construct an argument
- recognize that a good argument uses evidence to justify claims and that to oppose counterclaims, one needs to use evidence and not assertion

NGSS Reference

MS-LS2-4

Construct an argument supported by empirical evidence that changes to physical or biological components of an ecosystem affect populations.

   Clarification Statement: Emphasis is on recognizing patterns in data and making warranted inferences about changes in populations, as well as on evaluating empirical evidence supporting arguments about changes to ecosystems.

In this activity, students conduct a simulated field study in which they observe the condition of shells of pteropods collected off the West Coast of the United States. They count the number of pteropods that have undergone different levels of shell dissolution and compare their findings to estimates of shell dissolution in "preindustrial" oceans. Students represent and analyze their data and present arguments for whether pteropod shells look different than preindustrial times at their site. They have an opportunity to offer constructive feedback to their peers during a "gallery walk" at the conclusion of the activity.

Science Background

Content Knowledge

As fossil fuels are burned to create energy, the resulting carbon dioxide is released into the atmosphere, part of which settles into the world's oceans. As the ocean waters become more CO_2-enriched, the ocean's acidity increases, a process known as *ocean acidification*. The pH of the ocean in preindustrial times (before the year 1800) is estimated to be about 8.2—so, slightly basic. Currently, sensors measure the average ocean pH to be closer to 8.1. Given the increasing amount of CO_2 in the atmosphere, scientists estimate the pH will continue to decrease and the ocean will become increasingly more acidic.

   The organisms that live in the ocean are adapted to live at about pH 8.2. Even though 0.1 pH units does not seem like a dramatic decrease, this change is already causing problems for many species. Calcifying organisms (such as sea urchins, coral, and species with shells) are at risk because they depend on a stable ocean pH to build up their shells, which they use for protection.

Pteropods, meaning "winged foot" and sometimes called sea butterflies, are tiny, transparent marine snails. They use their foot to swim freely in the water, rather than to slug along the ground. They're also food for other fish, such as mackerel and herring. They are calcifying organisms—they use calcium carbonate dissolved in the ocean to form their shell. Recently, pteropods have been of interest to scientists because they may be indicators that the changing ocean pH is causing noticeable changes to organisms and ecosystems. This website has a picture of pteropod shells exposed to varying pH levels: http://ocean.si.edu/ocean-photos/shell-dissolves-seawater.

Knowledge for Teaching

pH is a notoriously difficult concept for students of science, because a *lower pH* means that a solution is *more acidic*. The disciplinary core idea is that changes to the physical environment cause changes to populations rather than acid-base chemistry, so it may be best to keep the explanation of the chemistry to a minimum and focus on the explanation that more atmospheric CO_2 is resulting in a more acidic ocean and that changes to ocean chemistry affect individuals, populations, and, ultimately, entire ecosystems.

A major focus of this activity is displaying data effectively and using data as evidence in a scientific argument. To keep the math simple, each group's sample has a total of 100 individuals; thus, the number of pteropods in each category of damage is also the percentage. Alter the expectations for data displays depending on students' comfort with calculating percentages and averages and graphing. For students or classes that need more support, calculate percentages together or brainstorm as a class how to display the data. It is not necessary to calculate the average number of pteropods in each category across sites; however, for a very advanced class, you could calculate mean and standard deviation and talk about the degree to which site samples differed.

Prior Knowledge for Students

Students should know about different types of graphs they could use to display their data (e.g., scatterplot, line graph, bar graph, pie chart).

Furthermore, ocean acidification is a fairly complex process to understand, so a general understanding of ecosystems and climate change will probably make this activity more meaningful for students. This activity might fit well toward the end of a unit on ecology.

Teaching Sequence
Materials

Projector for showing video clip and/or pictures of pteropods

Copies of student activity sheet (class set)

Chart paper (one per group) and markers, rulers

Stickys (two per student)

Pteropod "samples" from Sites 1 to 6. Each sample contains 100 pteropod cutouts.

- You will need to make 73 copies of Figure A.10.2 ("No dissolution"), 19 copies of Figure A.10.3 ("Minor dissolution"), 6 copies of Figure A.10.4 ("Type I"), 2 copies of Figure A.10.5 ("Type II"), and 2 copies of Figure A.10.6 ("Type III").
- Refer to the following table for how many of each type to include in each sample.

	No Dissolution	Minor Dissolution	Type I Dissolution	Type II Dissolution	Type III Dissolution
Preindustrial	80	18	2	0	0
Site 1: Washington Coast	74	18	6	1	1
Site 2: Northern Oregon Coast	75	18	4	2	1
Site 3: Southern Oregon Coast	69	20	5	3	3
Site 4: Northern California Coast	75	15	6	2	2
Site 5: Central California Coast	71	20	5	2	2
Site 6: Southern California Coast	71	20	6	2	1

Instructions for Activity

- **(7 min)** Show a brief video that explains the process of *ocean acidification:* http://science360.gov/obj/video/e6d75961-f294-4936-b365-8cab109bbb57/ocean-acidification.
- **(3 min)** Review the process of ocean acidification:
  - Levels of CO_2 are increasing in the atmosphere, as a result of the burning of fossil fuels, which has increased dramatically since the Industrial Revolution.
  - A lot of the CO_2 from the atmosphere is absorbed by the ocean.
  - When CO_2 dissolves in the ocean, it forms a weak acid (carbonic acid), which lowers the pH of the ocean (i.e., makes it more acidic).
  - The pH of the ocean prior to the Industrial Revolution is estimated to be about 8.2. The average ocean pH right now is closer to 8.1.
- **(5 min)** Introduce the following task:
  - Today we are going to do an activity in which we investigate whether there is a difference in the way a population looks at two time points: preindustrial times and present day. Scientists have estimated that the ocean pH differs between these two time points—8.2 (preindustrial) versus 8.1 (present day).
  - Pteropods are microscopic marine snails. They have a shell and tiny feet that they use to propel themselves around the ocean. They are an important food source for fish and other marine species.
  - Each group will be assigned a study site. The study sites are located off the West Coast of the United States. We are simulating a field study, where scientists would collect a sample of organisms from each field site.
  - Your group will get a sample of pteropods from your assigned site. It will be your job to examine your sample, group the organisms based on physical differences in their shells, and then construct an argument about whether there is a difference between the pteropods in the preindustrial ocean and the present-day ocean.

- ○ How do we know what preindustrial oceans looked like? Scientists have been able to "simulate" preindustrial ocean water by calculating backward based on the current pH and level of CO_2 in the atmosphere. Then, they grew pteropods in these simulated ocean conditions and observed them.

- ● **(10 min)** Whole-class data collection:
  - ○ Assign each group a study site. Groups could find their study site on a map of the United States.
  - ○ Pass out the student activity sheet.
  - ○ Pass out pteropod "samples" from each site to each group.
  - ○ Students have the following chart on their activity sheet:

Type of Damage	Description
No Dissolution	No pores are visible on the surface of the shell.
Minor Dissolution	10 or fewer small pores are visible on the surface of the shell.
Type I Dissolution	More than 10 small pores are visible on the surface of the shell.
Type II Dissolution	Larger areas of the shell surface are covered by dissolved patches. Many small and medium pores are visible on the shell.
Type III Dissolution	Large gaps on the surface of the shell. The shell is beginning to lose its structure due to damage.

- ○ Students count and record data in their own data tables.
- ○ Project the following data table onto the board or use Google Sheets to compile class data. Groups should record their data in the class data table.

Site	% No Dissolution	% Minor Dissolution	% Type I Dissolution	% Type II Dissolution	% Type III Dissolution
Preindustrial (estimated)	80	18	2	0	0
Site 1: Washington Coast					
Site 2: Northern Oregon Coast					
Site 3: Southern Oregon Coast					
Site 4: Northern California Coast					
Site 5: Central California Coast					
Site 6: Southern California Coast					

- **(10 min)** Groups of students summarize their own and/or class data in data displays (see student activity sheet) on chart paper. Below data displays, groups construct an argument that answers the question, "Is there a difference in the amount of dissolution of pteropod shells between preindustrial times and the present?"

- **(5 min)** Gallery walk: Students walk around and view other groups' work. They use one sticky to indicate something they learned from a poster and one sticky to offer critical feedback on a graph or an argument.

- **(5+ min)** Class debrief:

  - How did different groups choose to display their data?
  - Were some data displays more or less effective at showing the difference?
  - What made an argument more or less convincing?
  - If you had to provide a rebuttal to the argument that ocean acidification is causing pteropod shell dissolution, what would you say? [One idea: since we cannot be sure of what preindustrial pteropods looked like—although we have a pretty good idea based on fossils and simulation experiments—we cannot be absolutely positive that shell dissolution was not occurring prior to the more acidic ocean.]
  - Going beyond the activity: How might we design an experiment to show that the lower pH is causing pteropod shells to dissolve?

Student Activity: What Is Happening to Pteropods?

 An electronic copy of this activity is available on the companion website at https://resources.corwin.com/OsborneArgumentation.

Field Study Simulation

1. Your teacher will assign you a study site and give you your pteropod sample. Spread your pteropod sample out on your table.

2. Sort your sampled pteropods into groups based on how much dissolution you can observe on their shells. Refer to the following descriptions to sort your pteropods.

Type of Damage	Description
No Dissolution	No pores are visible on the surface of the shell.
Minor Dissolution	10 or fewer small pores are visible on the surface of the shell.
Type I Dissolution	More than 10 small pores are visible on the surface of the shell.
Type II Dissolution	Larger areas of the shell surface are covered by dissolved patches. Many small and medium pores are visible on the shell.
Type III Dissolution	Large gaps on the surface of the shell. The shell is beginning to lose its structure due to damage.

3. Count the number of pteropods in each group. Record your data in the following data table and on the class data table.

Site	% No Dissolution	% Minor Dissolution	% Type I Dissolution	% Type II Dissolution	% Type III Dissolution
Preindustrial (estimated)	80	18	2	0	0
Site 1: Washington Coast					
Site 2: Northern Oregon Coast					
Site 3: Southern Oregon Coast					
Site 4: Northern California Coast					

Site	% No Dissolution	% Minor Dissolution	% Type I Dissolution	% Type II Dissolution	% Type III Dissolution
Site 5: Central California Coast					
Site 6: Southern California Coast					

Displaying the Data

4. Pick a way to display data that compare the amount of pteropod shell damage in preindustrial times to pteropod shell damage today. Things to consider:

    - Do you want to summarize the class data or present the data from a single site only?
    - Which type of graph will be most effective in showing how pteropod shell damage compares (e.g., scatter plot, line graph, bar graph, pie graph)?
    - Construct your data display on chart paper. Give your data display a title and label your axes. Include a legend, if necessary.

Constructing Your Argument

5. Based on the simulated field study and your data analysis, you will now construct an argument that answers the question, "Is there a difference between the amount of pteropod shell dissolution between preindustrial times and the present?"

Write your argument below your data display on your chart paper. Be sure to include your claim, the evidence that supports your claim, and your reasoning.

Gallery Walk

6. Your teacher will tell you where to hang your chart paper with your data display and argument.

7. Rotate around the posters. You must post at least two sticky notes—one identifying something that you learned and one that poses a critique or a critical question.

Sentences starters for things you learned:

- This poster made me realize. . . .
- This poster made me think about. . . .
- This poster was different from mine because. . . .

Sentence starters for critical feedback:

- Your argument would be stronger if you included evidence on. . . .
- I disagree with this claim because. . . .
- I think this is not the best evidence because. . . .
- I think what is missing in the reasoning is. . . .
- This argument needs. . . .

Suggested Responses

There are many acceptable ways to display these data. Students may want to high-light a particular study site or, as in Figure A.10.1, average the samples from each site. Bar graphs (histograms) are a good way to show the data because there are particular "buckets" into which the data are sorted. Pie charts might also be effective in showing how populations differ across time and across sites.

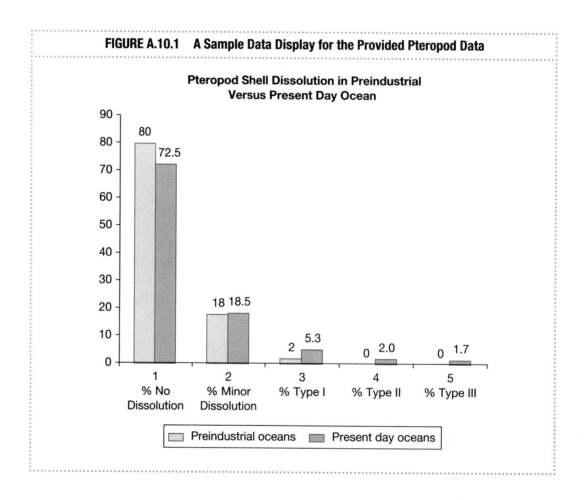

FIGURE A.10.1   A Sample Data Display for the Provided Pteropod Data

Students might also choose to display the increase in shells with Type II or III dam-age. In this case, it might be possible to do this effectively using a scatterplot, show-ing the difference between pre- and postindustrialization. However, a bar graph is still probably the most effective way to visualize the data.

CLAIM	REASONING clipart.com	EVIDENCE
There is a difference between the amount of pteropod shell dissolution in preindustrial times and the present.	Since the ocean is becoming more acidic (the pH has decreased from 8.2 to 8.1), pteropod shells are starting to dissolve more. There has always been some shell damage present (even in preindustrial times, some shells showed evidence of dissolution); however, the rate of Type I damage has doubled, and Type II and Type III damage is present (whereas there were no shells with that level of damage in preindustrial oceans).	On average, the number of pteropods with zero to minimal shell dissolution is lower in current ocean conditions than it was during preindustrial times. During preindustrial times, 80% of pteropod shells were pristine, whereas in the samples from the current study sites, only 72.5% shells were intact. The Southern Oregon Site had the lowest number of intact shells—only 69% of pteropod shells showed no dissolution. Type I damage has doubled between preindustrial times and present day. In preindustrial oceans, 2% of shells showed Type I damage; in the current study sites, 4% of shells showed Type I damage. Furthermore, Type II and Type III damage (the most severe dissolution) was only present in the current study sites. This type of damage was not present in preindustrial estimates of shell damage at these sites.

Additional Resources

Lethal Seas (NOVA video): http://www.pbs.org/wgbh/nova/earth/lethal-seas.html (52 minutes)

News article: http://www.pbs.org/newshour/rundown/acidity-increases-pacific-ocean-snail-shells-dissolving-faster-previously-thought/

Primary source article describing the pteropod study simulated in this activity: Bednaršek, N., Feely, R. A., Reum, J. C. P., Peterson, B., Menkel, J., Alin, S. R., & Hales, B. (2014). Limacina helicina shell dissolution as an indicator of declining habitat suitability owing to ocean acidification in the California Current Ecosystem. *Proceedings of the Royal Society of London B, 281*(1785), 20140123. http://doi.org/10.1098/rspb.2014.0123

Photograph of shell dissolution: http://ocean.si.edu/ocean-photos/shell-dissolves-seawater

Extension Activities

In this activity, students are not arguing about whether we can attribute the higher rate of pteropod shell damage to the, on average, lower pH of the ocean. However, the introduction to the lesson introduces the idea that because of the higher concentration of carbon dioxide in the atmosphere, more carbon dioxide dissolves into the ocean, and the pH of the ocean is, on average, lower than it was in preindustrial times, and this decrease is expected to continue. In subsequent lessons, students could read more about ocean acidification via the websites listed under "Additional Resources" and view the video *Lethal Seas,* which describes the biological implications of ocean acidification. They could continue exploring ocean acidification, the effect on pteropods, and possible solutions to the problem via the following extension activities:

Extension Activity 1: How would you design an experiment (in the field or the lab) that would provide evidence that lower pH *causes* the rate of pteropod shell dissolution to increase?

Extension Activity 2: How would you convince members of Congress that ocean acidification is happening and that the change in ocean chemistry will have negative effects for ocean species and humans?

- Prepare a poster and a speech.
- Prepare notecards that anticipate the questions Congress members might have and the responses you would give (i.e., anticipate rebuttals and prepare counterarguments).

 Electronic copies of Figures A.10.2 through A.10.6 are available on the companion website at https://resources.corwin.com/OsborneArgumentation.

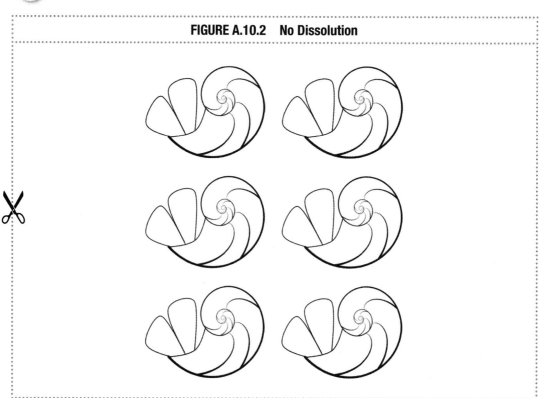

FIGURE A.10.2   No Dissolution

Source: Nautilus Shell, fletcherpenney.net, http://fletcherpenney.net/2008/08/context_free

FIGURE A.10.3   Minor Dissolution

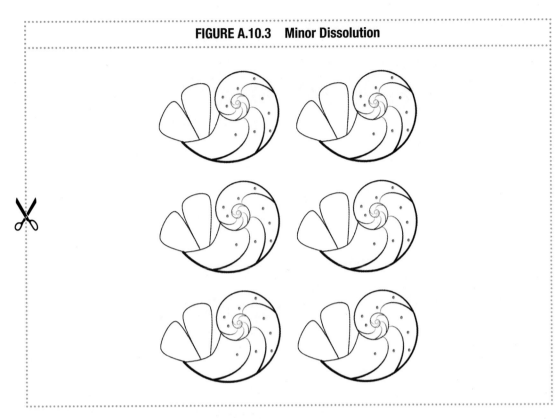

Source: Nautilus Shell, fletcherpenney.net, http://fletcherpenney.net/2008/08/context_free

FIGURE A.10.4   Type I Dissolution

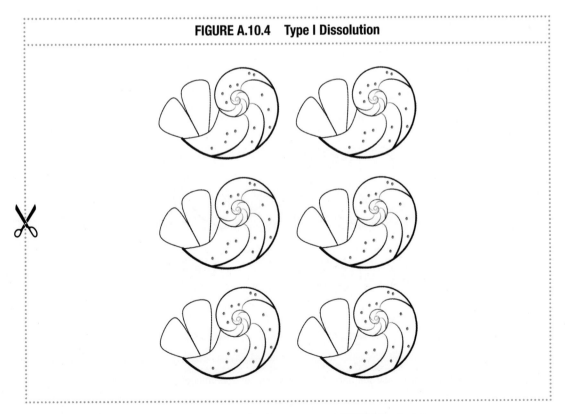

Source: Nautilus Shell, fletcherpenney.net, http://fletcherpenney.net/2008/08/context_free

FIGURE A.10.5 Type II Dissolution

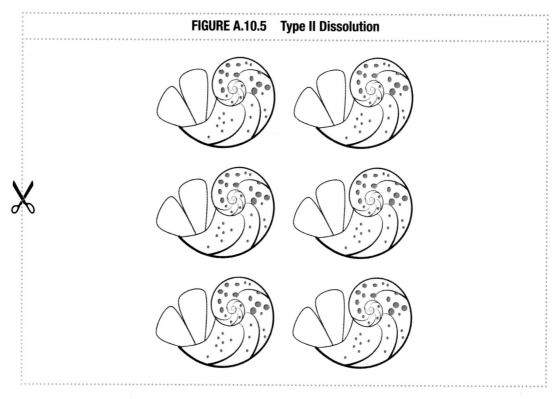

Source: Nautilus Shell, fletcherpenney.net, http://fletcherpenney.net/2008/08/context_free

FIGURE A.10.6 Type III Dissolution

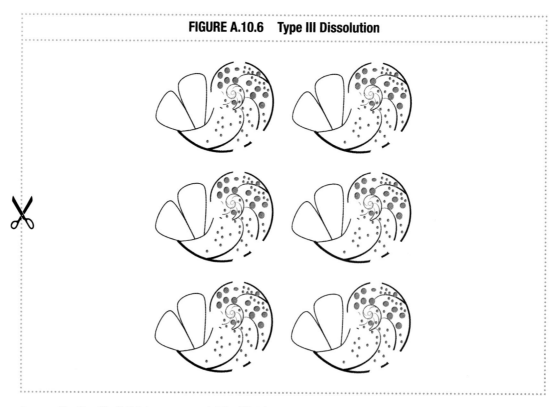

Source: Nautilus Shell, fletcherpenney.net, http://fletcherpenney.net/2008/08/context_free

What Factors Affect the Number of Moose on Isle Royale?

Learning Goals

The goals of this activity are for students to learn to

- examine how two populations interact with each other and with other biotic and abiotic factors in an ecosystem
- use evidence to justify claims
- understand that the quality of an argument is based on the amount of evidence supporting a claim
- recognize that effects in ecosystems can be observed on different time scales (i.e., that some changes can be observed in the short term, but more stable patterns emerge over longer time scales)
- learn and consolidate the concepts about ecosystems (e.g., interactions between abiotic and biotic factors, interdependence of species, predator-prey interaction, competition)

NGSS Reference

MS-LS2-1

Analyze and interpret data to provide evidence for the effects of resource availability on organisms and populations of organisms in an ecosystem.
   Clarification Statement: Emphasis is on cause-and-effect relationships between resources and growth of individual organisms and the numbers of organisms in ecosystems during periods of abundant and scarce resources.

MS-LS2-4

Construct an argument supported by empirical evidence that *changes to physical or biological components of an ecosystem affect populations*.
   Clarification Statement: Emphasis is on recognizing patterns in data and making warranted inferences about changes in populations and on evaluating empirical evidence supporting arguments about changes to ecosystems.

In this activity, students learn about an island that has been studied continuously for many years. They look at long-term data collected on the moose population on the island and the various biotic and abiotic factors that affect that population. Rather than simply asking students to argue about whether the wolves affect the moose population and support this argument using graphs of the predator and prey populations, this activity asks students to consider the many factors that might matter and make an argument for which factor is *most strongly associated with changes in the moose population*.

Science Background

Content Knowledge

The wolves and moose on Isle Royale, in Lake Superior, have been studied continuously from 1959 until now. In this activity, students learn about the moose and wolves that have lived on Isle Royale, interpret data about factors that affect the populations of moose and wolves, examine a graph displaying the population numbers for each species, and make claims about which factors are most strongly related to changes in the moose population. Wolves are predators of moose; however, the graph showing the populations of wolves and moose does not show the simple oscillating predator-prey pattern one might expect. The long-term pattern supports the predator-prey relationship, but smaller segments of the graph offer a more complicated picture.

Knowledge for Teaching

This activity addresses central concepts in population ecology such as predator-prey interactions and competition. It may be helpful to do this activity after students have learned about the components of ecosystems and how species interact.

Prior Knowledge for Students

This activity relies on students being able to interpret points plotted on an X-Y coordinate system. Furthermore, the wolves and moose are plotted on the same axis, so students may need support finding the two separate axis labels and interpreting the graphs. For classes or students who need more support interpreting graphs and tables, plan to spend more time with the background information and data cards. It is possible to use fewer cards. Furthermore, you may want to spend more time reading, interpreting, and discussing the graph.

Teaching Sequence

Materials

- Student activity sheets
- Background information and data cards
- Image of graph of "Moose & Wolves 1959–2009" to project
- Whiteboards or chart paper, markers

Instructions for Activity

- **(5 min)** Introduce the activity. Tell the students that they are going to work as teams of ecologists to interpret data about two species on Isle Royale: wolves and moose.
- **(10 min)** Put the students into groups and have them read the background information and data cards, using a reading strategy if desired. In groups, students use the background information and data cards and Figure A.11.1 to brainstorm about the biotic and abiotic factors that affect the growth of the populations of moose and wolves.
- Instruct students to look at "Moose and Wolf Populations, 1959–2009" on their student activity sheet. Project the graph for the class to see. Introduce the graph, explaining that these are the numbers of wolves and moose each year since 1959.
- **(5 min)** As a class, identify the important features of the graph:
  - Both moose and wolves are shown on the same graph (notice that the scale is different for each species, and there are always many fewer predators than prey).
  - Do you notice any patterns? We might expect to see a "predator-prey cycle"—when the number of prey decreases, the number of predators decreases also. Is that pattern visible on this graph?

○ There are exceptions to the expected predator-prey pattern (e.g., in 2002, the wolves began decreasing, but moose continued to decrease as well).

○ Which other factors did you identify that are related to the populations of moose and wolves (wolf inbreeding, weather, fir tree density, ticks, etc.)?

- **(15 min)** In groups, construct an argument that answers the following question: "Which abiotic or biotic factor is most strongly related to the population of moose on Isle Royale?" Construct your group's argument on large paper or a whiteboard.

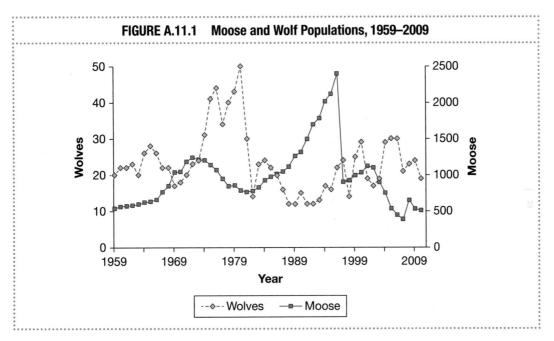

FIGURE A.11.1   Moose and Wolf Populations, 1959–2009

Source: Wolves & Moose of Isle Royale, http://www.isleroyalewolf.org/data/data/home.html, John A. Vucetich © 2016

CLAIM (_____ has the biggest effect on the population of moose.)	REASONING (This evidence supports my claim because. . . .)	EVIDENCE (List data that support your claim.)

- **(10 min)** Groups share their arguments. Other groups have the opportunity to ask questions or offer a critique of the evidence or reasoning.

Student Activity: What Factors Affect the Number of Moose on Isle Royale?

 An electronic copy of this activity is available on the companion website at https://resources.corwin.com/OsborneArgumentation.

Factors affecting the moose population on Isle Royale: In this activity, you will work with your team of ecologists to construct an argument that answers the question, "Which abiotic or biotic factor has the biggest effect on the population of moose on Isle Royale?"

1. Read background information and data cards.

2. Brainstorm factors that affect moose and wolves.

Population	Factors Affecting the Population
Moose	
Wolves	

3. With your class, look at the graph of wolf and moose populations between 1959 and 2009 (Figure A.11.2).

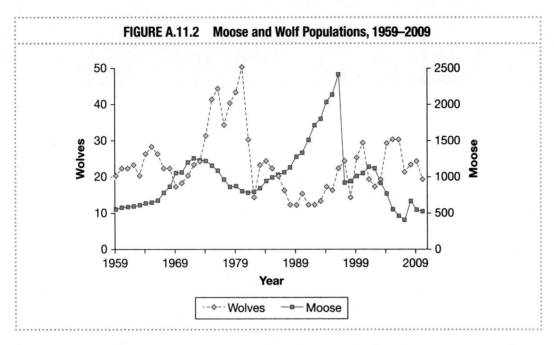

FIGURE A.11.2   Moose and Wolf Populations, 1959–2009

Source: Wolves & Moose of Isle Royale, http://www.isleroyalewolf.org/data/data/home.html, John A. Vucetich © 2016

4. Construct your argument on whiteboard or chart paper. Your argument should answer the question, "Which abiotic or biotic factor is most strongly related to the population of moose on Isle Royale?"

CLAIM (_____ is the most strongly related to changes in the moose population.)	REASONING (This evidence supports my claim because. . . .)	EVIDENCE (List data that support your claim.)

Isle Royale Data Cards

 Electronic copies of these cards are available on the companion website at https://resources.corwin.com/OsborneArgumentation.

Background Information: Isle Royale

Isle Royale is an isolated wilderness island in Lake Superior, which you can get to by boat from either Michigan or Minnesota. The weather is warm in the summer and very cold and snowy in the winter. The island has many deciduous trees and shrubs and also evergreen trees such as firs and balsams. The island also has animal species such as insects (notably, the *moose tick*), spiders, frogs, toads, various birds, squirrels, and beavers. The two species that are the focus of this activity are the *moose* and the *gray timber wolf*. These are the two largest species of the island and have been studied for many years.

Because the island is very small and is surrounded by water, it is an ideal place to study interactions between populations. The only changes in population numbers are due to births and deaths because animals cannot migrate to or from the island. Furthermore, there are no humans present on the island, so hunting and deforestation do not affect population numbers.

Background Information: Moose

Moose eat plants only, and they have to spend much of their time eating to get enough calories to live. During the summer, moose can consume 30 to 40 pounds of vegetation a day. That would be like you or me eating 7 pounds of salad every day! In preparation for winter, moose increase their body weight by as much as 25%.

During the winter, moose are not bothered by the cold, but they have difficulty getting food. During winter, moose mostly eat twigs from trees and shrubs and the twigs and needles of fir trees. It is also very difficult for them to gather food in the deep snow. Winter is also the time when moose ticks attach to their bodies and feed on their blood. The presence of the ticks makes the moose even weaker.

However, despite the difficulties of winter, many moose live to see the following spring. Female moose give birth to their babies in May, when the mothers are still quite malnourished from the winter. However, their babies need time to grow before the harsh winter begins again.

Background Information: Wolves

Wolves live together in groups called packs. Members of the same pack are often cooperative, and members of other packs are usually enemies (although there are exceptions). Wolves spend much of their day walking. They walk for two reasons: to capture food and to defend their territories. Wolf territories on Isle Royale average about 75 square miles. To patrol and defend their territory, wolves must walk constantly.

Isle Royale wolves eat only moose. They typically only attack 1 out of every 10 moose that they chase down and they kill 8 or 9 of every 10 moose they decide to attack. They might decide not to attack if the moose is too strong or the wolf determines that it might get injured during the attack. Wolves typically eat almost all parts of the moose. Starvation is a common cause of death for wolves, since killing prey requires a lot of energy and often results in injury.

Inbreeding is a problem for the wolves on Isle Royale. Since there are so few of them on the island and there are few examples of wolves from the mainland being able to get to Isle Royale, the wolves end up mating with close relatives. Inbreeding results in a decrease in fitness and, ultimately, higher wolf death.

Data: Harsh Winters

The winter is always cold and snowy on Isle Royale, but some winters over the past 50 years have been harsher (colder and snowier) than others. The 3 years listed in the following table are the harshest winters on record on Isle Royale.

Harshest Winters on Isle Royale 1959–2009

Year	Description
1991	Winter low temperature: –10°F Snowfall: 30 inches
1997	Winter low temperature: –12°F Snowfall: 31 inches
2002	Winter low temperature: –15°F Snowfall: 28 inches

The data above are not authentic and were created for teaching purposes only.

Data: Average Number of Ticks on Moose per Year

Ticks are parasites of moose. They attach to the moose in the fall and feed on their blood through the winter. The presence of ticks weakens moose and makes them less likely to survive tough winters. Between 1996 and 2009, scientists estimated the number of ticks on the average moose.

Year	Average Number of Ticks on Moose
1996	125,000
1997	150,000
1998	100,000
1999	90,000
2000	80,000
2001	145,000
2002	140,000
2003	110,000
2004	90,000
2005	89,000
2006	80,000
2007	78,000
2008	80,000
2009	79,000

The data above are not authentic and were created for teaching purposes only.

Data: Fir Tree Density on Isle Royale

Fir trees do not drop their leaves in the winter like deciduous trees do. Fir trees are an important food source for the moose on Isle Royale because they are a plant that the moose can eat year round. The number of trees on Isle Royale changes from year to year. Scientists have been counting the number of fir trees per hectare on Isle Royale since 1960. They conduct a tree survey every 5 years. The data are shown in the following table.

Year	Fir Tree Density on Isle Royale (Trees/Hectare)
1960	3,000
1965	2,800
1970	2,400
1975	2,000
1980	1,600
1985	1,800
1990	1,900
1995	1,400
2000	1,800
2005	1,800
2010	1,900

The data above are not authentic and were created for teaching purposes only.

Suggested Response

Cases can be made for all the different factors significantly affecting the moose population in individual years or across the entire period studied. Arguments for factors that explain the *pattern over time,* rather than single data points, will be superior. Thus, claims that identify *fir tree density* and *wolf predation* are able to be supported with data from across the years studied. *Tick load* and *weather* explain dramatic decreases of moose in single years, but there may not enough data to properly support these claims.

CLAIM (_____ is most strongly related to changes in the moose population.)	REASONING (This evidence supports my claim because. . . .)	EVIDENCE (List data that support your claim.)
Changes in the population of wolves on Isle Royale are most strongly related to changes in the moose population.	From 1959 until 2009, there are several times when an increase in wolves is associated with a decrease in moose and vice versa. While harsh winters and tick counts may explain some of the variation in the moose population, they only explain variation at single time points. Thus, wolves are probably the most significant factor associated with changes in the moose population.	On the graph of wolves and moose between 1959 and 2009, there are many examples of an increase in wolves that is associated with a decrease in moose. For example, as the wolf population increased between 1969 and 1979 from about 18 individuals to more than 50 individuals, the moose population fell steadily from about 1,200 moose to about 700 moose. Following a drop in the wolf population after 1979, the deer population began to recover. Also, between 2004 and 2007, the wolf population increased from 20 to 30 and the deer population began to fall.

Additional Resources

A website dedicated to providing information and data about the Isle Royale ecosystem: http://www.isleroyalewolf.org/.

Additional information about the effects of winter ticks on the moose on Isle Royale can be found at http://www.isleroyalewolf.org/node/44 and http://news.nationalgeographic.com/2015/06/150601-ghost-moose-animals-science-new-england-environment/.

	Extension Activities	
	"Should We Reintroduce the Wolf to Isle Royale?" activity (this book)	

ACTIVITY 12

Should We Reintroduce the Wolf to Isle Royale?

Learning Goals

The goals of this activity are for students to learn to

- use evidence to justify claims
- recognize that a good argument uses evidence to justify claims and that it also opposes counterclaims through the use of evidence rather than assertion
- learn and consolidate the concepts about ecosystems (e.g., interactions between abiotic and biotic factors, interdependence of species, predator-prey interaction, competition, biodiversity and ecosystem services)
- understand that there are multiple trade-offs involved in decisions made about what to do about ecosystems

NGSS Reference

MS-LS2-5

Evaluate competing design solutions for maintaining biodiversity and ecosystem services.
  Clarification Statement: Examples of ecosystem services could include water purification, nutrient recycling, and prevention of soil erosion. Examples of design solution constraints could include scientific, economic, and social considerations.

The aim of this exercise is to explore the benefits and costs of reintroducing a species that is disappearing from an ecosystem.

Science Background

Content Knowledge

The wolves and moose on Isle Royale, in Lake Superior, have been studied continuously since 1959. Isle Royale is usually only accessible by boat (an ice bridge sometimes forms during especially cold winters), making it an ideal place to study the interactions between species, because none of the changes in population are due to immigration, emigration, hunting, or deforestation.

Since 2009, the population of wolves has been declining on Isle Royale. In 2015, the annual survey of wolves showed that there were only three wolves remaining on the island. Ecologists disagree about what to do about the wolf population.

An important concept explored in this activity is the interdependence of species in a food web. Every ecosystem has producers, consumers, and decomposers. Primary consumers eat plants; secondary consumers eat other animals. Tertiary consumers, or top predators, prey on primary and secondary consumers. Wolves are top predators in the Isle Royale ecosystem. They eat moose, deer, and other primary consumers.

Another important concept explored in this activity is the idea of maintaining biodiversity and ecosystem services. Biodiversity refers to the number and types of organisms present in an ecosystem. The more different types of organisms are in an ecosystem, the higher the biodiversity. Biodiversity may be important for maintaining ecosystem stability. Furthermore, loss of biodiversity means potential loss of ecosystem services. Ecosystem services are specific services that humans rely on from ecosystems such as the water filtration provided by wetlands or the hurricane storm surge protection provided to tropical coastal cities by local mangroves.

Knowledge for Teaching

The strategy for engaging students in argumentation is a "town hall meeting." To avoid making this event simply a series of group presentations, post sentence starters for clarifying questions and critiques. Consider including questions and critiques into your assessment of students' participation in the town hall meeting. Point out the difference between a "counterargument" and a critique—in a counterargument, students present an alternative claim. A critique is the identification of a weakness in the evidence or reasoning. Both forms of argumentation have a place at the town hall meeting; however, point out that all groups will have an opportunity to present their argument, so their counterargument will be heard. Thus, during the question/discussion periods, it may be most beneficial to their cause to offer a pointed critique, rather than simply reiterating their own position.

This activity will take two class periods. Students need one class to read background information and case studies and construct their own arguments. The town hall meeting and debrief will take a second class period.

Prior Knowledge for Students

Students should have prior experience with food webs and exposure to the idea that the interdependence of organisms in a food web means that when a species is added to or leaves a food web, there are effects in other parts of the food web.

Students should understand the concepts of natural capital and ecosystem services. Briefly, ecosystems provide resources that humans need. Ecosystem services are any positive benefits that ecosystems provide to people. For example, although we obtain much of our food via agriculture, our oceans contain natural fisheries, which we rely on for food.

Teaching Sequence

Materials

- Identity cards
- Information cards
- Computer access for additional resources (optional)
- Whiteboards or charter paper, markers

Instructions for Activity

- Consider doing Activity 11 prior to this activity to provide students more background knowledge about Isle Royale, moose, and wolves.
- **(5 min)** Discuss the declining wolf population on Isle Royale (see previous section on "Content Knowledge"). Display "Moose and Wolf Populations, 1959–2015" (Figure A.12.1) for students to view. Introduce the idea that scientists disagree about whether or not to introduce additional wolves to the ecosystem.
- **(2 min)** Tell the students that they are going to work in teams to decide whether to introduce new wolves to Isle Royale. They will first meet in a group composed of members with the same position in the argument. Then, all the groups will come together in a "town hall meeting," in which each group will present their claim, evidence, and reasoning. Other groups will have the opportunity to ask questions and offer rebuttals.

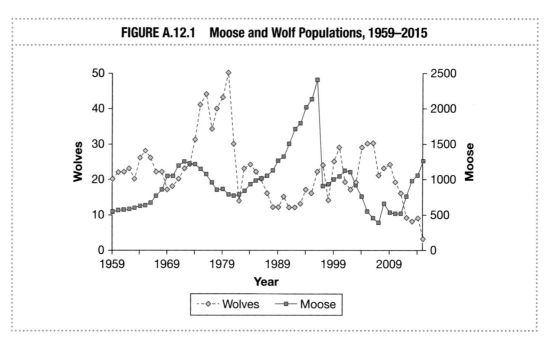

FIGURE A.12.1 Moose and Wolf Populations, 1959–2015

Source: Wolves & Moose of Isle Royale, http://www.isleroyalewolf.org/data/data/home.html, John A. Vucetich © 2016

- **(2 min)** Divide students into groups of four to six. Pass out identity cards to each group:

  - Ecologists who support the reintroduction of the wolf
  - Ecologists who do not support the reintroduction of the wolf
  - Isle Royale park rangers
  - Wolf biologists
  - Moose biologists
  - Plant biologists
  - Representatives from the timber industry

- **(15 min)** Using the student activity sheet, groups of students categorize the two case studies ("Reintroduction of Wolves to Yellowstone" and "Reintroduction of Red Kites to Britain") based on whether the case supports reintroduction or not. Then, they decide whether, in their assigned role, they should use the case to support their position.

- **(20 min)** Groups of students construct their arguments using case studies, information cards, and additional web resources. Groups should prepare a whiteboard or poster that outlines their argument, including their claim, evidence, and reasoning.

- **(45 min)** Hold a town hall meeting. Students should sit in a large circle, possibly around tables pushed together. Groups should sit together. Structure of meeting:

  - The chosen moderator opens the meeting with a description of the problem.
  - Group 1 presents their argument (2 minutes). Moderator keeps time.
  - Other groups may ask clarifying questions (2 minutes).
  - Other groups offer rebuttals, in which they identify weaknesses in the evidence or in the reasoning. Encourage students to offer critiques of evidence or reasoning, rather than simply reiterating their opposing claims (3–5 minutes).
  - Repeat this sequence for all groups.
  - Moderator opens the floor for general discussion, in which groups can make final arguments or respond to additional questions.
  - Students vote, by secret ballot, to pursue reintroduction of the wolf.
  - Possible reflection prompts:
    The most convincing evidence for me was _____.
    My thinking changed during the activity because _____.

Isle Royale Identity Cards

 Electronic copies of these cards are available on the companion website at https://resources.corwin.com/OsborneArgumentation.

Ecologists Who Support Reintroduction

You are a group of ecologists that has studied the Isle Royale ecosystem and has decided that the reintroduction of the wolves is the decision that will benefit the ecosystem. You need to convince the other groups that reintroduction of the wolf is in the best interest of the whole Isle Royale ecosystem.

Ecologists Who Do Not Support Reintroduction

You are a group of ecologists that has studied the Isle Royale ecosystem and has decided that the reintroduction of the wolves is not the right decision. You need to convince the other groups that reintroduction of the wolf is not in the best interest of the whole Isle Royale ecosystem.

Isle Royale Park Rangers

As park rangers, your concern is the people visiting Isle Royale. Does the reintroduction of wolves benefit or harm potential visitors?

Wolf Biologists

You are a group of biologists that specializes in the study of gray wolves. Your concern in this argument is the size and health of the *wolf population only*. However, keep in mind that *more* wolves does not necessarily mean *healthier* wolves. You should spend time examining why the wolves declined in the first place and whether reintroduction is the right move for the wolves.

Moose Biologists

You are a group of biologists that specializes in the study of moose. Your concern in this argument is the size and health of the *moose population only*. You should spend time looking at patterns of moose and wolf interactions in the past and determine whether reintroduction is the right move for the wolves.

Plant Biologists

You are a group of biologists that specializes in the study of plants. Your concern in this argument is the number and distribution of vegetation (trees and plants) on Isle Royale. You should spend time examining the effects of possible reintroduction on the number of plants on the island.

Representatives of the Timber Industry

Cutting down trees for lumber is not allowed on Isle Royale because it is currently a national park. However, as representatives of the timber industry, you are always on the lookout for potential sources of trees that can be cut down. You feel that the argument about whether to reintroduce wolves might have an effect on the future of the trees on Isle Royale.

Student Activity: Should We Reintroduce the Wolf to Isle Royale?

 An electronic copy of this activity is available on the companion website at https://resources.corwin.com/OsborneArgumentation.

My group's role is: _____

Step 1. Read background information cards.

Step 2. Read Comparison Case Study 1: Reintroduction of Wolves to Yellowstone National Park and examine the graph of Moose and Wolf Populations 1959–2009.

- What were the positive outcomes of reintroduction (if any)?
- What were the negative outcomes of reintroduction (if any)?
- In your role, which part of this case study (if any) will you use to support your position?

Step 3. Read Comparison Case Study 2: Reintroduction of Red Kites to Britain.

- What were the positive outcomes of reintroduction (if any)?
- What were the negative outcomes of reintroduction (if any)?
- In your role, which part of this case study (if any) will you use to support your position?

Step 4. Construct your argument.

As _____, we **do/do not** support reintroduction of wolves to
(your group's assigned role)
Isle Royale.

Our evidence is

Our evidence supports our claim because

Isle Royale Information Cards

Isle Royale

Isle Royale is an isolated wilderness island in Lake Superior that you can get to by boat from either Michigan or Minnesota. The weather is warm in the summer and very cold and snowy in the winter. The island has many deciduous trees and shrubs and also evergreen trees such as firs and balsams. The island also has animal species such as insects (notably, the *moose tick*), spiders, frogs, toads, various birds, squirrels, and beavers. The two species that are the focus of this activity are the *moose* and the *gray timber wolf*. These are the two largest species of the island and have been studied for many years.

Because the island is very small and is surrounded by water, it is an ideal place to study interactions between populations. The only changes in population numbers are due to births and deaths because animals cannot migrate to or from the island. Furthermore, there are no humans present on the island, so hunting and foresting do not affect population numbers.

The island has been designated as a national park. Visitors come to Isle Royale to experience a relatively untouched ecosystem and to view the wildlife (occasionally catching site of the rare gray wolf).

Wolves

Wolves live together in groups called packs. Members of the same pack are often cooperative, and members of other packs are usually enemies (although there are exceptions). Wolves spend much of their day walking. They walk for two reasons: to capture food and to defend their territories. Wolf territories on Isle Royale average about 75 square miles. To patrol and defend their territory, wolves must walk constantly.

Isle Royale wolves eat only moose. They typically only attack 1 out of every 10 moose that they chase down, and they kill 8 or 9 of every 10 moose they decide to attack. They might decide not to attack if the moose is too strong or the wolf determines that it might get injured during the attack. Wolves typically eat almost all parts of the moose. Starvation is a common cause of death for wolves, because killing prey requires a lot of energy and often results in injury.

Moose

Moose eat plants only, and they have to spend much of their time eating to get enough calories to live. During the summer, moose can consume 30 to 40 pounds of vegetation a day. That would be like you or me eating 7 pounds of salad every day! In preparation for winter, moose increase their body weight by as much as 25%.

During the winter, moose are not bothered by the cold, but they have difficulty getting food. During winter, moose mostly eat twigs from trees and shrubs and the twigs and needles of fir trees. It is also very difficult for them to gather food in the deep snow. Winter is also the time when moose ticks attach to their bodies and feed on their blood. The presence of the ticks makes the moose even weaker.

However, despite the difficulties of winter, many moose live to see the following spring. Female moose give birth to their babies in May, when the mothers are still quite malnourished from the winter. However, their babies need time to grow before the harsh winter begins again.

Wolves are the only predators of moose.

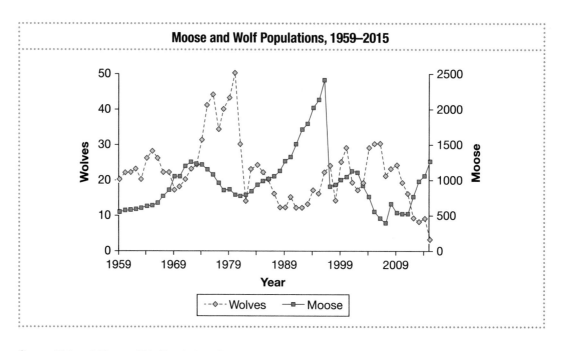

Moose and Wolf Populations, 1959–2015

Source: **Wolves & Moose of Isle Royale,** http://www.isleroyalewolf.org/data/data/home.html, John A. Vucetich © 2016

COMPARISON CASE STUDY 1: REINTRODUCTION OF WOLVES TO YELLOWSTONE NATIONAL PARK

Yellowstone National Park is located in the state of Wyoming. The climate (temperature and weather) is similar to that of Isle Royale. However, Yellowstone is not an island, so species can migrate into and out of the park. Furthermore, Yellowstone is surrounded by farms and ranches, where animals are raised for food. The wolf population became critically low in Yellowstone due to farmers, ranchers, and hunters shooting wolves for attacking livestock. However, the decrease in wolves resulted in a dramatic increase in their prey (deer) and cascading effects on other species. For example, the vegetation that the deer ate was almost completely eliminated. The decision was made to reintroduce the wolves, and in 1995, wolves were reintroduced into Yellowstone National Park from Canada. With the introduction, the conflict between the wolves, ranchers, and hunters began again. However, the number of deer in the park began to stabilize and vegetation returned.

COMPARISON CASE STUDY 2: REINTRODUCTION OF RED KITES TO BRITAIN

The red kite is a bird of prey that is native to Europe. Red kite populations got smaller and smaller leading up to the beginning of the 19th century—the birds were considered pests and people were encouraged to hunt and kill them. The population remained low up until the 20th century, and by the 1960s, there were only about 20 mating pairs of birds left in Britain. In 1989, a reintroduction program was started in England and Scotland. Young red kites were removed from other parts of Europe and reintroduced into Britain. Today the population is flourishing, with thousands of mating pairs. The red kite is no longer considered threatened. However, the growing population of red kites is starting to take a toll on native songbird populations in Britain. Although red kites are typically scavengers, eating the remains of dead animals, they do also eat songbird eggs and nestlings. It is unclear how big an effect the growing population of red kites is having on songbird populations, but birdwatchers have begun to notice declining populations.

Additional Resources

Background information and data about the species on Isle Royale: http://www.isleroyalewolf.org/.

Research paper about the challenges of reintroducing predators: http://www.jyi.org/issue/a-review-of-management-problems-arising-from-reintroductions-of-large-carnivores/.

		Extension Activities
		If students vote to reintroduce the wolf, an extension activity is to design a plan for the reintroduction of the wolves (number of wolves, timing, monitoring plans, etc.).

Notes

_____

_____

_____

_____

_____

_____

_____

_____

_____

_____

_____

_____

_____

Is Rotifer Reproduction Sexual or Asexual?

Learning Goals

The goals of this activity are for students to learn to

- use evidence to justify claims that a population is reproducing sexually or asexually
- use evidence to evaluate models of inheritance for a reproducing population

NGSS Reference

MS-LS3-2

Develop and use a model to describe why asexual reproduction results in offspring with identical genetic information and sexual reproduction results in offspring with genetic variation.

Clarification Statement: Emphasis is on using models such as Punnett squares, diagrams, and simulations to describe the cause-and-effect relationship of gene transmission from parent(s) to offspring and resulting genetic variation.

There are three aims to this lesson. The first is to help students understand that sexual and asexual reproduction work through different models of inheritance. The second is to help students link genetic models of inheritance in sexually and asexually reproducing species to patterns of genetic variation in a population of organisms. Third, these activities encourage students to argue about the strengths and weaknesses of different genetic models of inheritance to explain patterns in genetic data.

Science Background

Content Knowledge

This lesson explores the genetics behind sexual and asexual reproduction. Sexual reproduction produces genetic variation in a population for a variety of reasons. First, there is the fact that sexually reproducing parents each contribute half of their genetic material to their offspring. Also, the independent assortment of alleles during meiosis and homologous recombination ensures that there is genetic variation across the gametes (sperm or egg cells) produced by parents. Asexual reproduction, on the other hand, does not produce genetic variation because it involves the cloning, or replication, of parental DNA. Genetic variation can be produced through asexual reproduction because of mutations and copying errors during DNA replication. However, asexual reproduction tends to result in a population of genetic clones.

Research suggests that an organism, called a rotifer, is capable of both sexual and asexual reproduction. When the environment is homogeneous, the rotifers tend to clone themselves. Yet, when the environment of the rotifer is heterogeneous, populations of rotifers tend to engage in sexual reproduction. The evolutionary reasoning for this phenomenon is that homogeneous environments do not change, and therefore, once an optimal phenotypic variation of rotifer gets established in such an environment, it is not evolutionarily advantageous, in terms of survival or reproduction, to differ from the optimal phenotype. Because sexual reproduction increases variation, it also increases the probability that individuals not well suited to the homogeneous environment will die. Therefore, asexual reproducers have a competitive advantage in homogeneous environments. In constantly changing environments, or heterogeneous environments, genetic variation in offspring is an advantage because it increases the likelihood that offspring will be able to survive and reproduce. Thus, sexual reproduction is favored in rotifer populations when the environment is changing, or heterogeneous. For a link to the study this lesson is based on, see the following URL: http://doi.org/10.1038/nature09449.

Knowledge for Teaching

Prominent misconceptions about genetics that are common in student populations and that may be elicited through these activities or influence thinking during these activities include the following: (1) each trait is influenced by one Mendelian locus, and (2) each locus has only two alleles. For more details on these misconceptions and how to address them, please refer to http://evolution .berkeley.edu/evolibrary/misconceptions_faq.php. Also, there are some academic and scientific language demands in this lesson such as the words *conclusive, inconclusive, variation, gene, allele, homozygous recessive, homozygous dominant, heterozygous, carrier, genotype, phenotype,* and *locus.*

Prior Knowledge for Students

Genetically, students will need to know a fair amount about Mendelian genetics to complete this lesson. For instance, they should know that different gene forms are called alleles. They should know that multiple alleles may be present at any given locus (e.g., more than just two). And, last, they should have a clear understanding of the common dominant-recessive relationships discussed within Mendelian genetics along with the genotypic and phenotypic ratios commonly observed in monohybrid crosses. In addition to these Mendelian concepts, students should know some molecular genetics, such as the structure of DNA. They should know that genes are sequences of nucleotides and that different gene forms, or alleles, correspond to different nucleotide sequences at the same locus. Reproductively, students should know the differences between asexual and sexual reproduction. They should know that sexual reproduction produces genetic variation through processes such as independent assortment of alleles and homologous recombination. And, they should know that asexual reproduction tends not to produce genetic variation; rather, at best, it can only conserve or pass on the genetic variation that already exists in a population. Students should be capable of describing their knowledge of these concepts using scientific vocabulary such as *heterozygous, homozygous, dominant, recessive, genotype,* and *phenotype.* They should also be familiar with words such as *homogeneous* and *heterogeneous.*

Teaching Sequence

Lesson 1: How Do These Rotifers Reproduce?

- **(10 min)** Have students read independently about the disagreement between Alan and Jimmy. Then, pair them off into groups of two and ask the students to look at the evidence and discuss whether it supports Alan's or Jimmy's claim.
- **(10 min)** Next, lead a debate using an argument line on this question: "Do the data better support Alan's claim of sexual reproduction or Jimmy's claim of asexual reproduction? What makes you say that?"
- **(10 min)** Have the students complete the graphic organizer summarizing the arguments on both sides of the debate.

Lesson 2: Extension Activity—Proposed Explanations for the Data

- **(10 min)** Introduce students to the reproductive models that Alan and Jimmy use to explain the genetic evidence they collected. Alan uses a heterozygote cross. Jimmy uses a cloning model to explain the data.
- **(10 min)** Ask the students to discuss the prompt at the end of the worksheet and to come up with an answer in pairs.
- **(20 min)** After everyone has finished, use an argument line to debate, "Does Alan or Jimmy have a better model to explain the data? What makes you say that?"

Lesson 3: Extension Activity—Collecting More Data to Resolve the Debate

- **(5 min)** Explain to the students that both models account for the pattern in the data so we cannot determine which model is better. We need to collect more data to determine an answer to our question.
- **(5 min)** Introduce the new data that Alan and Jimmy collected to resolve their debate.
- **(5 min)** Have the students work in groups of four to discuss the new evidence and whether it supports Alan's or Jimmy's claims about sexual and asexual reproduction.
- **(20 min)** Use the four corners activity to discuss the strengths and weaknesses of each argument.
- **(20 min)** Have the students come up with an argument about why the other person's argument is flawed.
- **(10 min)** Lead a debate using an argument line with the whole class to conclude the debate. At the end, explain the strengths and weaknesses you, as a teacher perceive, in Alan's and Jimmy's arguments.

Student Activity: Is Rotifer Reproduction Sexual or Asexual?

 An electronic copy of this activity is available on the companion website at https://resources.corwin.com/ OsborneArgumentation.

How Do These Rotifers Reproduce?

There is a species called a rotifer that is capable of sexual or asexual reproduction (Figure A.13.1). The rotifer tends to reproduce asexually when it lives in a homogeneous environment, and it tends to reproduce sexually when it lives in a heterogeneous environment.

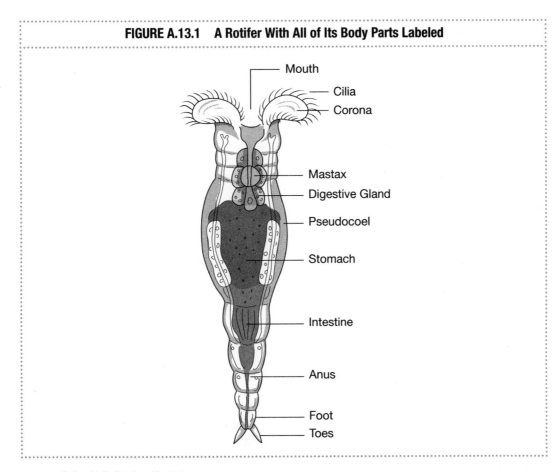

FIGURE A.13.1   A Rotifer With All of Its Body Parts Labeled

Source: © David R. Dudley, Illustrator.

Alan and Jimmy have just sampled 100 individual rotifers from a pond near their homes. They want to know if the rotifer population in the pond is reproducing sexually or asexually. To answer this question, they collect a DNA sample from each of the 100 rotifers. Then, they compare each rotifer's DNA sequence at the same location in their DNA. They find the following:

- 27% have this sequence of DNA (TCCA/TCCA)
- 49% have this sequence of DNA (TCCA/TGCA)
- 24% have this sequence of DNA (TGCA/TGCA)

After looking at these data, Alan claims that the rotifers are sexual reproducers. Jimmy claims that the rotifers are asexual reproducers.

	Alan	**Jimmy**
Claim	The rotifers are sexual reproducers.	The rotifers are asexual reproducers.
Does the genetic evidence support this claim? If so, then why? If not, then why?		

Proposed Explanations for the Data

Alan's Reproductive Model

Heterozygote Cross		**Parent 1**	
		TCCA	**TGCA**
Parent 2	TCCA	TCCA/TCCA	TCCA/TGCA
	TGCA	TCCA/TGCA	TGCA/TGCA

Alan's argument: When two heterozygous individuals reproduce sexually, there is a 25% chance of producing homozygous-dominant offspring, a 50% chance of producing offspring with a heterozygous genotype, and a 25% chance of producing offspring with a recessive genotype that is homozygous. If the rotifers were heterozygous and sexually reproducing, it would explain why 27% of the rotifers had the DNA sequence TCCA/TCCA. The genotype TCCA/TCCA is a recessive genotype that is homozygous. If the parents were heterozygotes, it also explains why 49%, or nearly half, of the rotifers had the heterozygous genotype, TCCA/TGCA. Finally, if the parents were heterozygotes and reproduced sexually, it would explain why 24% of the rotifers had a homozygous-recessive genotype, TGCA/TGCA. Because the proportion of genotypes in our sample fits the 1:2:1 ratio predicted by a heterozygote cross in a Punnett square, the rotifers must be sexual reproducers.

Jimmy's Reproductive Model

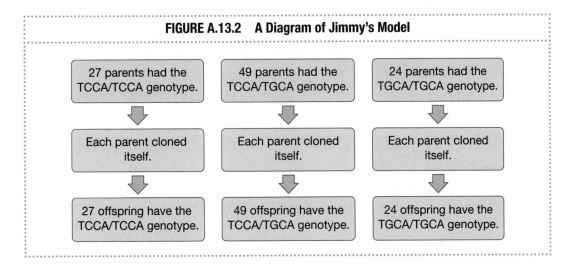

FIGURE A.13.2   A Diagram of Jimmy's Model

27 parents had the TCCA/TCCA genotype.	49 parents had the TCCA/TGCA genotype.	24 parents had the TGCA/TGCA genotype.
Each parent cloned itself.	Each parent cloned itself.	Each parent cloned itself.
27 offspring have the TCCA/TCCA genotype.	49 offspring have the TCCA/TGCA genotype.	24 offspring have the TGCA/TGCA genotype.

Jimmy's argument: I disagree with your argument, Alan. I think that the reason we see a 1:2:1 ratio of genotypes in our sample is because the individuals cloned themselves. For example, 27 of the homozygous-dominant parents cloned themselves, 49 of the heterozygous-dominant parents cloned themselves, and 24 of the homozygous-recessive parents cloned themselves (Figure A.13.2). I also think there is a flaw in your argument. The Punnett square model predicts 25 homozygous-dominant individuals, 50 heterozygous individuals, and 25 homozygous-recessive individuals. But we did not observe these numbers. Instead, we observed two more homozygous-dominant individuals than expected, one less heterozygous individual than what was expected, and one less homozygous-dominant individual than was expected. So you must be wrong because the data do not fit your model.

Discussion question: Who do you think has a better explanation for the patterns of genotypes found in the data? What makes you say that?

Collecting More Data to Resolve the Debate

Alan and Jimmy decide that both of their explanations are consistent with the data. So, they decide to collect more data to determine if the rotifers in their pond are sexual or asexual reproducers. Instead of looking at just one locus, Alan and Jimmy analyze the genotypes of their rotifers at five different locations. They also collect data on the availability of food in the environment of the pond. Their findings are presented in the section that follows.

Genetic Data

Alan and Jimmy find that the rotifers in the pond have different sequences of DNA at each locus in their DNA. For example, when they look at the first locus, they find three different alleles in the population of rotifers. When they look at the second locus, they find that the sample of rotifers has a total of three different alleles as well. The following table summarizes how many alleles were found at each locus in the sample of rotifers and the proportion of rotifers that have this allele.

Locus	Alleles Found in the Sample at Each Locus
1	TTT (34%), TCT (33%), TCA (33%)
2	GGG (50%), GGC (23%), CGG (27%)
3	AAT (60%), TAT (40%)
4	TTTTG (90%), GTTTT (5%), GGTTT (3%), GGGTT (1%), TTTTC (1%)
5	AAAA (100%)

Environmental Data

Alan and Jimmy find that quality and quantity of food vary across the pond. At the surface of the pond, there is more food for the rotifers. But, as you go deeper, there is less food available. The quality of the food, in terms of caloric content, also gets lower as one moves away from the shore of the lake. Figure A.13.3 presents two drawings summarizing these patterns.

Quality and Quantity of Food in the Pond

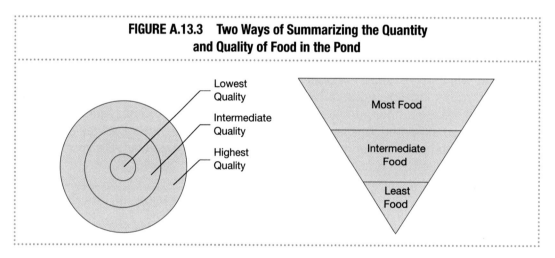

FIGURE A.13.3   Two Ways of Summarizing the Quantity and Quality of Food in the Pond

At first glance, do you think these new data support the claim that the rotifers are reproducing sexually or the claim that they are reproducing asexually? What makes you say that?

Four Corners Discussion

Each corner of the room represents a different point of view. The first corner represents the strengths of the argument for sexual reproduction, and the second represents the weaknesses in the argument for sexual reproduction. The third corner represents the strengths in the argument for asexual reproduction, and the fourth represents the weaknesses in the argument for asexual reproduction. As you rotate through each corner of the room, discuss the strengths or weaknesses of each argument with your group.

Constructing Your Argument

Do the data better support Alan's claim that the rotifers in the pond are sexual reproducers or Jimmy's claim that the rotifers are asexual reproducers?

CLAIM	REASONING	EVIDENCE

If you think these data support Alan's argument, then why do you think Jimmy's claim is flawed? Conversely, if you think the data support Jimmy's argument, then why do you think Alan's argument is flawed?

Argument Line

Are the rotifers in the pond sexual or asexual reproducers? Use your argument above to pick a position on the line and to argue for your position.

Suggested Responses

Beneath are an indication of the possible responses to this activity that would demonstrate a good understanding of the science. The students might not use this language in their work, but you would still want to look for these concepts in their work.

- **Lesson 1:** An exemplary response for Lesson 1 would involve stating that the evidence is inconclusive. The data appear to support the claim that the rotifers are reproducing sexually because there is genotypic variation that corresponds to the expected genotypic ratio in a population of sexually reproducing heterozygous individuals. Because we have genetic variation at a single locus, the data are consistent with Alan's claim that the rotifers are sexual reproducers. But the data are not inconsistent with Jimmy's claim that the rotifers are asexually reproducing. For example, it is possible for asexually reproducing lines of rotifers to exhibit a 1:2:1 ratio of genotypes if the initial founding population exhibited the same variability.
- **Lesson 2:** An exemplary response for Lesson 2 would involve stating that the evidence is still inconclusive for the same reasons stated in Lesson 1. However, students who have thought deeply about the debate might point out that the genetic data correspond very closely to the predicted genotypic ratio from a heterozygous cross. Furthermore, students might point out that Jimmy's counterargument that the data do not perfectly fit a heterozygous cross is misguided, because Punnett squares are probability models.
- **Lesson 3:** An exemplary response for Lesson 3 would involve stating that the evidence more strongly supports the claim of sexual reproduction. First, there is genetic variation at all loci in the sampled genome of the rotifers. This evidence supports the claim of sexual reproduction because sexual reproduction generates genetic variation. Therefore, we would expect a sexually reproducing species to exhibit variation at multiple loci. Second, there is variability in the quality and quantity of food throughout the pond. In the introduction, the students are told that rotifers tend to reproduce sexually when living in a heterogeneous environment. Thus, the environmental data are consistent with a sexually reproducing population. Given that the environmental and genetic data are consistent with a sexual model of reproduction, Alan appears to have won the debate.

Notes

_____

_____

_____

_____

Why Don't Lions Have Stripes?

Learning Goals

The goals of this activity are for students to learn to

- understand how a phylogenetic tree shows evolutionary relationships between organisms
- use similarities and differences in the morphology of cats to make claims about the evolution of coat coloration in cats

NGSS References

MS-LS4-2

Apply scientific ideas to construct an explanation for the anatomical similarities and differences among modern organisms and between modern and fossil organisms to infer evolutionary relationships.

    Clarification Statement: Emphasis is on explanations of the evolutionary relationships among organisms in terms of similarity or differences of the gross appearance of anatomical structures.

The first lesson engages students in argumentation to help them explore the properties of phylogenetic trees and to use phylogenetic trees to make inferences about the ancestral relations between different species of cats. In the second lesson, students are asked to make arguments about where and when characteristic patterns of coat coloration evolved in cats.

Science Background

Content Knowledge

Teachers will need to be familiar with the different kinds of coat coloration in cats. A flecked coat is another way of saying a spotted coat. Find a picture of a Canada lynx to see what it looks like. A uniform coat is one that lacks any patterns. Find a picture of a mountain lion or a jaguarundi to see what it looks like. A striped coat can be found on tigers and is attached as an image to this lesson, because the lesson is about why lion's don't have stripes. Show the students the attached picture of the tiger if needed. A rosette coat can be seen on a leopard. It consists of rose-like, or flowery, shaped spots (see Figure A.14.4 on page 165). Familiarize yourself with these coat colorations and find pictures of them for your students.

    As for phylogenetic trees, you should know that the number of shared nodes between two different species tells you something about how related two species are. Since nodes represent common ancestors, two species separated by two nodes are more closely related than two species separated by three nodes.

    Beyond the different forms of coat coloration and the basics of the tree node, one also needs to know how a phylogenetic tree is constructed. The methods that scientists use to construct phylogenies are typically mathematical, and they rely on molecular genetic data or character data (i.e., phenotype data). Today, scientists conduct pairwise comparisons of the DNA sequences counting up the number of differences in the nucleotide sequence between different species.

After counting the genetic differences, scientists create a distance matrix that records the total number of nucleotide differences between the organisms in their sample. By applying a molecular clock based on a known mutation rate, population genetic theory, and statistical methods, scientists are able to construct phylogenetic trees and assign a probability to them. Yet, there is always more than one way to skin a cat—so to speak. Therefore, scientists often argue about which phylogeny represents the data the best. When different groups of scientists use different genetic or phenotypic measures and/or different statistical methods on the same sample of organisms and produce the same phylogenetic tree, then it probably means that they have inferred an evolutionarily accurate tree. Nevertheless, as scientists collect more data, their phylogenetic maps change too. Thus, scientists tend to argue about the phylogeny that best fits the data. The original study that constructed the phylogeny in this lesson can be found at the following URL: http://online library.wiley.com/doi/10.1111/j.1095-8312.1997.tb01632.x/full.

Once a tree has been constructed, it can be used to make inferences about the evolution of phenotypic characteristics in and across species. That is what the second lesson in this activity is focused on. It asks students to make claims about where the different kinds of coat coloration evolved on the phylogeny.

Knowledge for Teaching

Prominent misconceptions about evolution that may be elicited through these activities or may influence thinking during these activities include the following: (1) taxa that are adjacent to each other are more closely related to one another than they are to taxa further away from them on the tips of the phylogeny, (2) taxa that appear near the top right-hand side of a phylogeny are more evolutionarily advanced than those appearing below them, and (3) a long branch on a phylogeny indicates that a taxon has changed very little over the course of time. For more details on these misconceptions and how to address them, please refer to http://evolution.berkeley.edu/evolibrary/misconceptions_faq.php.

Prior Knowledge for Students

Students should already be familiar with the idea that a phylogenetic tree shows evolutionary relationships between organisms. They should know that the nodes on a phylogenetic tree label the hypothesized common ancestor of the organisms downstream from that node. They should also know that the length of the lines on a tree represent time, and therefore, species separated from their most recent common ancestor by longer lines are more distantly related than species separated from their common ancestor by shorter lines. Last, students should know that phylogenetic trees can be constructed by scientists using phenotypic or genetic data from extant organisms.

Teaching Sequence
Lesson 1: Evaluating Claims About the Relationships
Between Organisms on a Phylogenetic Tree

- **(5 min)** Introduce students to the phylogenetic tree in the student materials. Say the names of each cat out loud and show the students pictures of these animals, pointing out each species' distinct characteristics.
- **(5 min)** Show students the phylogenetic tree of cats and explain that it shows evolutionary relationships between species in its branching pattern. Explain that as you move from right to left, you go back in time. Explain how the tree was constructed by scientists and it represents an evidence-based hypothesis for the evolutionary relationships between cats.

- **(5 min)** Have the students read aloud the four claims listed for the "four corners debate." Explain to students they will be using the tree in Figure A.14.1 to debate the accuracy of the four claims. Go over the rules of the four corners discussion, explaining that in each corner, the students will discuss the strengths and weaknesses of each claim. Students will have 5 to 7 minutes per corner to discuss the claim and decide whether they agree or disagree with it. They will need to provide evidence from the phylogenetic tree and reasons to support their claim in the graphic organizer provided to them.
- **(20–30 min)** Have students perform the four corners debate.
- **(5 min)** Big reveal: Explain how Claim 1 is wrong because the snow leopard and leopard have a more recent common ancestor than the jaguar and jaguarundi. Explain how Claim 2 is incorrect because time is not represented from top to bottom in the phylogeny; rather, it is represented from left to right. Explain how Claim 3 is correct because the jaguarundi has a more recent common ancestor with the snow leopard than it does with the bobcat. Explain how Claim 4 is incorrect because the tiger has a more recent common ancestor with the jaguar than it does with the snow leopard.

Lesson 2: Extension Activity—Arguing About
the Origin of Traits on an Evolutionary Tree

- **(5–10 min)** Explain each of the different kinds of coat coloration to students and show them the data in Table A.14.1. Introduce students to Figure A.14.2 and explain how each letter represents a possible spot in the evolutionary tree where a specific kind of coat coloration could have evolved. Explain that it is their task to use the data in Table A.14.1 to make claims about out where each trait evolved on the tree.
- **(20–30 min)** Have the students work in groups of four to complete the graphic organizer for their arguments about where each trait evolved and then have the students label the places on the blank tree where they believe each trait evolved.
- **(10 min)** Pair students from different groups together and have them identify any differences in their trees and discuss the reasons for these differences.
- **(10 min)** Have students reconvene in their original group and make changes to their tree. Ask students to explain their reasons for making any changes in writing in response to the prompt below the phylogeny.
- **(5 min)** Have students answer the following question: Why don't lions have stripes?

Student Activities: Why Don't Lions Have Stripes?

 An electronic copy of this activity is available on the companion website at https://resources.corwin.com/OsborneArgumentation.

Lesson 1

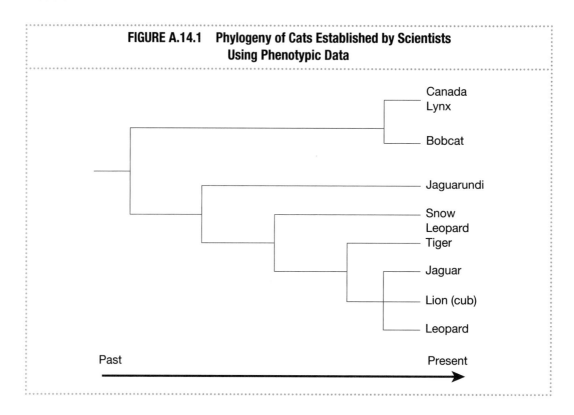

FIGURE A.14.1   **Phylogeny of Cats Established by Scientists Using Phenotypic Data**

Four Corners Debate

Which of these four claims is supported by the phylogenetic tree and the evidence in the data table?

- **Claim 1:** The jaguar and the jaguarundi are more closely related to each other than the leopard and the snow leopard are.
- **Claim 2:** The Canada lynx evolved into the bobcat, which evolved into the jaguarundi, which evolved into the snow leopard, which evolved into the tiger, which evolved into the jaguar, which evolved into the lion, which evolved into the leopard.
- **Claim 3:** The jaguarundi is more closely related to the snow leopard than it is to the bobcat.
- **Claim 4:** The leopard is more closely related to the lion than it is to the jaguar.

Instructions: Each corner of the room represents one of the four claims above. As you move to each corner of the room, discuss each claim in reference to the phylogeny in Figure 5.15 and the data in Table 5.1. As a group, discuss whether the phylogeny support or reject each claim. As a group, state whether you agree or disagree with each claim and outline the reasons that led you to this conclusion.

	Claim 1	Claim 2	Claim 3	Claim 4
My group agrees with. . .				
My group disagrees with. . .				
Our reasons are. . .				

Lesson 2

In pairs, use the data in Table 5.1 and the phylogenetic tree in Figure 5.16 to construct an argument for where each of the five following traits evolved.

TABLE A.14.1   Evidence: Phenotypes of Each Species

	Canada Lynx	Bobcat	Jaguarundi	Snow Leopard	Tiger	Jaguar	Lion (Cub)	Leopard
Short Tail	Yes	Yes	No	No	No	No	No	No
Long Tail	No	No	Yes	Yes	Yes	Yes	Yes	Yes
Flecked Coat	Yes	Yes	No	No	No	No	No	No
Uniform Coat	No	No	Yes	No	No	No	No	No
Striped Coat	No	No	No	No	Yes	No	No	No
Rosette Coat	No	No	No	Yes	No	Yes	Yes	Yes

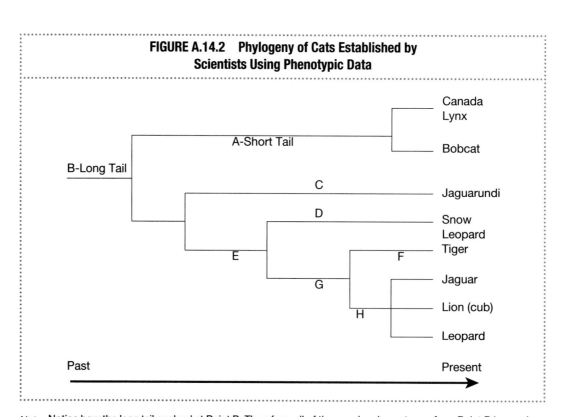

FIGURE A.14.2   Phylogeny of Cats Established by Scientists Using Phenotypic Data

Note: Notice how the long tail evolved at Point B. Therefore, all of the species downstream from Point B have a long tail with the exception of the Canada lynx and bobcat. These species evolved a short tail at Point A. Therefore, only the lynx and the bobcat have a short tail.

FIGURE A.14.3   A Tiger With Its Characteristic Striped Coat

Source: © David R. Dudley, Illustrator.

FIGURE A.14.4   A Snow Leopard With Its Characteristic Rosette Coat

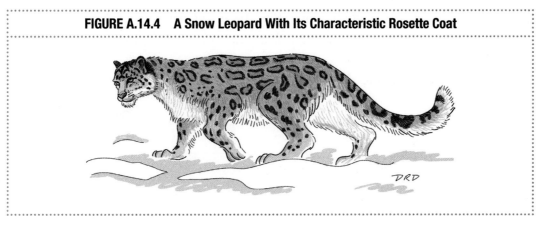

Source: © David R. Dudley, Illustrator.

CLAIM	REASONING	EVIDENCE
We hypothesize that the flecked coat evolved over time somewhere along the branch labeled with the letter:		
We hypothesize that the rosette coat evolved over time somewhere along the branch labeled with the letter:		

(Continued)

(Continued)

CLAIM	REASONING	EVIDENCE
We hypothesize that the uniform coat evolved over time somewhere along the branch labeled with the letter:		
We hypothesize that the striped coat evolved over time somewhere along the branch labeled with the letter:		

In Figure A.14.5, label the branch on the tree where you believe each trait evolved over time.

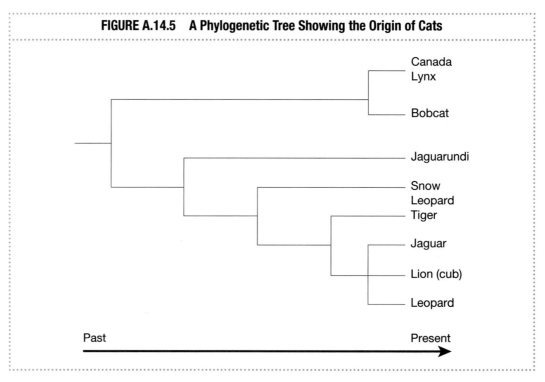

FIGURE A.14.5   A Phylogenetic Tree Showing the Origin of Cats

Source: © David R. Dudley, Illustrator.

Explain any changes that you made to your tree based on your discussion with someone from another group. Why did you make these changes?

What is your explanation for why lions don't have stripes?

Suggested Responses

Beneath are an indication of the possible responses to this activity that would demonstrate a good understanding of the science:

Lesson 1: An exemplary response for Lesson 1 would argue that (a) Claim 1 is incorrect because the leopard and snow leopard have a more recent common ancestor than the jaguar and jaguarundi, and (b) Claim 2 is incorrect because, for example, the bobcat and Canada lynx evolved from the same common ancestor. Students might also argue that neither the Canada lynx nor the bobcat shows more relatedness to the other cat species. Therefore, it cannot be the case that the lynx evolved into the bobcat, which evolved into the other cats. (c) Claim 3 is correct because the jaguarundi has a more recent common ancestor with the snow leopard than the bobcat, and (d) Claim 4 is incorrect because the leopard, lion, and jaguar all diverged from the same common ancestor.

Lesson 2: An exemplary response for Lesson 2 would argue that the flecked coat evolved first at Point B. Then, it was lost at Points C and E. Given that only the jaguarundi has a uniform coat, uniform coats probably evolved at Point C. Given that snow leopards, jaguars, lions, and leopards all have a rosette coat, the rosette coat probably evolved at Point E. However, because only the tiger has a striped coat, the rosette coat was probably lost at Point F when striped coats evolved in the line leading to the tigers. If these claims are correct, then lions do not have stripes for two main reasons. The first is that the evolutionary line leading to tigers broke away from the evolutionary line leading to jaguars, lions, and leopards before stripes evolved. Stripes evolved after tigers had separated from the other big cats.

Notes

_____

_____

_____

_____

_____

_____

_____

How Do You Design a Test of Evolutionary Theory?

Learning Goals

The goals of this activity are for students to learn

- how scientists design studies to test hypotheses about evolution
- about the social processes involved in the funding of scientific research
- to apply evolutionary ideas, such as variation, inheritance, selection, and time, to evaluate a biological study
- to construct arguments about the quality of a scientific study design

NGSS References

MS-LS4-4

Construct an explanation based on evidence that describes how genetic variations of traits in a population increase some individuals' probability of surviving and reproducing in a specific environment.

Clarification Statement: Emphasis is on using simple probability statements and proportional reasoning to construct explanations.

In this lesson, students will design a study to test the evolution of larger feet in a species of lizard. In the first lesson, students engage in argument to design a study in a small group to test a hypothesis based in evolutionary theory. In the second lesson, students engage in argument in a peer-review process to evaluate how well another group's study tests evolutionary theory.

Science Background

Content Knowledge

This lesson demands a lot of content knowledge about evolution, adaptation, and the nature of science. The present lesson tests a hypothesis that is based in the theory of evolution by natural selection. Theories explain a wide variety of phenomena and are supported by a broad range of scientific evidence. Hypotheses, on the other hand, are the predictions made by a theory. The present case discusses how one ought to test a hypothesis about lizard evolution.

The case debated in this lesson revolves around the rapid evolution of two species of lizard, *Anolis carolinensis* and *Anolis sagrei,* which can be found along the subtropical islands of Florida. The actual scientific study that this case is based on can be found at the following URL: http://doi .org/10.1126/science.1257008.

In the present case, scientists are testing the hypothesis that competition between closely related species of *Anolis* lizards (*A. carolinensis* and *A. sagrei*) will lead to the evolution of larger feet in *A. carolinensis,* as individuals of this species begin to forage higher in trees to reduce competition with the other lizard, *A. sagrei*. The reasoning for this hypothesis is that for adaptation to occur, there needs to be sufficient variation in foot size within both species. Furthermore, this variation needs to be heritable, or genetically encoded, so that it can be passed from parent to offspring through reproduction. Then, there needs to be selection pressure. In the present case, scientists impose selection pressure by increasing interspecific competition. Under competition with *A. sagrei*, *A. carolinensis* individuals with larger feet have a competitive advantage over *A. carolinensis* individuals, who have smaller feet, because they can get more food by climbing higher in the trees to forage. This behavior reduces competition, and it also favors individuals with larger feet. Thus, over time, the frequency of *A. carolinensis* with large feet on islands where both species coexist should increase. Or, put differently, on islands where both species coexist, *A. carolinensis* individuals should have bigger feet, on average, and forage higher in trees, on average, than *A. carolinensis* individuals living on islands where *A. sagrei* is absent.

Knowledge for Teaching

Prominent misconceptions about evolution that may be elicited through these activities or may influence thinking during these activities include the following:

1. Evolution is a theory about the origin of life.

2. Evolution results in progress.

3. Individual organisms can evolve during a single life span.

4. Evolution only occurs slowly and gradually.

5. Natural selection involves organisms trying to adapt.

6. All traits of organisms are adaptations.

7. Evolution is not science because it is not observable or testable.

8. Evolution is "just a theory."

For more details on these misconceptions and how to address them, please refer to http://evolution .berkeley.edu/evolibrary/misconceptions_faq.php, or to http://www.ucmp.berkeley.edu/ncte/twb/ misconceptions.html. Also, there are some academic and scientific language demands in this lesson such as the words *variation, inheritance, selection, peer-review, theory, hypothesis, competition,* and *assumption.*

Prior Knowledge for Students

There is a high degree of prior knowledge assumed in this lesson. Regarding the nature of science, students should know the difference between a hypothesis and a theory. Ecologically, students should know that competition between two species that share the same niche is intense. Last, but not least, evolutionarily, students should know that the theory of evolution by natural selection claims that species evolve provided that four criteria are met: (1) There is phenotypic variation in a population, (2) the different phenotypes in a population are inherited through genes, (3) selective factors in the environment cause some individuals with certain kinds of phenotypes to survive and reproduce more than individuals with other kinds of phenotypes, and (4) there is a sufficient amount of time for selection to act on a population to change the frequency of individuals with certain phenotypes. In addition, students should know that adaptations evolve through the process of natural selection.

Teaching Sequence

Lesson 1: Sorting Studies on Lizard Feet to Construct a Proposed Study

- **(10 min)** Introduce the reading entitled "Lizard Feet." Read the case aloud as a class. Highlight how the case is about testing whether evolution is occurring because of competition between two closely related species that share the same niche. Explain to students that they are tasked with designing a study to test the hypothesis in the case.
- **(20 min)** Have students work in groups of four to sort each study onto the provided graphic organizer. Use a modified version of the listening triads method to structure group participation. The reader is the person who will read the study description. The revoicer is the person who will describe what was just read in his or her own words. The decider is the person who will categorize the study on the graphic organizer and provide a reason for his or her choice. The seconder will listen to the decider's reasons and provide a reason for why he or she agrees or disagrees with the decider's opinion (as in, "I second the motion to place the study there, because. . . ."). Students are to cycle through each study design on each of the eight cards, rotating through different roles as they evaluate the design on each card.
- **(10 min)** Have the students in each group decide upon three studies that they think will provide the best test of the hypothesis. Ask students to glue or tape the chosen cards into the provided graphic organizer (entitled "My Study Proposal") and have them write an explanation that summarizes how the three studies provide a test of the hypothesis.

Lesson 2: Evaluation of the Proposed Study Through the Peer-Review Process

- **(5 min)** Introduce the reading entitled "Peer-Review Process." Read the introduction aloud as a class. Highlight how the goal of the activity is to pretend to be a grant review committee. The goal of the committee is to evaluate a research proposal of another group of scientists who are testing a hypothesis about the evolution of lizard feet based in the theory of evolution by natural selection.
- **(15 min)** Hand out the worksheet entitled "Proposed Study." Have each student read the study and circle any passages that describe the different components of evolution by natural selection: (a) variation, (b) inheritance, (c) selection, and (d) time. You may want to have the students use a different color pencil for each term.
- **(5 min)** Explain that every group will evaluate the "Proposed Study" to determine whether it is grounded in the four components of evolutionary theory. Explain that the study should only be funded if it tests all four components of evolutionary theory.
- **(20 min)** For four corners discussion, in each corner of the room, put up signs that say "Variation," "Inheritance," "Selection," and "Time." Tell students that they will rotate around each corner and evaluate whether the proposal tests each of the four components of evolutionary theory. Ask students to fill out the graphic organizer associated with each corner as they rotate through.
- **(5 min)** Using an argument line, have students discuss whether to fund or deny funding for the study based on their evaluation of its theoretical quality.
- **(5 min)** Have students independently write down their decision to fund or not fund the project, as well as their reasons, and suggestions for improving the study.

Student Activities: How Do You Design a Test of Evolutionary Theory?

 An electronic copy of this activity is available on the companion website at https://resources.corwin.com/OsborneArgumentation.

Lizard Feet

Studies have found that evolution can occur rapidly when natural selection is strong. One way that natural selection can be strong is when two closely related species compete with each other for the same resources. Evolutionary biologists have hypothesized that closely related species can evolve to become more genetically different from one another if they have a lot of negative interactions with each other, such as when they compete for food. In the islands surrounding the state of Florida, two species of closely related lizards tend to interact negatively with each other because they compete for the same food sources. One species is called *A. sagrei,* and the other is called *A. carolinensis* (Figure A.15.1). Studies suggest *A. sagrei* has a life span of less than 18 months, whereas *A. carolinensis* lives from 2 to 8 years.

You want to know whether competition between *A. sagrei* and *A. carolinensis* is causing these two closely related species to become more genetically different from one another in areas where the two species coexist. One way that these species might become more different from one another is in the size of their feet. Both species hunt for insects in the trees. But when the two species of lizards share the same habitat, *A. carolinensis* tends to look for food higher in trees than *A. sagrei,* because it reduces competition for food. Because larger feet help lizards climb trees better, you think it would be a good idea to explore whether competition between *A. sagrei* and *A. carolinensis* is causing *A. carolinensis* to climb higher into the trees, which, in turn, will cause populations of *A. carolinensis* to evolve bigger feet.

FIGURE A.15.1 *A. carolinensis* (Top) and *A. sagrei* (Bottom)

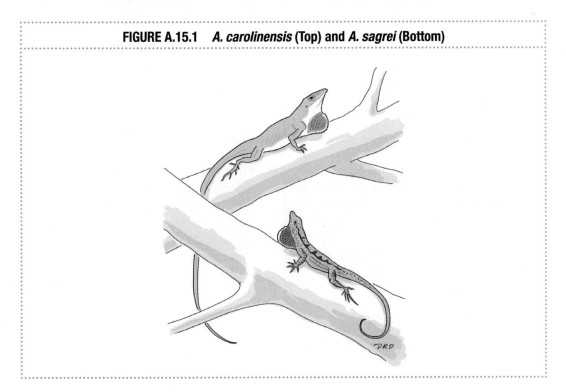

Source: © David R. Dudley, Illustrator.

Study Sort

Each of the following studies costs money and takes a lot of time to conduct. Read each study carefully. To come to a conclusion about which studies to conduct, cut out each square and sort them into the following table to identify those studies that test your full hypothesis, those studies that do not test your hypothesis, and those studies that partially test your hypothesis.

Hypothesis: Competition between *A. sagrei* and *A. carolinensis* will cause *A. carolinensis* to forage higher in trees and evolve larger feet over time.

A. Find islands where only *A. carolinensis* is present and islands where both species of lizard are present. Collect observations on how high the lizards forage for food in the trees. Measure the size of lizard feet. Collect these data for a year.	B. Go to islands that contain either one species of lizard or the other. At each island, collect eggs from the lizard species. Raise these offspring in the same laboratory environment with the same amount of food. See if the foot size of the offspring in the lab is identical to the foot size of the parents in the wild.
C. Create lizard traps and distribute them on different islands to collect a bunch of lizards. Measure the foot size of *A. carolinensis* individuals on islands where both species exist. Compare this to the foot size of *A. carolinensis* individuals on islands where there is no population of *A. sagrei*. Collect these data for 20 years.	D. Introduce *A. sagrei* individuals to islands where *A. carolinensis* individuals live alone. Then, measure how high each individual forages for food in the trees and its foot size. Do this for a period of 20 years. Collect the same measures on islands where only *A. carolinensis* individuals are present. Compare the data from the two different islands.
E. Introduce *A. sagrei* individuals to islands where only *A. carolinensis* individuals live. Then, collect observations on how high each species forages for food in the trees and the foot size of individuals. Collect these data for 20 years.	F. Find islands where both species of lizards have been living together for many years. Collect DNA from each lizard on the island and measure how many genetic differences exist between individuals from different species.
G. Collect eggs from individuals from both species on islands where both species exist. Raise these offspring in the same laboratory environment with the same amount and kind of food. See if the foot size of the offspring in the lab is identical to the foot size of the parents in the wild.	H. Find islands where both species of lizards have been living together for many years and islands where only *A. carolinensis* individuals are present. Measure how genetically different the populations of *A. carolinensis* are on different islands.

Hypothesis: Competition between *A. sagrei* and *A. carolinensis* will cause *A. carolinensis* to forage higher in trees and evolve larger feet over time.

Place studies that fully test the hypothesis to the left of the line. Place studies that do not test the hypothesis to the right of the line. Place studies that partially test the hypothesis on the line.

Studies That Fully Test Hypothesis	Studies That Do Not Test Hypothesis

My Study Proposal

Instructions: Based on your sorting of the studies, pick three studies that you think will provide the best test of your hypothesis. Then place these three studies into the graphic organizer in the order you will conduct them.

Hypothesis: Competition between *A. sagrei* and *A. carolinensis* will cause *A. carolinensis* to forage higher in trees and evolve larger feet over time.		
Order	Place your chosen studies into the boxes below in the order that you will conduct them.	Explain how these three studies provide a test of your hypothesis.
1		
2		
3		

Proposed Study

The hypothesis is the following: Competition between *A. sagrei* and *A. carolinensis* will cause *A. carolinensis* to forage higher in trees and evolve larger feet over time. Below is our study design.		
1	Find islands where only *A. carolinensis* is present and islands where both species of lizard are present. Collect observations on how high the lizards forage for food in the trees. Measure the size of lizard feet. Collect these data for a year.	The first study will provide us with baseline data about the lizards. It will tell us how high the lizards forage in the trees (perch height) and what the average foot size is for each species across islands. It will help us understand if there is variation in foot size and perch height in populations of *A. carolinensis,* which can be acted upon by selection. However, this study will not tell us whether the different perch heights and foot sizes were caused by competition between the species. The second study allows us to test this claim about selection.
2	Introduce *A. sagrei* individuals to islands where *A. carolinensis* individuals live alone. Then, measure how high each individual forages for food in the trees and its foot size. Do this for a period of 20 years. Collect the same measures on islands where only *A. carolinensis* individuals are present. Compare the data from the two different islands.	When we introduce *A. sagrei* lizards to the islands where only *A. carolinensis* is present, we can measure if *A. carolinensis* begin to forage higher in the trees for food. Also, we can see if individuals in the population of *A. carolinensis* with bigger feet reproduce more often and become more common in the population. Therefore, this study allows us to manipulate selection by adding competition to see if it changes which individuals survive and reproduce over long periods of time. If we find that the population of *A. carolinensis* forages higher in the trees and develops bigger feet, then this suggests that the population is evolving. If our hypothesis is correct, then we would expect *A. carolinensis* to have larger feet on the islands where both species are present compared to the islands where only *A. carolinensis* is present. The one problem with this design is that it does not allow us to figure out whether foot size and foraging behavior of *A. carolinensis* is heritable. That is, we do not know whether foot sizes differ because individuals with genes for big feet are surviving and reproducing more often.
3	Select eggs from individuals from both species from islands where both species exist and raise these offspring in the same laboratory environment with the same amount and kind of food. See if the foot size of the offspring in the lab is identical to the foot size of the parents in the wild.	Study 3 allows us to test whether foot size and foraging behavior are heritable because if big-footed parents produce big-footed offspring in a completely different environment where all lizards get the same amount and kind of food, then it is probably because they inherited genes for big feet from their parents.

Peer-Review Process

To do scientific research, you need to have money to carry out your research plans. When scientists conduct research, they write a proposal to a funding agency to get money for the research. At the funding agency, each proposal is read by a panel of people, called reviewers, who argue about which research studies are worth funding. Reviewers tend to fund research projects if they meet two criteria: (1) the research needs to test a hypothesis that is firmly rooted in theory; (2) the research needs to involve methods that provide a convincing test of the hypothesis. The hypothesis we are working with in this lesson is rooted in the theory of evolution by natural selection. To establish that evolution by natural selection has occurred, scientists need to produce evidence to support each of the following claims:

1. **Variation:** The organisms within a population vary genetically and phenotypically.

2. **Inheritance:** Phenotypic traits are inherited from parents and are passed on to offspring through DNA.

3. **Selection:** Organisms with traits that are favorable for survival and reproduction are more likely to pass on the genes for these traits to the next generation.

4. **Time:** Evolutionary change can happen in a few generations, but major change, such as speciation, often takes many thousands of generations.

Make an argument that the study you are reviewing tests these four claims of evolution by natural selection.

CLAIM	REASONING	EVIDENCE FROM STUDY DESIGN
Corner 1: The study tests the **variation** assumption: Yes or No		
Corner 2: The study tests the **inheritance** assumption: Yes or No		
Corner 3: The study tests the **selection** assumption: Yes or No		

CLAIM	REASONING	EVIDENCE FROM STUDY DESIGN
Corner 4: The study tests the **time** assumption: *Yes or No*		

I think this study should be (circle one) **Funded** or **Denied Funding**.

My reason for this decision is. . . .

To improve this study, I suggest that you. . . .

Suggested Responses

Beneath are an indication of the possible responses to this activity that would demonstrate a good understanding of the science:

Lesson 1: An exemplary response for Lesson 1 would involve a study design and justification similar to the study design used in the second lesson, entitled "Proposed Study."

Lesson 2: An exemplary response for Lesson 2 would involve the argument to fund the study because it clearly tests all four assumptions of evolutionary theory. For example, the proposed set of studies tests the variation assumption because baseline data will be collected to establish how high the lizards forage for food in the trees and how large their feet are in Study 1. The inheritance assumption is tested in Study 3. The selection assumption is tested in Study 2 because the researchers plan to introduce *A. sagrei* lizards to the islands where only *A. carolinensis* are present to measure if *A. carolinensis* begin to forage higher in the trees for food. Also, they plan to see if individuals in the population of *A. carolinensis* with bigger feet reproduce more often and become more common in the population. Therefore, Study 2 manipulates selection by adding competition. Because the total duration of study is 20 years, and because the life span of both species of lizard is much less than the duration of study, there should be enough time to detect evolution if it occurs quickly. The study is based on the idea that evolution can occur extremely quickly when two closely related species compete with one another. Thus, the time assumption is tested in all three studies.

	Extension Activities
	Conduct Lesson 2 by having the students evaluate their classmates' proposed studies.

Notes

_____

_____

_____

_____

_____

What Is Killing the Cats in Warner County?

Learning Goals

The goal of this activity is for students to learn that evolution occurs when selection causes a change in the frequency of a heritable trait in a population over time.

NGSS References

MS-LS4-6

Use mathematical representations to support explanations of how natural selection may lead to increases and decreases of specific traits in populations over time.
  Clarification Statement: Emphasis is on using mathematical models, probability statements, and proportional reasoning to support explanations of trends in changes to populations over time.

This activity encourages students to think about what constitutes evidence for evolution. Students are asked to evaluate a claim about the evolution of cats by sorting individual pieces of evidence from a fictional case study. Then, students are asked to envision mathematical representations of data that could be used to support a claim about the evolution of cats. Finally, students are asked to construct a scientific argument about evolution based on the evidence they have envisioned. In essence, this lesson requires students to apply evolutionary theory to data to evaluate a claim about evolutionary change in a population.

Science Background

Content Knowledge

This activity explores evolution by natural selection and the concept of adaptation. For evolution to occur, it requires (a) the existence of genetically encoded phenotypic variation in a population and (b) selection pressure on a population over time that increases the fitness of some phenotypic variants relative to others in the population. Thus, a mark of evolution by natural selection is a change in the frequency of a heritable trait over time in a population. When natural selection occurs, it can produce adaptation. Adaptations are heritable traits produced by natural selection, which confer a fitness advantage. That is, adaptations evolve in a population through natural selection because they are traits that increase the probability of survival and reproduction.

  In this lesson, selection comes in the form of a fictional disease called feline acquired immunodeficiency syndrome, or FAIDS. This disease is killing cats, and therefore, it is possibly acting as a selective force that is reducing the cat population of Warner County, Wisconsin. The FAIDS epidemic is spread from mice to cats, and there appears to be a genetic variation in the cat population that reduces the probability of dying of FAIDS. The implicit question of this activity, then, is whether or not this genetic mutation is an evolved adaptation.

Knowledge for Teaching

Prominent misconceptions about evolution that may be elicited through these activities or may influence thinking during these activities include the following:

1. Individual organisms can evolve during a single life span.

2. Evolution only occurs slowly and gradually.

3. Organisms are always getting better through evolution.

4. Natural selection involves organisms trying to adapt.

5. Natural selection acts for the good of the species.

6. Natural selection gives organisms what they need.

Please refer to http://evolution.berkeley.edu/evolibrary/misconceptions_faq.php for more details on these misconceptions and how to address them. Also, there are some academic and scientific language demands in this lesson such as the words *eradicate, eradication, transmitted, transmission, conclusive, inconclusive, acquired immunodeficiency syndrome (AIDS),* and *mutation.*

Prior Knowledge for Students

Mathematically, students will need to know how to read and interpret bar and line graphs, and they must also be proficient in the construction of these graphs. Biologically, students will need to know a basic definition of evolution, such as descent with modification. Students should be familiar with evolution by natural selection and thus should know that evolution occurs when selection acts upon heritable variation in a population over time. In addition, students should know about different sources of genetic variation that underlie phenotypic variation in a population, such as mutation, independent assortment of alleles, or homologous recombination. In essence, students need to know how variation, selection, inheritance, and time interact to cause the frequency of traits in a population to change through time.

Teaching Sequence

Lesson 1: The Puzzle of Feline Acquired Immunodeficiency
Disease: Are the Cats of Warner County Evolving?

- **(20 min)** Elicit prior knowledge about evolution by having students complete a Frayer model for the concept of evolution. Review how variation, selection, inheritance, and time interact to cause the frequency of traits in a population to change through time (optional).
- **(15 min)** Have students read the case study. While students read, have them underline information in the text, such as (a) anything that discusses variation in a population in green, (b) anything that discusses selection pressure in red, (c) anything that discusses inheritance of traits in blue, and (d) anything that discusses changes in the frequency of traits in black.
- **(20–30 min)** In small groups of two to four, have students complete the graphic organizer for the evidence sort.
- **(10 min)** When finished with the evidence sort, lead students through a whole-class discussion using an argument line for the question: "Tom and Jerry disagree about whether the cat population in Warner County is evolving a genetic resistance to FAIDS. Do you think the evidence conclusively supports this claim, conclusively rejects this claim, or is the evidence inconclusive? What makes you say that?"

- **(5 min)** Big reveal: Explain how the evidence for evolution is inconclusive because while some evidence supports Tom, much of the evidence supports Jerry. For example, the fact that cats with the mutation are less likely to die of FAIDS and the fact that this mutation is heritable supports the claim that the cat population could evolve a genetic defense against FAIDS. But it does not definitively show that the cats have evolved. House cats usually live for only 15 years. Since FAIDS has only been around for 20 years, there has not been enough time for cats to reproduce so that the mutation can sweep through the population in Warner County. This is reflected in the data on the proportion of cats with the mutation. Basically, the proportion of cats with the beneficial mutation has not changed, which is inconsistent with the claim that the cat population is evolving. Furthermore, the rival argument that the rat eradication program is preventing the spread of the disease is a good one, because the time at which the eradication program began (2005) perfectly coincides with the start of the decline of the disease.

Lesson 2: Extension Activity—Envisioning the Perfect Data

- **(20 min)** Having established that evolution is not occurring, ask the students to envision what the data in each of the four graphs would have to look like to definitively support Tom's claim that the cat population is evolving a genetic defense against FAIDS. Have the students work in groups of four to complete this task. Assign each student in each group to complete one of the four graphs.
- **(15 min)** When students have finished constructing the graphs, jigsaw them into different groups so there is a representative from each of the original groups in each new group. Ask students to discuss the similarities and differences in their graphs and ask them to choose the best set of graphs to support Tom's claim.
- **(10 min)** Once students have generated the best-looking data for Tom's claim, have them use the graphic organizer to outline their argument for how the data support Tom's claim that the cats are evolving a genetic resistance to FAIDS.
- **(5 min)** Big reveal: Explain what the perfect data would look like. First, the time scale for each line graph would have to be long enough for multiple generations of cats. Figure 5.22 could stay exactly the same because it already shows that cats with the mutation survive more than cats without the mutation. Figure 5.23 would have to show an increasing proportion of cats with the mutation through time. Figure 5.24 could show that the rat eradication program is not working, so either the rat population stays the same or it increases through time. The point is that the graph should not show a decrease in the rat population, because this would reduce the selection pressure on the cats.

Student Activities: What Is Killing the Cats in Warner County?

 An electronic copy of this activity is available on the companion website at https://resources.corwin.com/OsborneArgumentation.

Lesson 1: The Puzzle of Feline Acquired Immunodeficiency Disease

House cats can live for 15 years or more. But recently a newly discovered disease is cutting this life span short. A strange new disease is killing cats in the county of Warner, Wisconsin. For the past 20 years, many cats in Warner County have been taken to local veterinarians with symptoms similar to the acquired immunodeficiency disease (AIDS) in humans. Scientists call this disease feline acquired immunodeficiency disease, or FAIDS.

Cats infected with the FAIDS virus have weakened immune systems that are not able to fight off common infections. Therefore, when cats contract the FAIDS virus, they are more likely to die of secondary infections such as pneumonia. Furthermore, scientists have discovered that cats get infected with the FAIDS virus after contact with rats. The virus does not appear to harm the rats, but when cats kill a rat infected with the FAIDS virus, the virus gets transmitted to the cat. The transmission occurs when infected blood from the rat enters into the cat through a mucous membrane such as the cat's nose or mouth.

Almost every cat that contracts the virus that causes FAIDS ends up dying. Yet, some infected cats do not die, which is a big puzzle for scientists. Another puzzling trend is that over the past decade, the amount of infected cats dying of the FAIDS virus has decreased.

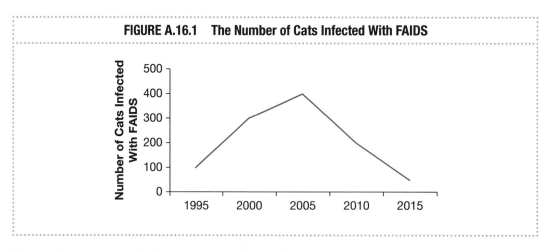

FIGURE A.16.1   The Number of Cats Infected With FAIDS

The data above are not authentic and were created for teaching purposes only.

Recently, two biologists have begun to explore these puzzles. Professors Tom Gatto and Jerry Souris have spent the last year exploring two issues. First, they want to understand why fewer cats are dying of FAIDS. Second, they want to know why a small proportion of cats infected with the FAIDS virus survive. They hypothesize that the cats in Warner County are beginning to evolve a genetic defense against FAIDS.

To test this hypothesis, Tom and Jerry have collected a variety of data. For example, the vets in Warner County have taken blood samples from all of the infected cats. So, Tom and Jerry are able to analyze the DNA in the blood of each cat to see whether the small proportion of surviving cats is genetically different from the cats that have died of FAIDS. They find that cats that have a mutation in a gene that affects the immune system are less likely to die of FAIDS than cats who do not have this mutation. Tom and Jerry have also found that this mutation can be passed from an infected cat to its offspring.

FIGURE A.16.2   The Number of Cat Deaths in Warner County

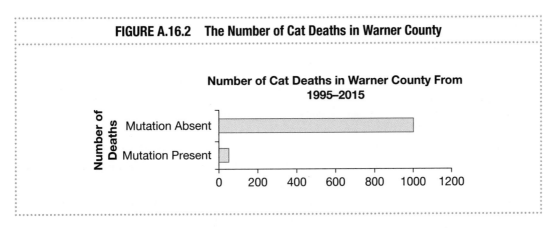

The data above are not authentic and were created for teaching purposes only.

Tom and Jerry also have found that very few cats in Warner County have this mutation and that, over time, the amount of cats with this mutation has not changed a lot.

FIGURE A.16.3   The Proportion of Cats With the Genetic Mutation

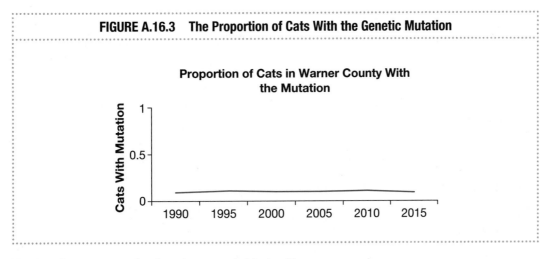

The data above are not authentic and were created for teaching purposes only.

Tom and Jerry have also collected data from the department of pest control in Warner County on the number of rats infected with FAIDS. When Tom and Jerry look over these data, they find that the rat population in Warner County is decreasing over time. In addition, the rat population dropped significantly after Warner County started a program to kill rats in 2005.

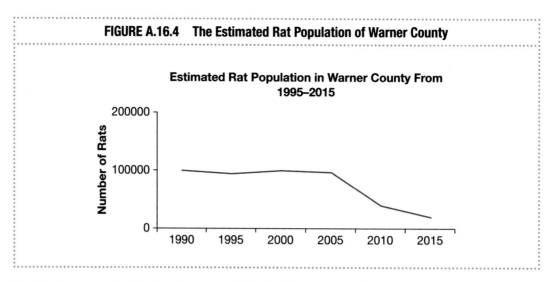

FIGURE A.16.4   The Estimated Rat Population of Warner County

The data above are not authentic and were created for teaching purposes only.

Evidence sort: Based on these data, Tom and Jerry have come to different conclusions about whether or not the cats in Warner County are evolving a genetic defense to FAIDS.

Tom's claim: "The population of cats is evolving a genetic defense against FAIDS."

Jerry's claim: "The rat eradication program is preventing cats from getting infected by the disease."

Which evidence supports Tom's claim and which evidence supports Jerry's claim?

Evidence	Supports Tom	Supports Jerry	Inconclusive	What Is Your Reason for Your Answer?
House cats typically live for 15 years.				
Figure A.16.1. The number of cats infected with the FAIDS virus has decreased over the past 10 years.				
Figure A.16.2. Fewer infected cats have died that have a mutation in a gene that affects immune system function.				

Evidence	Supports Tom	Supports Jerry	Inconclusive	What Is Your Reason for Your Answer?
Figure A.16.3. The proportion of cats with the special mutation has not changed much over a 20-year period.				
Figure A.16.4. The rat population in Warner County has decreased dramatically since 2005.				

Argument line: Tom and Jerry disagree about whether the cat population in Warner County is evolving a genetic resistance to FAIDS. Do you think the evidence conclusively supports this claim, conclusively rejects this claim, or is the evidence inconclusive? What makes you say that?

Lesson 2: Extension Activities—Envisioning the Perfect Data

Draw what the data would look like if they perfectly supported Tom's claim that the cats have evolved a genetic resistance to FAIDS. Be sure to specify the scale of each axis.

- What would Figure A.16.1 look like if Tom's claim was correct?

- What would Figure A.16.2 look like if Tom's claim was correct?

- What would Figure A.16.3 look like if Tom's claim was correct?

Proportion of Cats
With the Mutation

Time

- What would Figure A.16.4 look like if Tom's claim was correct?

Estimated Rat
Population

Time

- How does the evidence in the graphs you just created support Tom's claim that the cats are evolving a genetic resistance to FAIDS?

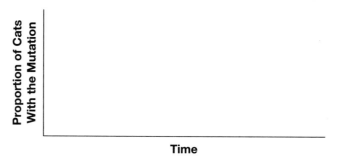

CLAIM	REASONING	EVIDENCE
Cats are evolving a genetic resistance to FAIDS.		

Suggested Responses

Beneath are possible responses to this activity that would demonstrate a good understanding of the science:

Lesson 1: An exemplary response for Lesson 1 would involve arguing that some of the evidence supports Tom's claim and some supports Jerry's claim, but neither claim is conclusively supported by the data. Even though some of the evidence, such as that presented in Figure A.16.2, is clearly consistent with the claim of evolution, much more evidence appears to be consistent with Jerry's claim that the cats are not evolving.

Evidence	Supports Tom	Supports Jerry	Incon-clusive	What Is Your Reason for Your Answer?
House cats typically live for 15 years.		X		This evidence does not support the claim of evolution because evolution by natural selection requires many generations of reproduction to occur. Evolution can occur quickly at times, but if house cats live for 15 years and there is only 30 years of data, then there is, at most, only two to four generations of cats present in the data set. It is not likely that the cat population can evolve in 30 years given the reproduction rate of the cats.
Figure A.16.1. The number of cats infected with the FAIDS virus has decreased over the past 10 years.			X	This evidence could support either claim and is therefore inconclusive. On one hand, the fact that the amount of cats with FAIDS is decreasing could reflect the evolution of a genetic resistance to the disease.

(Continued)

(Continued)

Evidence	Supports Tom	Supports Jerry	Incon-clusive	What Is Your Reason for Your Answer?
				But, when one considers that the eradication program coincides with the decline in the FAIDS epidemic, it seems more likely that there are less cases of FAIDS because there are less infected mice around to infect the cats. Furthermore, if cats are dying of FAIDS, then there are fewer cats around to be infected. Therefore, we would expect the number of cats infected with the FAIDS virus to decrease as the population of cats is reduced.
Figure A.16.2. Fewer infected cats have died that have a mutation in a gene that affects immune system function.	X			This evidence supports Tom's claim of evolution because it appears that the mutation confers a selective advantage to the cats who inherit it. In addition, the immune response phenotype associated with this mutation is hypothetically on the causal pathway responsible for the disease.
Figure A.16.3. The proportion of cats with the special mutation has not changed much over a 20-year period.		X		This evidence is strongly inconsistent with the claim of evolution. If evolution were to occur, we would expect a change in the proportion of individuals within the population who have the genetic mutation that reduces the risk of FAIDS. When there is strong selective pressure and a phenotype confers a selective advantage, it should spread

Evidence	Supports Tom	Supports Jerry	Incon-clusive	What Is Your Reason for Your Answer?
				through a population. However, if the mutation is exceedingly rare, it might take a long time to reach a high enough frequency in the population where natural selection can act upon it. Therefore, given the consistently low proportion of individuals with the beneficial mutation, it might be the case that sufficient time has not occurred for selection to increase the frequency of the mutation in the population. In either case, this piece of evidence is not consistent with the claim that cats of Warner County are presently evolving a resistance to the virus that causes FAIDS.
Figure A.16.4. The rat population in Warner County has decreased dramatically since 2005.		X		Given that the eradication program perfectly coincides with the decline in the FAIDS epidemic, this evidence would support Jerry's claim that the rat eradication program is really driving the decrease in the proportion of cats with FAIDS. But because correlation is not causation, this evidence inconclusively supports Jerry's claim.

Lesson 2: An exemplary response for Lesson 2 would involve, at the very least, redrawing Figure A.16.3 to show an increase in the proportion of cats who have the beneficial mutation. Then, students would need to argue that the evidence clearly supports the claim that the mutation is beneficial, heritable, and increasing in the population. Students cannot change the life span of a house cat, but they could change the time scale on each graph to show that there has been a sufficient amount of time for cats with the mutation to reproduce and increase in proportion. Figure A.16.1 could be changed to support the claim of evolution by including two lines. One line would show a decreasing amount of cats with the beneficial mutation dying of FAIDS. The other line would show an increasing or unchanging amount of cats dying of FAIDS who do not have the beneficial mutation. If students make all of the above changes to the graph, then Figure A.16.4 becomes less important. Students might choose to show that the rat eradication program is not decreasing the rat population.

CHAPTER 6

Physical Sciences

How Do Forces Affect the Way an Object Moves?

Learning Goals

The aim of this exercise is to build a deeper understanding of the force of gravity, that it always acts toward the center of the Earth, and the nature of forces in general. The goals of this activity are for students to learn that

- the force of the Earth's gravity is always directed toward the center of the Earth, which is called "down"
- it is possible for force to be in the opposite direction to motion
- there can be forces acting on an object even if it is not moving

NGSS References

MS-PS2-4

Construct and present arguments using evidence to support the claim that gravitational interactions are attractive and depend on the masses of interacting objects.

Clarification Statement: Examples of evidence for arguments could include data generated from simulations or digital tools and charts displaying mass, strength of interaction, distance from the Sun, and orbital periods of objects within the solar system.

Assessment Boundary: Assessment does not include Newton's law of gravitation or Kepler's laws.

This activity encourages the use of argument to think about the action of forces on a moving object. The students are asked to work in groups to discuss two competing interpretations of the forces acting when a ball is thrown in the air.

Science Background

Content Knowledge

The two forces in this situation are gravity, which is only an attractive force and pulls the object downward all the time, and electromagnetic forces. The latter exhibit themselves as contact forces when one set of matter (containing charged particles) comes into contact with another. In this example, this is when there is contact between the hand and the object as it is moved upward. However, as soon as the object leaves the hand, there is no contact and thus there is no force by the hand on the object. There is still contact between the ball and the air it is moving through—a force commonly referred to as "air resistance"—but it is minimal at these speeds and does not need to be discussed unless a student raises it. There are only four types of forces in the universe: electromagnetic; gravitational; strong nuclear interactions, which only take place within the nucleus; and the weak interaction, which is responsible for radioactive decay and interactions between particles called neutrinos.

Knowledge for Teaching

This activity explores a very standard misconception students have that force is in the direction of motion. The reality is that this is not always so. Obvious examples of where it is not are a car or bike braking where the force is very definitely not in the direction of motion. Other examples are force on an object moving in a circle where the force is at right angles to the direction of motion and toward the center of a circle. This idea arises because students confuse the momentum of an object with the force acting. Resolving the distinction requires an activity like this, which highlights the difference.

Prior Knowledge for Students

Students need to know that gravity is a force that acts downward on the surface of the Earth and that the force is the same as the weight of the object. They should also know that the forces exerted by one object on another such as the push of a hand on a door requires the two objects to be in contact, but they are likely to forget that in this task.

Teaching Sequence

The main point of this activity is to explore a very standard difficulty that students have with gravity and forces. Students traditionally tend to associate force with the direction of motion. This activity challenges that and helps to challenge students' conception and get them to think more carefully about forces.

- There are a variety of ways in which this activity can be done. Hand out the student activity sheet and ask the students to circle what they think is the right answer without sharing with anybody else for when the ball is on the way up, at the top, and on the way down. Research would suggest that most students will ring (b), (c), and then (a), which reflects a belief that force is in the direction of movement and, that when there is no movement, there is no force. You can choose to elicit the answers publicly or use an electronic student response system like BrainCandy (www.braincandy.org), Socrative (http://socrative.com/), or Kahoots (https://getkahoot.com/) to poll the answers. These polling systems have the advantage of allowing students to participate anonymously, which encourages both greater and more candid participation.
- Now that they have decided on their answer, ask students to work in groups of three and discuss the two arguments put forward by Joe and Salma for a maximum of 10 minutes. Either during or at the end of their discussion, they should summarize the points that have emerged from their discussion on the table provided. The summary should provide reasons for supporting Joe or Salma.
- Now repeat the poll. Hopefully, more students should know or understand the scientific position. If not, you will have to point to the arguments for the scientific idea and why the commonsense assumption is incorrect.

If students are having problems with discussing this task, try asking the following questions:

What are the forces on a moving car/football/ship going through the water?

Are any of those in the opposite direction to the movement?

Why does a bicycle stop if you stop pedaling?

Can you have a force without objects being in contact? What kinds of forces are those?

Another way is to play devil's advocate in the discussion and whatever the students are arguing, take the contrary view—even if it means taking the nonscientific explanation—and challenge the students to respond. Being able to argue why you are wrong matters as much as being able to argue why you are right.

Student Activity: How Do Forces Affect the Way an Object Moves?

 An electronic copy of this activity is available on the companion website at https://resources.corwin.com/OsborneArgumentation.

A student throws a tennis ball straight up in the air just a small way. The following questions are about the *total* force on the ball (see Figures A.17.1–A.17.4).

FIGURE A.17.1   A Ball Thrown Into the Air

1. If the ball is on the way up, then the *force* on the ball is shown by which arrow?

FIGURE A.17.2   A Possible Illustration of the Total Force Acting on a Ball Thrown Into the Air

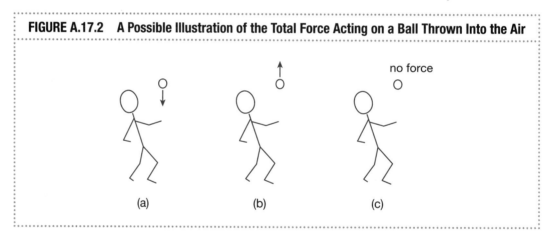

2. If the ball is at the top of its flight, then the *force* on the ball is shown by which arrow?

FIGURE A.17.3   A Second Possible Illustration of the Total Force Acting on a Ball Thrown Into the Air

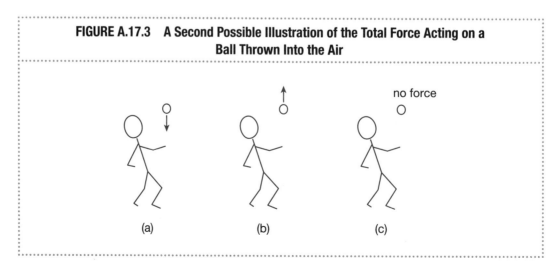

3. If the ball is on the way down, then the *force* on the ball is shown by which arrow?

FIGURE A.17.4   A Third Possible Illustration of the Total Force Acting on a Ball Thrown Into the Air

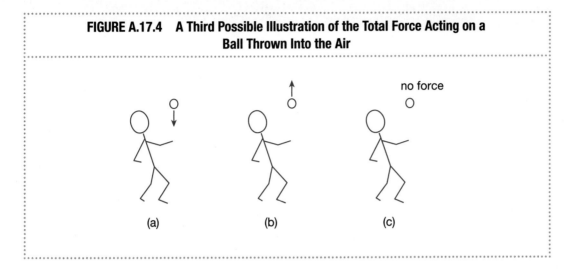

(a)   (b)   (c)

Joe and Salma are discussing the questions shown in Figures A.17.1 through A.17.4. This is what they say:

Joe: *I think the right answer is that the force in the first one is up; when it gets to the top, the upward force and gravity balance out, and then gravity is larger so it starts to drop again.*

Salma: *No, there is only ever one force and that is gravity, which is always acting down toward the center of the Earth. So in all three cases, the answer is (a).*

In your discussion, you might find it useful to consider the following questions:

1. Does gravity ever switch off?

2. What kinds of forces are there?

3. Which forces need objects to be in contact for there to be a force?

Arguments for Joe	Arguments for Salma

Suggested Responses

The most common choices by students are (b), (c), and (a), which shows that they believe that the force is in the direction of motion. The correct scientific response is (a), (a), and (a).

The following table offers some of the responses that might be made to the second part.

Arguments for Joe	Arguments for Salma
To make something move, you have to push it. To make it go up, you have to push it upward. When it is not moving, it follows that there is no force on it. When it is falling, it is going down so gravity must be pulling it down. Gravity is always acting, but on the way up, the "push up" is greater than gravity.	Gravity always acts downward. Gravity does not switch off just because something is moving upward. Push forces require objects to be in contact. Once the ball has left your hand, it is not being pushed. Just because something is not moving does not mean there is not force on it.

Activity Extensions

 An electronic copy of this activity is available on the companion website at https://resources.corwin.com/OsborneArgumentation.

FIGURE A.17.5   Book on a Table

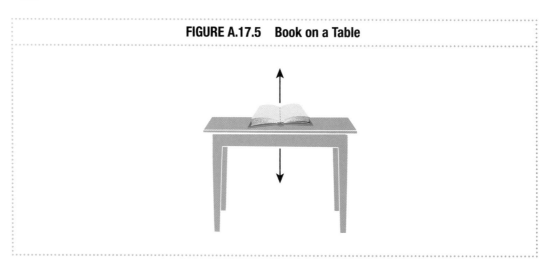

Show the students a picture of a book on a table (Figure A.17.5).
Provide the following statement.

The book does not move because the force of gravity is balanced by the push back of the table.

Put the students back in their groups and ask them to discuss this statement.

What evidence would suggest that the statement is true?

What evidence would suggest that the argument is flawed?

Is There Gravity Beyond the Earth?

Learning Goals

The primary learning goal of this exercise is to develop students' understanding of the nature of gravitational forces and recognition that although an object may appear weightless, a force of gravity is still acting on it. Thus, students will learn that

- our weight is the force of the pull of gravity on us
- gravity is a force that acts over long distances
- the size of the force of gravity depends on the size of the interacting masses and the distance between the masses
- because an object appears weightless does not mean that gravity is not acting

NGSS References

MS-PS2-4

Construct and present arguments using evidence to support the claim that gravitational interactions are attractive and depend on the masses of interacting objects.

    Clarification Statement: Examples of evidence for arguments could include data generated from simulations or digital tools and charts displaying mass, strength of interaction, distance from the Sun, and orbital periods of objects within the solar system.

    Assessment Boundary: Assessment does not include Newton's law of gravitation or Kepler's laws.

This activity encourages the use of argument to think about the action of gravitational forces in space. The students are asked to work in groups to discuss two physical instances that are provided and justify the choices for the explanations they think are correct.

Science Background

Content Knowledge

This activity seeks to explore the concept of gravity by looking at its effects in unfamiliar situations. The first is on the Moon, where there is gravity as the Moon has mass, but as the Moon is only about one sixth of the mass of the Earth, the force of gravity is about one sixth. This means that humans are able to jump further and that the thrust of a spacecraft required to lift off the Moon, such as when astronauts went there in the late 1960s, is much less. As there is no atmosphere on the Moon, it is essential to wear a spacesuit, which maintains normal atmospheric pressure around the body.

    The second situation explores the concept of weightlessness. Myriad videos of people in space make it look as if there is no gravity in orbit. People appear to be "floating." There is gravity in space, and it is not greatly reduced at the low Earth orbit that many of these shots are taken at. The reason it looks as if there is not any gravity is because both the space vehicle and the astronauts are falling toward the Earth at the same rate. It is exactly the same as being in an elevator if the cord were to break. Both you and the elevator would be falling toward the ground at the same rate and you would feel weightless. The nearest we get to experiencing this on Earth is when we jump off a diving board (see https://www.youtube.com/watch?v=6E2wMKc0En0 for an example of this). The reason they don't fall to the ground is that they are also in orbit going sideways as well falling toward the ground at exactly the same rate that the ground curves away from them so that they stay at the same height above the Earth.

Knowledge for Teaching

Both of these activities seek to explore difficulties with the concept of gravity. Students may think, for instance, that there is no gravity on the Moon and that the special suit is required to hold the astronaut to the surface of the Moon. The big point that needs to be understood as an outcome of this activity is that weight is simply the force of gravity on us.

In the case of the second example, it looks to all effects that the astronauts are weightless. This is a common perception and a familiar picture from movies such as *2001: A Space Odyssey* and *The Martian*. However, given that they are in low Earth orbit, there is still much gravity there.

Prior Knowledge for Students

Students need to know that weight is the force of gravity on a body and that the force of gravity diminishes as you go away from the center of the Earth. At a distance that is equal to two times the radius of the Earth—that is, at 4,000 miles/6,400 km—it would have one quarter of the strength that it does on the surface of the Earth. Low Earth orbits are only 100 miles/160 km above the surface of the Earth.

Teaching Sequence
Instructions for Activity 1

- Introduce the activity. Tell the students that they are going to work in groups to discuss what forces are acting when we are on another planet. It may be helpful to show YouTube clips of astronauts on the Moon or clips from films such as *2001* and say that this is an opportunity to discuss the science.
- Put the students into groups of three or four and give out the Activity 1 sheet. Ask them to follow the instructions.
- Allow them up to 10 minutes to complete the sheet. Emphasize that it is important that they fill in as much information as possible in the Evidence/Reasons column as they will need this for the activity at the end.
- After 10 minutes, run a whole-class discussion. Take each statement and ask who thinks it is "True." Ask them to explain why. Ask for those who think that it is "False" or "Don't Know." Ask them to explain why.
- If you think that the students are unconvinced by the scientific argument, you will have to insert additional arguments/evidence. See the background notes for more information.

Instructions for Activity 2

- This activity uses an argument line. Tell the students that they are going to discuss the issue of whether there is gravity in space. Those who think there is should go to one side of the room. Those who think there is not should go to the other side of the room. Those who think it depends should go to the middle of the room.

- When the students are in their places, they should then discuss the evidence statements and work out which ones support their position. They should also work out why they think students who have gone to another position are wrong.
- Give them up to 10 minutes for this discussion. At the end, call a halt and ask a spokesperson for each group to explain why he or she thinks this is the correct position. In response, ask somebody from another position to explain why he or she thinks the other person's argument is wrong. Continue this cycle for several times or until you think it has been exhausted.
- Now tell students that they can change their position after having listened to the arguments.
- Finish by making sure that the students have the scientific arguments presented for the argument that there is gravity in space.

Students can be provided with the following evidence statements:

- The picture shows people floating in space.
- When the shuttle came back to Earth, it did not use its engines.
- If airplane engines fail, it will fall to Earth.
- The Moon is in orbit falling toward the Earth.
- Satellites stay in orbit and do not fall to the Earth.
- If you are in an elevator and the cord breaks, both you and the elevator will fall and you will think you are weightless.
- Things still fall in an airplane at 30,000 feet.
- Gravity at 4,000 miles above the Earth is one quarter of the strength it is at the surface.
- Low Earth orbits are typically 100 miles above the surface of the Earth.

Clearly, the quality of argumentation will improve the more background knowledge that students can bring to the discussion. Thus, it will help if students have discussed what weight is before this activity. Students need to grasp that gravity is a very strong force holding us to the ground and that it does not switch off as soon as you leave the Earth. For instance, ask students what keeps the Moon going round the Earth. Ask them too how far away the Moon is and whether that is nearer or further than the orbit of a space station. What does this imply about gravity in orbit?

Questions that students could discuss for further exploration of this topic are as follows:

1. If every object attracts every other object, why are we all not drawn to each other?

2. Do you weigh more at the equator or the North Pole?

Student Activity 1: Is There Gravity on the Moon?

An electronic copy of this activity is available on the companion website at https://resources.corwin.com/OsborneArgumentation.

Figure A.18.1 shows an astronaut standing still on the surface of the Moon.

Source: Image http://history.nasa.gov/ap11ann/kippsphotos/5903.jpg; NASA Media Usage Guidelines http://www.nasa.gov/multimedia/guidelines/index.html

Production

- Work in groups of three or four.
- Start by reading the statements and deciding whether you think the statements are "True," "False," or you "Don't Know."
- Now see what others in your group have put down and discuss each possible solution.
- Now complete the final column, giving as many reasons as possible for which choice you decided on.

Statement	True	False	Don't Know	Evidence/ Reasons
There's no gravity but he's weighted at heavier than normal weight to keep his feet stuck on the ground.				
There is gravity on the Moon but it's not as strong as on the Earth.				
If he or she is standing still, there are no forces acting on him.				
The space helmet is needed because the atmosphere on the Moon is poisonous.				
There is no atmosphere on the Moon so there is no gravity.				

Student Activity 2: Weightless in Space

 An electronic copy of this activity is available on the companion website at https://resources.corwin.com/OsborneArgumentation.

FIGURE A.18.2   Astronauts in Extra-Vehicular Activity in Low Earth Orbit

Source: ©istock/essentialscollection

Argument line: This is an argument line activity (Figure A.18.3). Decide which of these statements you think is correct. Then go to that side of the room.

FIGURE A.18.3   An Argument Line

There is no Gravity in Space   There is Gravity in Space

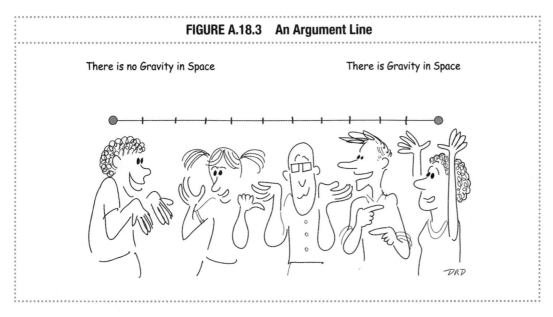

Source: © David R. Dudley, Illustrator.

Your task is to work with your fellow students on your side of the room to

1. Construct an argument for why you are in the correct place

2. Explain why the students on the other side of the room are in the wrong place

Here are some statements of fact that you may want to use as evidence for your argument.

- The picture shows people floating in space.
- When the shuttle came back to Earth, it did not use its engines.
- If airplane engines fail, the airplane will fall to Earth.
- The Moon is in orbit falling toward the Earth.
- Satellites stay in orbit and do not fall to the Earth.
- If you are in an elevator and the cord breaks, both you and the elevator will fall and you will think you are weightless.
- Things still fall in an airplane at 30,000 feet.
- Gravity at 4,000 miles above the Earth is one quarter of the strength it is at the surface.
- Low Earth orbits are typically 100 miles above the surface of the Earth.

Suggested Responses

Statement	True	False	Don't Know	Evidence/Reasons
There's no gravity but he's weighted at heavier than normal weight to keep his feet stuck on the ground.		FALSE		There is gravity on the moon. It is one sixth of that here on the surface of the Earth. The astronaut's boots are simply part of his spacesuit and do not grip him to the surface. If they did, he would walk with a strange gait, which is not supported by videos of men on the Moon.
There is gravity on the Moon but it's not as strong as on the Earth.	TRUE			The force of gravity depends on the masses of the object and the distance between them. The Moon is one sixth of the mass of the Earth and so the force is reduced.
If he or she is standing still, there are no forces acting on him.		FALSE		This is not true. It would mean that the force of gravity had switched off. The force of gravity is still acting.
The space helmet is needed because the atmosphere on the Moon is poisonous.		FALSE		There is no atmosphere on the Moon. The spacesuit is needed to keep air at normal pressure around his body. If he lost his helmet, he could not breathe, the gas in his blood would "boil," and he would die a very nasty death. The effect would be similar to what divers experience when they get the bends.
There is no atmosphere on the Moon so there is no gravity.		FALSE		Although this is false, it is understandable. Gravity is what stops the gases in the atmosphere leaving a planet. The reason they have in the case of the Moon is that the gravity has not been strong enough.

Extension Activities

As a further activity, you could ask your students to write an answer about how they would explain the difference between weight and weightlessness. Are the two the same thing or are they different, and how would they justify their reasoning?

What Has Energy Got to Do With Movement?

Learning Goals

The goals of this activity are for students to learn to

- identify and justify whether data support the claim that "changing the speed of anything requires a transfer of energy"
- identify where energy is associated with movement
- show how kinetic energy can be transferred between objects

NGSS References

MS-PS3-5

Construct, use, and present arguments to support the claim that when the kinetic energy of an object changes, energy is transferred to or from the object.

Clarification Statement: Examples of empirical evidence used in arguments could include an inventory or other representation of the energy before and after the transfer in the form of temperature changes or motion of object.

Assessment Boundary: Assessment does not include calculations of energy.

This activity encourages the use of argument to think about phenomena that involve the change of energy—specifically the transfer of kinetic energy to other forms. The activity consists of a set of description of phenomena—each of which has to be examined to see if it involves a transfer of kinetic energy. By the end of the activity, students should understand that there is energy associated with movement and kinetic energy can be transferred to other objects.

Science Background

Content Knowledge

This activity explores the concept of energy and how it can be used to explain a phenomenon. The concept of energy is not easy as it is essentially an abstraction, and it is impossible to demonstrate conservation of energy in the classroom. Rather, as Richard Feynman argued,

> It is important to realize that in physics today, we have no knowledge of what energy *is*. We do not have a picture that energy comes in little blobs of a definite amount. It is not that way. However, there are formulas for calculating some numerical quantity, and when we add it all together it always gives the same number. It is an abstract thing in that it does not tell us the mechanism or the *reasons* for the various formulas (Feynman, Leighton, & Sands, 2013).

So this exercise is an attempt to use the concept qualitatively and to build an understanding of the mechanisms. Water at the bottom of Niagara Falls is warmer than that at the top because the potential energy it has is transferred to kinetic energy of movement, which then gets transferred to the molecules of water when the water smashes into the rock at the bottom. Faster moving molecules have more kinetic energy and hence a higher temperature. Students who can construct this kind of qualitative understanding should be able to apply it to a range of other phenomena.

There are essentially only two kinds of energy: "potential energy," which is stored in a "spring-like" manner, and kinetic energy, which is a property of moving objects. In any process or event, energy is transferred between these two by pushing or pulling.

Knowledge for Teaching

Energy is a difficult concept, mainly because it is not tangible. It is associated with movement, stored in chemicals, carried by electrical charges, and transferred by radiation, but it is an abstraction. Coming to an understanding of the concept of energy means asking students to look at phenomena and begin to use the appropriate scientific language. This exercise provides an opportunity for students to share their thinking and to learn from their peers and you about what is the scientific description of these phenomena using the concept of energy.

For students, the concept of energy is often difficult to understand. Energy is commonly associated with some kind of fuel—the gas you put in your car or the food you eat to keep you going. The idea that something has energy just because of its vertical position or because it is moving is often challenging as there is no visible substance associated with either the position or the movement.

Prior Knowledge for Students

Students will need to have been introduced to the concept of energy. They should have had some teaching and learning experiences about the types of energy that exist—especially the idea that energy can be stored as potential energy and that there is energy associated with moving objects called kinetic energy.

Teaching Sequence

Instructions for Activity

- This activity is best done after some other work on energy. Students will need to have been introduced to the concept of energy beforehand and be familiar with different forms of energy.
- Introduce the activity by saying that it is an activity designed to get them thinking and using the idea of energy. We recommend eliciting prior knowledge such as the meaning of potential energy and kinetic energy. The table on page 209 contains examples of six phenomena. Each of these may or may not involve energy associated with a moving object (kinetic energy), which may or may not be transferred to another object.
- Working in small groups of three or four students, students should start by working individually first and deciding whether the phenomenon in the box on the left is evidence to support the statement or not.
- When they have done this, they should come together and discuss their arguments for why it is or why it is not. Each student should then fill in the justification that he or she would give in the box on the right. Students can use drawings if they want or additional paper to support their argument. Allow 10 to 15 minutes for this activity.
- When they have finished, hold a whole-class discussion. Ask one group to put forward their view about a phenomenon. When they have finished, ask if there is another group that disagrees. Call on them to explain their disagreement. Then encourage a discussion by asking if other groups would like to respond. If there is no disagreement, ask if there is any group that would like to add on or elaborate further.

- Then repeat these for each phenomenon in the table. Finish by asking each student to go back and revise his or her justification in light of what he or she has heard.

Suggestions for Improving the Quality of the Argumentation

One way of improving students' thinking is to play devil's advocate in the discussion, and whatever the students are arguing, take the contrary view—even if it means taking the nonscientific explanation—and challenge the students to respond. Being able to argue why you are wrong matters as much as being able to argue why you are right.

Student Activity: What Has Energy Got to Do With Movement?

 An electronic copy of this activity is available on the companion website at https://resources.corwin.com/OsborneArgumentation.

Which of the following phenomena would support the view that changing the speed of anything requires a transfer of energy? For each statement, place an "X" in the column "Supports" or "Does Not Support." Use the final comment to provide reasons to justify your choice.

Statement	Supports	Does Not Support	Justification
Water at the bottom of Niagara Falls is warmer than that at the top.			
A tennis ball becomes warm after being hit lots of times.			
A satellite orbiting the Earth keeps going at constant speed.			
The brakes on a car get hot on a long descent.			
A falling object speeds up.			
Rubbing your hands together makes them warmer.			

Suggested Responses

Beneath are an indication of the possible responses to this activity that would demonstrate a good understanding of the science.

Statement	Supports	Does Not Support	Justification
Water at the bottom of Niagara Falls is warmer than that at the top.	X		The water gains kinetic energy/speed as it falls. On smashing onto the rocks beneath, the movement of the water is transferred to the individual molecules, which move faster, causing the temperature rise. And there is no other way the water could have been warmed in falling from the top to the bottom.
A tennis ball becomes warm after being hit lots of times.	X		Each time the tennis ball is hit, some of the kinetic energy of the racket is transferred to the ball. Most of this goes to movement, but some of it causes the molecules in the ball to move faster so they get warmer.
A satellite orbiting the Earth keeps going at constant speed.		X	The satellite is moving, but it is not transferring its energy to any other objects.
The brakes on a car get hot on a long descent.	X		Friction between the brakes and the wheels slows the car. The brakes are rubbing against the disc, transferring kinetic energy from the moving disc to the molecules in the brakes and the disc itself, which move faster and get warm.
A falling object speeds up.	X		Objects have energy by virtue of being above the ground. Once they are let go, the stored energy is transferred to kinetic energy.
Rubbing your hands together makes them warmer.	X		Your hands have kinetic energy. As they rub against each other, some of that kinetic energy is transferred to speeding up the molecules in your hand, raising their temperature.

Extension Activities

Instruct students to write additional statements with examples of phenomena where kinetic energy is and is not transferred to other forms. Then, students should exchange statements and identify whether they think the statements are examples of the transfer of kinetic energy and evaluate each other's responses.

If You Fall From a Plane, Will You Go Faster and Faster?

Learning Goals

The goals of this activity are for students to

- justify how statements about gravity and motion are correct or incorrect
- analyze what forces are acting on objects and construct an argument for their effect

NGSS References

MS-PS3-1

Construct and interpret graphical displays of data to describe the relationships of kinetic energy to the mass of an object and to the speed of an object.

Clarification Statement: Emphasis is on descriptive relationships between kinetic energy and mass separately from kinetic energy and speed. Examples could include riding a bicycle at different speeds, rolling different sizes of rocks downhill, and getting hit by a wiffle ball versus a tennis ball.

This is an activity that requires students to construct an explanation about the way in which an object falls through the atmosphere and produce reasons to justify their explanation. The activity is carefully structured and can be done by pairs of students working together who can then compare their answers. The activity develops students' understanding of forces and the concept of terminal velocity.

Science Background

Content Knowledge

This activity explores what happens to the kinetic energy of a falling object and its speed as an object falls. The kinetic energy is proportional to the square of the velocity, so a doubling of the speed leads to a quadrupling of the kinetic energy. This is what is known as a nonlinear relationship. Likewise, the force of air resistance is proportional to the square of the velocity. The force of gravity—the weight of a skydiver, for example—is constant. Once the speed is high enough, the force of gravity will be balanced by air resistance and the box will no longer speed up. At this point, the box will have reached what is known as its terminal velocity.

Knowledge for Teaching

The main difficulty for students here is that the relationship between kinetic energy and speed, and the relationship between air resistance and speed, is nonlinear. The purpose of the activity is to help students develop a better understanding of this relationship, but students will need to have been introduced to what the relationship between velocity and kinetic energy is at least in qualitative terms, likewise for air resistance. Such relationships are best explored through looking at patterns—that is, when the speed doubles, the kinetic energy quadruples; if it triples, it goes up by nine times. What would be the next step?

Prior Knowledge for Students

Students should have been introduced to the concept of kinetic energy and done some work on forces. They will also need to have done some work with graphs of velocity-time, displacement-time, and force-time so that the graphical representations are not unfamiliar.

Teaching Sequence

Instructions for Activity

- Frame the activity by telling the students that they are going to build on their knowledge of kinetic energy and forces to construct an argument for the effect of forces on a falling object.
- Start by dropping a piece of paper and then a book. Get the students to describe what happens. Ask them what the difference is and tell them that they should be able to explain why the book and piece of paper fall differently by the end of class.
- Then, put the students into groups of three. Hand out the sheets.
- Tell them that this activity is designed to get them thinking about what happens when an object falls through the air. The particular focus is on the changes in energy and what forces are acting.
- Tell them that they must write whether the statement is correct or incorrect and put reasons to justify their choice in each box. In addition, they should put reasons why the other choices are wrong.
- Give them 15 minutes to begin with to see where they are.
- When they have all finished, hold a class discussion to compare answers. You might use a polling system (e.g., Socrative, Polleverywhere) or facilitate an argument for statements that appear to be contentious, where one line is for students who think the statement is correct and another line for students who think the statement is incorrect. Play devil's advocate for the scientific case if a flawed argument seems to be dominating.
- Then ask them to do the graphing activity. Again, you might use a polling system or facilitate an argument line, where one line corresponds to each graph. For Question 3, you might invite students to write their answers on the board.
- Finish by holding a whole-class discussion of the answers. Draw on groups who have different answers, asking them to explain not only why they think they are right but also why other answers are flawed.

Student Activity: If You Fall From a Plane, Will You Go Faster and Faster?

An electronic copy of this activity is available on the companion website at https://resources.corwin.com/OsborneArgumentation.

Imagine somebody who jumps out of an airplane, flying at a height of 1,000 meters (Figure A.20.1). This person falls to the ground. The statements in the boxes that follow link together to explain how this person falls.

Some boxes contain more than one statement. In each of these boxes, pick the statement that you think is correct. Then justify why you think this is the correct one. Also, provide a justification for why you think the others are wrong.

Continue until you have chosen one statement from every box, to produce a complete explanation and supporting arguments for the way the person falls.

FIGURE A.20.1   A Man Freefalling to the Ground

Source: © David R. Dudley, Illustrator.

1 There is a force of gravity on the person.

↓

2 This acts downward.

↓

	Justification
3a Gravity is roughly the same size throughout the fall.	
3b Gravity is biggest when the person is high up and gets a lot smaller as he falls.	

3c Gravity is biggest when the person is high up and gets a lot smaller as he falls.	

↓

	Justification
4a This force makes the person begin to accelerate downward.	
4b This force makes the person begin to move downward at a steady speed.	

↓

5 As the person begins to move, the kinetic energy increases.	

↓

	Justification
6a As the speed doubles, the kinetic energy doubles.	
6b As the speed doubles, the kinetic energy quadruples.	
6c As the speed doubles, the kinetic energy gets eight times bigger.	

↓

7 Also, as the person starts to move, there is air resistance.	

↓

	Justification
8a This acts downward, in the direction the person is going.	
8b This acts upward, in the opposite direction to the person's motion.	

↓

	Justification
9a The air resistance force on the person is much smaller than the force of gravity, and so it can be ignored.	
9b The air resistance force on the person becomes quite large and has to be taken into account.	

↓

	Justification
10a So the total force on the person is equal to the force of gravity and is constant.	

10b The total force on the person is the sum of the gravity force and air resistance, and this gets gradually less as he falls, because the air resistance increases.	

↓

	Justification
11a Therefore, the person has a uniform acceleration throughout his fall.	
11b Therefore, acceleration of the person is biggest to begin with and gets gradually less. Once the air resistance force becomes equal to the force of gravity, the acceleration is zero and the person then falls at a steady speed.	
11c Therefore, the person falls at a steady speed throughout his fall.	

Question 1

Which graph (Figure A.20.2 or Figure A.20.3) best represents the change in speed with time as the person falls to the ground?

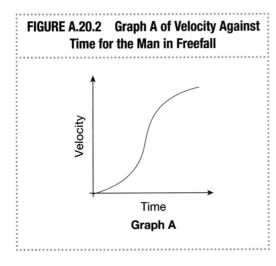

FIGURE A.20.2   Graph A of Velocity Against Time for the Man in Freefall

Graph A

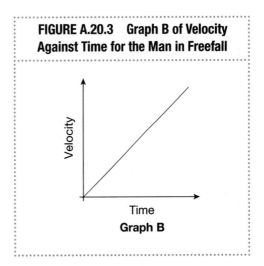

FIGURE A.20.3   Graph B of Velocity Against Time for the Man in Freefall

Graph B

How would you justify your choice?

Question 2

Which graph (Figure A.20.4 or Figure A.20.5) best represents the change in kinetic energy with time as the person falls to the ground?

How would you justify your choice?

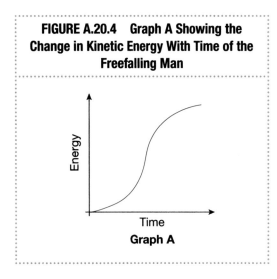

FIGURE A.20.4 Graph A Showing the Change in Kinetic Energy With Time of the Freefalling Man

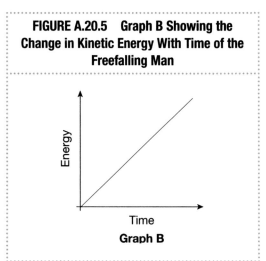

FIGURE A.20.5 Graph B Showing the Change in Kinetic Energy With Time of the Freefalling Man

Question 3

Use Figure A.20.6 to sketch how the force of air resistance will vary with time.

How would you justify what you have drawn?

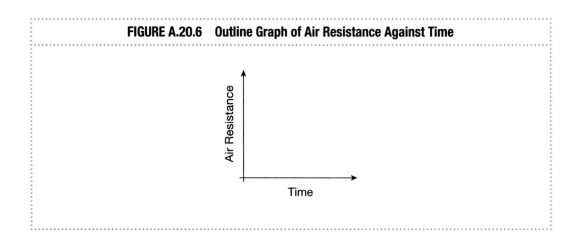

FIGURE A.20.6 Outline Graph of Air Resistance Against Time

Suggested Responses

Beneath are an indication of the possible responses to this activity that would demonstrate a good understanding of the science.

1 There is a force of gravity on the person.

2 This acts downward.

	Justification
3a Gravity is roughly the same size throughout the fall.	This is true. The force of gravity is lower higher up, but the change over a 1,000 meters is not much.
3b Gravity gets bigger as you get closer to the Earth.	This is true, but the difference is negligible.
3c Gravity is biggest when the person is high up and gets a lot smaller as he falls.	This is not true as gravity falls off the further apart two objects are.

	Justification
4a This force makes the person begin to accelerate downward.	Gravity is a force downward. This force will make the person speed up.
4b This force makes the person begin to move downward at a steady speed.	This is not true; objects can be seen to speed up rapidly when dropped.

5 As the person begins to move, his kinetic energy increases.

↓

	Justification
6a As the speed doubles, the kinetic energy doubles.	This is not true. Kinetic energy depends on the velocity squared. Doubling the speed requires four times as much energy.
6b As the speed doubles, the kinetic energy quadruples.	This is correct for the reason above.
6c As the speed doubles, the kinetic energy gets eight times bigger.	This is not true. If it were, kinetic energy would depend on the velocity cubed.

↓

	Justification
8a This acts downward, in the direction the person is going.	As the name implies, air resistance is a force that acts in the opposite direction to motion.
8b This acts upward, in the opposite direction to the person's motion.	This is correct—see above.

↓

	Justification
9a The air resistance force on the person is much smaller than the force of gravity, and so it can be ignored.	This is true at low speeds. However, it is not true once we are going over about 15 mph. You can feel it when you are on a bike, and cars and airplanes are streamlined to reduce air resistance.
9b The air resistance force on the person becomes quite large and has to be taken into account.	True—see above.

↓

	Justification
10a So the total force on the person is equal to the force of gravity and is constant.	This is not true. Total force is the sum of all the forces acting—in this case, gravity and air resistance.
10b The total force on the person is the sum of the gravity force and air resistance, and this gets gradually less as it falls, because the air resistance increases.	This is true. The air resistance increases to the point where it balances the force of gravity.

↓

	Justification
11a Therefore, the person has a constant acceleration throughout his fall.	This is not true. Constant acceleration requires a constant net force, and it is not constant.
11b Therefore, acceleration of the person is biggest to begin with and gets gradually less. Once the air resistance force becomes equal to the gravity force, the acceleration is zero and the person then falls at a steady speed.	This is correct.
11c Therefore, the person falls at a steady speed throughout his fall.	This is not true as the net force is not zero. And when he jumps out of the plane, he is not moving to start with.

Extension Activities

Further work on motion and its graphical representation can be done by downloading the program Graphs and Tracks from http://www.opensourcephysics.org/items/detail.cfm?ID=12023.

This is a Java file and takes a few minutes to work out how it functions. The way to use it is to adjust the track and then ask the students to work in pairs to sketch what they think the graph will look like when you run it. Listen to their justifications and try and get several alternatives on the table before running it. When you have run the program, ask the students to explain *not* why those who were correct were correct by why the others were wrong.

Notes

Two Models to Explain the Behavior of Matter—Which Is the Best?

Learning Goals

The goals of this activity are for students to

- use evidence to justify which model of liquid water particles is best
- use evidence to critique and refine a model of liquid water particles

NGSS References

MS-PS1-4

Develop a model that predicts and describes changes in particle motion, temperature, and state of a pure substance when thermal energy is added or removed.

Clarification Statement: Emphasis is on qualitative molecular-level models of solids, liquids, and gases to show that adding or removing thermal energy increases or decreases kinetic energy of the particles until a change of state occurs. Examples of models could include drawings and diagrams. Examples of particles could include molecules or inert atoms. Examples of pure substances could include water, carbon dioxide, and helium.

This activity is intended to build a deeper understanding of the arrangement and movement of particles, particularly in the liquid state. Two competing models of liquid water are provided for students. Next, students are asked to use evidence and reasoning to determine which of the models is best. Finally, students engage in model revision, which is a practice central to science.

Science Background

Content Knowledge

The arrangement of particles of a substance relates to its state of matter. Typically, the speed of the particles, their disorder, and the distance between them increase from solid to liquid to gas. Adding or removing thermal energy changes the temperature of the substance and the kinetic energy of its particles until a change of state occurs (i.e., boiling, condensing, freezing, melting).

Knowledge for Teaching

In Part 1, the observation that a solid has a rigid structure is evidence of highly ordered particles. The observation that a liquid pools and flows is evidence of disordered particles. Olivia's model is better than Jayden's model in the sense that hers shows particles near each other (i.e., not filling the space of the container). However, Olivia's model shows the particles as moving faster than Jayden's, which is problematic because particles of a substance move slower in the liquid state compared to the gaseous state. Thus, students can justify why either model is better depending on whether they prioritize the arrangement or speed of the particles.

Prior Knowledge for Students

Students should know the macroscopic properties of solids, liquids, and gases (e.g., liquids take the shape of a container, gases take both the shape and fill a container). In addition, they should know that matter is made of tiny invisible pieces called "particles." It is important that students know the speed of particles increases as temperature increases and from solid to liquid to gas. The optional activity "Model of Particle Motion" (see Extension Activities) is intended to facilitate students' understanding of the relationship between temperature and particle motion. Finally, it would be helpful for students to know some purposes of scientific models: They represent a system (or parts of a system), explain phenomena, and communicate ideas to others. In addition, models are based on evidence and are modified when new evidence is uncovered that the models can't explain. As for the models in this activity, students should be familiar with representations of particles, such as those shown in Part 1.

Teaching Sequence

Materials: large pieces of paper or whiteboards and markers

- **(2 min) Frame the activity:** Elicit students' background knowledge of the properties of solids, liquids, and gases. Explain that the goal of this activity is to represent the particles of substances in the different states of matter.
- **(15 min) Part 1:** Facilitate a human bar graph activity, where the two lines correspond to Olivia's and Jayden's claims. Here are some suggested questions and possible student responses (*italics*):
  - "What is the evidence that supports your claim that (Olivia's/Jayden's) model is better?" (*"We see a pool of water on a surface, which fits with how Olivia's representation shows particles on the bottom of the box." "Jayden's model shows the liquid particles moving faster than the solid particles, but not too fast."*)
  - "What is a problem with (Olivia's/Jayden's) model?" (*"Olivia's model shows the particles as moving too fast." "Jayden's model doesn't show the particles on a surface, which doesn't fit with us seeing the liquid water on a surface."*)
  - Prompt students to respond to each other's claims using talk moves such as, "Could someone restate what [student name] just said?" and "Do you agree/disagree with [student name's] idea? Explain your thinking." "What has someone else said that has changed your thinking?"
- **(30 min) Part 2:** Explain that the goal of Part 2 is to work together to make the best liquid model, which is similar to how scientists try to improve models. Groups should construct a model using paper or whiteboards and explain why it is better than Olivia's and Jayden's model. Then, facilitate a fishbowl discussion where students share their models, compare and contrast them, and propose a "best model" for the class. The outer circle should take notes about how members of the inner circle use evidence and reasoning and respond to each other's ideas. Here are some suggested questions/prompts:
  - "Please ask the other groups how they represented liquid water and for their justification."
  - "How is your model different from [group name's] model?"
  - "How is your model similar to [group name's] model?"
  - "Are there any models, including your own, that could be improved? If so, how?"
  - "Which model fits best with the evidence and our knowledge of states of matter? Explain your thinking."

Student Activity: Two Models to Explain the Behavior of Matter—Which Is Best?

 An electronic copy of this activity is available on the companion website at https://resources.corwin.com/ OsborneArgumentation.

PART 1: Models of Liquid Water

An ice cube is left out on a table for the afternoon and it melts to become liquid

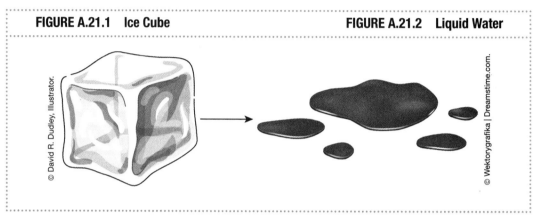

FIGURE A.21.1   Ice Cube

© David R. Dudley, Illustrator.

FIGURE A.21.2   Liquid Water

© Wektorygrafika | Dreamstime.com.

water (Figure A.21.1 and Figure A.21.2).

Olivia and Jayden draw models to show the particles of water as a solid and as a liquid. They draw the same model of matter for the solid water, but their models of the liquid water are different (Figure A.21.3 and Figure A.21.4).

Which model do you think is a better representation of the liquid water? Justify

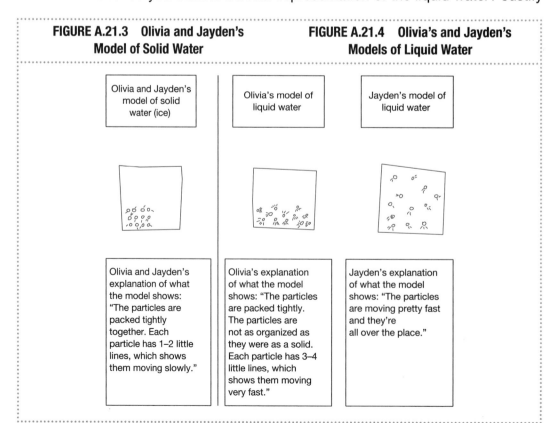

FIGURE A.21.3   Olivia and Jayden's Model of Solid Water

FIGURE A.21.4   Olivia's and Jayden's Models of Liquid Water

Olivia and Jayden's model of solid water (ice)

Olivia's model of liquid water

Jayden's model of liquid water

Olivia and Jayden's explanation of what the model shows: "The particles are packed tightly together. Each particle has 1–2 little lines, which shows them moving slowly."

Olivia's explanation of what the model shows: "The particles are packed tightly. The particles are not as organized as they were as a solid. Each particle has 3–4 little lines, which shows them moving very fast."

Jayden's explanation of what the model shows: "The particles are moving pretty fast and they're all over the place."

your answer using reasoning and evidence.

PART 2: **Improving a Model**

Evidence

- Solid particles move slower than liquid particles.
- Liquid particles do not fill a container.
- Gas particles move faster than liquid particles.

Use the evidence above to explain a problem in Olivia's model or Jayden's model.

Whose model do you want to talk about? _____

Use the evidence to explain at least one problem with the model you chose in the space beneath.

Help Olivia and Jayden! Draw a model of liquid water in the space beneath. Then, use evidence to justify why your model is better than their models.

Suggested Responses

Beneath are an indication of the possible responses to this activity that would demonstrate a good understanding of the science.

PART 1: Models of Liquid Water

Which model do you think is a better representation of the liquid water? Justify your answer using reasoning and evidence.

Olivia's model is better because it shows the particles at the bottom of the box, which fits with the observation that water makes a puddle on a surface.

Jayden's model is better because it shows the particles moving faster than the solid particles, and we have learned that liquid particles move faster than solid particles.

PART 2: Improving a Model

Evidence

- Solid particles move slower than liquid particles.
- Liquid particles do not fill a container.
- Gas particles move faster than liquid particles.

Use the evidence above to explain a problem in Olivia's model or Jayden's model. Whose model do you want to talk about? ___Jayden's___

Use the evidence to explain at least one problem with the model you chose.

A problem with Jayden's model is that it shows the particles filling the box. Liquid water makes a small pool on a surface, so the particles should be at the bottom of the box.

Use the evidence above to explain a problem in Olivia's model or Jayden's model. Whose model do you want to talk about? ___Olivia's___

Use the evidence to explain at least one problem with the model you chose.

A problem with Olivia's model is that the particles are moving very fast. Liquid particles move faster than solid particles, but she shows the particles moving very fast, which would make more sense for a gas.

Help Olivia and Jayden! Draw a model of liquid water. Then, use evidence to justify why your model is better than their models (Figure A.21.5).

FIGURE A.21.5   Model of Liquid Water (Suggested Response)

This model is better than Olivia's because I show the liquid particles as moving slower than hers. In addition, my model is better than Jayden's model because it shows the particles on the bottom, which makes sense since liquid water is on a surface.

Additional Resources

States of Matter (https://phet.colorado.edu/en/simulation/states-of-matter-basics)

Eureka Molecules in Solid (https://www.youtube.com/watch?v=5jpA1H1adII)

Eureka Molecules in Liquid (https://www.youtube.com/watch?v=ppdTvr0FDBg)

Tips for modeling in science (https://www.cfa.harvard.edu/smg/Website/UCP/classroom/modeling.html)

Tools for Ambitious Science Teaching: Models and modeling introduction (http://ambitiousscienceteaching.org/wp-content/uploads/2014/09/Models-and-Modeling-An-Introduction1.pdf)

Extension Activities

Model of Particle Motion

This is an optional activity to precede the model of states of matter activity. It will help students to develop the understanding that particles at a higher temperature move faster than particles at a lower temperature. You will drop blue food coloring in the cool water and red food coloring in the hot water. The motion of particles increases as temperature increases, causing the substance to expand and decrease in density. Thus, the warm water is at lower density than the cool water. In addition, there is a greater temperature and density difference between the warm water and the food coloring compared to the cool water and food coloring. Due to the density difference, convection and mixing occurs at a higher rate in the warm water compared to the cool water.[1] You do not necessarily need to facilitate students' understanding of the convection explanation for the phenomenon. This activity could solely be used to provide evidence of the relationship between temperature and rate of motion. Students should represent the red food coloring particles as discrete (i.e., versus a blob of color) and farther from each other compared to the blue food coloring particles in the same time interval. This activity assumes students know that substances are made of tiny pieces called particles.

---

1   There is a common misconception that diffusion is the primary cause of the mixing. See Dou, R., Hogan, D., Kossover, M., Spuck, T., & Young, S. (2013). Defusing diffusion. *The American Biology Teacher*, *75*(6), 391–395.

Materials

- Red and blue food coloring, two cups or beakers with water (one hot and one cold), large pieces of paper or whiteboards and markers to represent the particles, sticky notes
- Student sheet beneath

Instructions

- Frame the activity: Elicit students' background knowledge of the properties of solids, liquids, and gases. Remind students that substances are made of tiny pieces called particles. Explain that the goal of this activity is to represent the particles of substances at different temperatures.
- Tell the students that you will drop blue food coloring in the cool water and red food coloring in the hot water. Ask students to predict what will happen. Drop the food coloring in the appropriate cup/beaker. After students observe the demonstration, have them represent the arrangement and speed of the particles using large pieces of paper or whiteboards and markers. Then, remind students to include their justification of how the model fits with the evidence.
- Optional scaffold (simplifies the task): Provide the particle models for 1 second after dropping the food coloring in the water.
- Note: Students commonly represent the food coloring particles as a colored blob rather than as discrete particles. If this occurs, facilitate a discussion to reconcile the different representations or play devil's advocate by drawing the food coloring particles as discrete.
- Use a gallery walk to have students comment on the following: (1) What is good about the other groups' models? (2) Questions or suggestions for improvement.
- Finally, have students read the feedback from their peers, revise their models, and reflect on how their models changed.

Student Activity: Model of Particle Motion

 An electronic copy of this activity is available on the companion website at https://resources.corwin.com/OsborneArgumentation.

Represent the food coloring particles at different temperatures.

Low Temperature

1 second after food coloring is dropped in water

10 seconds after food coloring is dropped in water

High Temperature

1 second after food coloring is dropped in water

10 seconds after food coloring is dropped in water

Justify how your model fits with your observations of the food coloring.

Reflect: What did you learn from the feedback of your peers?

What Particle Model for Boiling Water Fits Best With the Evidence?

Learning Goals

The goals of this activity are for students to

- use evidence and reasoning to justify claims about the motion and arrangement of particles during boiling
- use evidence and reasoning to justify claims about a model for water particles as it boils

---

NGSS References

MS-PS1-4

Develop a model that predicts and describes changes in particle motion, temperature, and state of a pure substance when thermal energy is added or removed.

    Clarification Statement: Emphasis is on qualitative molecular-level models of solids, liquids, and gases to show that adding or removing thermal energy increases or decreases kinetic energy of the particles until a change of state occurs. Examples of models could include drawings and diagrams. Examples of particles could include molecules or inert atoms. Examples of pure substances could include water, carbon dioxide, and helium.

Activity 21 is designed to precede this activity, but it does not need to. This activity is intended to build a deeper understanding of the arrangement and movement of particles during boiling. Students are provided with two competing claims about particles during boiling, and they are asked to engage in an evidence-based argument to determine which of these claims is better. In Part 2 of the activity, students will construct an argument for which of four particle models of boiling water is best, and they will critique an alternative model.

Science Background

Content Knowledge

During a change of state (melting, boiling, freezing, condensing), there is no change in temperature, assuming constant pressure and volume. Temperature is a measure of the average kinetic energy of a system, and kinetic energy depends on the mass and velocity of particles in the system. Because temperature does not change during a phase change and the mass of the particles does not change either, we can also infer that the average velocity of the particles remains constant during a change of state. During a change of state, thermal energy that is added or removed from the system affects the arrangement of the particles (i.e., rather than their velocity). As a substance melts and boils, particles move farther from each other and become less ordered in their arrangement. Conversely, as a substance condenses and freezes, particles typically move nearer to each other and become more ordered in their arrangement.

Knowledge for Teaching

There is a common misconception that temperature changes during boiling, but as noted, temperature remains constant during a change of state. In Part 1, the energy from the flame causes the molecules of water to become less ordered and farther from each other as they transition from liquid to gas. Since the temperature of the boiling water remains constant during boiling, the average speed of the molecules does not change either. Thus, in Part 1, Naomi's claim is better than Mia's claim. In Part 2, Representation D is best because it represents the molecules as moving at the same speed as those at 1 minute.

Prior Knowledge for Students

Students should know that matter is made of tiny invisible pieces called *particles*, which are in constant random motion. Atoms are the smallest fundamental particles of elements (atoms are composed of subatomic particles, but these particles are not, in and of themselves, elements). Molecules are composed of two or more atoms, and they are the smallest fundamental particles of compounds, including water. It would be helpful for students to know some purposes of scientific models: They represent a system (or parts of a system), explain phenomena, and communicate ideas to others. In addition, models are based on evidence, and they are modified when new evidence is uncovered that the models can't explain. As for the models in this activity, students should be familiar with representations of particles for different states of matter, such as those shown in Part 2. Students should also know that particles of a substance move faster, are less ordered, and are farther apart in the gaseous state compared to the liquid state and the liquid state compared to the solid state. Last, students should be able to analyze the temperature-time graph included in this activity.

Teaching Sequence and Points

- **(5 min) Frame the activity, eliciting prior knowledge:** Ask students what they have learned about the motion and arrangement of particles in different states. Remind the students that the smallest particles of water are called *molecules*. Then, tell them that the goal of this activity is to build on their knowledge to argue for which representation of water molecules during boiling is best.
- **(10 min) Part 1:** Have students complete the question about which idea is better.

CLAIM	REASONING	EVIDENCE

- **(15 min) Facilitate an argument line activity,** and then have students revise their argument. Here are some suggested questions:
  - ○ "What is the evidence that supports your claim that Mia's/Naomi's claim is better?"
  - ○ "What is a problem with Mia/Naomi's claim?"
  - ○ Prompt students to respond to each other's claims using talk moves such as, "Could someone restate what [student name] just said?" and "Do you agree/disagree with [student name's] idea? Explain your thinking." "What has someone else said that has changed your thinking?"
- **(15 min) Part 2:** Have students compare and contrast Models A to D with the t = 1-minute representation, perhaps using the following graphic organizer.

	Model A	**Model B**	**Model C**	**Model D**
Are there any differences between the models of the water after it has been boiling for 4 minutes and 1 minute? If so, what are the differences?				

- Then, facilitate a four corners activity, where each corner corresponds to a representation. Use talk moves to elicit evidence and reasoning. See "Suggested Responses" for possible student answers. Finally, have students write an argument and critique a model of their choice on the handout.

Student Activity: What Particle Model for Boiling Water Fits Best With the Evidence?

 An electronic copy of this activity is available on the companion website at https://resources.corwin.com/OsborneArgumentation.

FIGURE A.22.1   Boiling Water

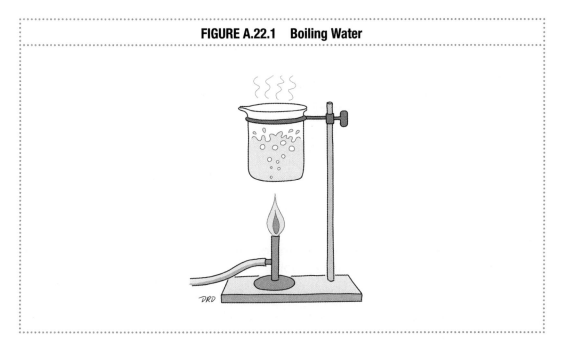

Source: © David R. Dudley, Illustrator.

PART 1

Two students make claims about the movement and arrangement of molecules of water during boiling (Figure A.22.1).

- Naomi says, "The molecules get farther from each other as the water boils."
- Mia says, "The molecules move faster after a lot of time boiling than just a little time boiling."

Evidence

1. The fire is near the bowl of water while it boils.

2. Particles of a substance move faster when temperature increases.

3. The particles of a liquid are nearer to each other than particles of gas.

4. Figure A.22.2 presents a graph of the temperature of the water during boiling.

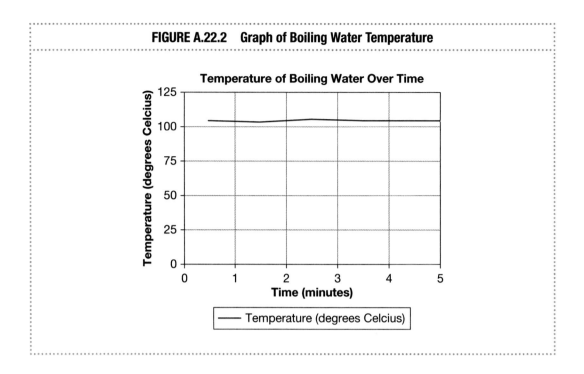

FIGURE A.22.2   Graph of Boiling Water Temperature

Do you agree with Mia, Naomi, both, or neither? Support your answer with reasoning and evidence in the space below.

PART 2

Naomi and Mia are asked to draw pictures to show the movement and arrangement of molecules as the water boils (Figure A.22.3). They have drawn models of the water molecules when the water has been boiling for 1 minute. The small lines show the speed of the molecules. How should they represent the water molecules when the water has been boiling for 4 minutes?

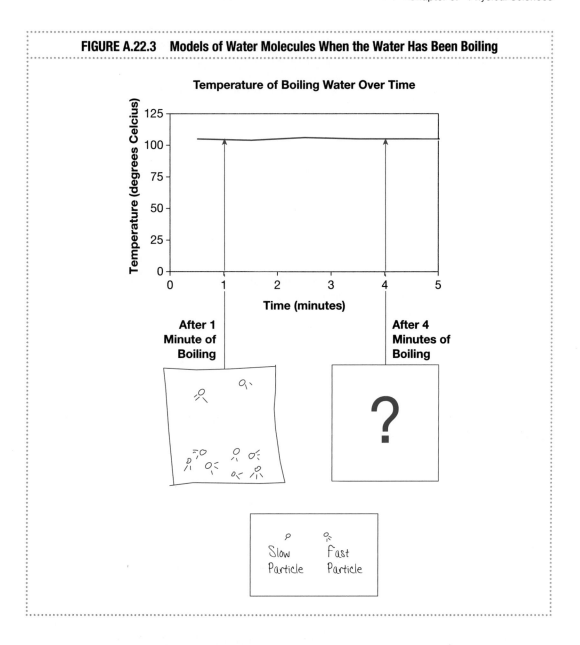

FIGURE A.22.3   Models of Water Molecules When the Water Has Been Boiling

1. Which model (Figures A.22.4–A.22.7) best shows the speed and arrangement of molecules when the water has been boiling for 4 minutes? Circle the model you think is best.

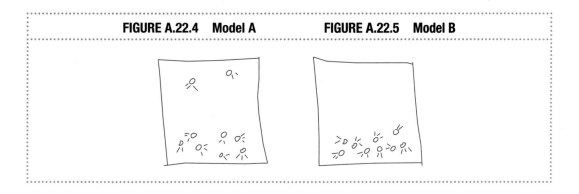

FIGURE A.22.4   Model A   FIGURE A.22.5   Model B

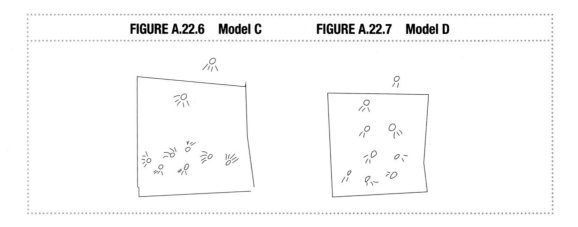

FIGURE A.22.6   Model C   **FIGURE A.22.7   Model D**

Use evidence and reasoning to support your claim about which drawing is the best model of water after it has been boiling for 4 minutes.

2. Choose one of the other models and explain why it is not as good as the one you chose.

   Which model will you critique (A, B, C, or D)? _____

   Why is this model not as good as the diagram you think is best?

Suggested Responses

Beneath are an indication of the possible responses to this activity that would demonstrate a good understanding of the science.

Which Model of Boiling Water Fits Best With the Evidence?

PART 1

Do you agree with Mia, Naomi, both, or neither? Support your answer with reasoning and evidence.

I agree with Naomi. The speed of particles goes up when the temperature goes up. Since the graph shows the temperature as staying the same over time, the speed of the water molecules stays the same during boiling. The evidence also says "the particles of a liquid are nearer to each other than particles of gas." When water boils, it turns from a liquid to a gas, so the gas molecules are farther from each other than the liquid molecules.

PART 2

Use evidence and reasoning to support your claim about which drawing is the best model of water after it has been boiling for 4 minutes.

I think Model D is best because it shows the molecules more spread out than the other representations. When water boils, it turns from a liquid to a gas and because gas particles are farther from each other than liquid particles, Model D fits with the evidence.

2. Choose one of the other models and explain why it is not as good as the one you chose.

Which model will you critique (A, B, C, or D)? _____
Why is this model not as good as the diagram you think is best?
Here are some example critiques of the other representations:
Model A: This diagram does not show changes in the arrangement and motion of the molecules. The water has been boiling, and during boiling, liquid transitions to gas. Particles are farther from each other as a gas than as a liquid. Therefore, particles need to be farther from each other at $t = 4$ minutes than $t = 1$ minute.
Model B: This diagram shows all of the molecules at the bottom of the box. During boiling, there is more gas (and less liquid) over time. Because gas particles are free, there should be fewer particles on the bottom over time.
Model C: This representation shows the particles moving faster, but this does not fit with the evidence that temperature stays the same during boiling and particles move faster when temperature increases.

Additional Resources

Tips for modeling in science: https://www.cfa.harvard.edu/smg/Website/UCP/classroom/modeling.html

Tools for Ambitious Science Teaching: Models and modeling introduction: http://ambitiousscience-teaching.org/wp-content/uploads/2014/09/Models-and-Modeling-An-Introduction1.pdf

Extension Activities

Have students construct and/or critique models of water or other substances that experience a change of state other than boiling (i.e., melting, freezing, condensing).

Notes

_____

_____

_____

_____

_____

_____

_____

_____

_____

_____

_____

_____

_____

Is Matter Always Conserved?

Learning Goals

The goals of this activity are for students to

- determine the change in mass of substances before and after a chemical reaction and analyze a class set of these data
- construct an argument for whether or not data support the law of conservation of matter
- critique a claim stating that atoms disappear during a chemical reaction

NGSS References

MS-PS1-5

Develop and use a model to describe how the total number of atoms does not change in a chemical reaction and thus mass is conserved.

    Clarification Statement: Emphasis is on law of conservation of matter and on physical models or drawings, including digital forms, that represent atoms.

    Assessment Boundary: Assessment does not include the use of atomic masses, balancing symbolic equations, or intermolecular forces.

The goal of this exercise is to build a deeper understanding of the idea that atoms rearrange and do not disappear during chemical reactions, as shown by the evidence that the total mass of the system stays the same. In the activity, students will conduct an investigation to determine the change in mass for the reaction of Epsom salt with ammonia. Then, they will analyze the class data and construct an argument for whether the evidence supports the law of conservation of matter.

Science Background

Content Knowledge

Scientists have found that matter is not created or destroyed, and this principle is known as the law of conservation of matter. In a chemical reaction, atoms rearrange to form new substances, and the total number of atoms does not change. Evidence for the conservation of matter in a chemical reaction is that the mass of substances before a chemical reaction (i.e., reactants) is the same as the mass of substances after a chemical reaction (i.e., products).

Knowledge for Teaching

In this activity, students collect data for the mass of substances before and after a precipitation reaction (i.e., where an insoluble salt is formed in a chemical reaction), which allows them to calculate the change in mass of the substances. Students should conclude that there is not a change in mass, or if there is, the change in mass can be explained by measurement error. Thus, the data from the activity are consistent with the law of conservation of matter.

The following chemical equation describes the chemical reaction that occurs in the activity. Magnesium sulfate (Epsom salt) reacts with ammonia to produce ammonium sulfate and magnesium hydroxide (the precipitate).

$$MgSO_{4\ (aq)} + 2NH_{3\ (aq)} + 2H_2O_{(l)} \rightarrow (NH_4)_2SO_{4\ (aq)} + Mg(OH)_{2\ (s)}$$

magnesium sulfate + ammonia + water $\rightarrow$ ammonium sulfate + magnesium hydroxide

When ammonia is in an aqueous solution, it is in equilibrium with ammonium hydroxide, as shown in the following chemical equation:

$$NH_{3\ (aq)} + H_2O_{(l)} \rightleftharpoons NH_4(OH)_{(aq)}$$

ammonia + water $\rightleftharpoons$ ammonium hydroxide

Magnesium sulfate, ammonium sulfate, and ammonium hydroxide are ionic compounds that break into ions (Mg^{2+}, SO_4^{2-}, and NH_4^+, OH^-) when dissolved in water, as they have been in this activity.

Prior Knowledge for Students

Students need to know that atoms are the smallest fundamental particles of elements (atoms are composed of subatomic particles, but these particles are not, in and of themselves, elements). Students should also be able to determine the mean of a set of measurements. The calculation of the mean value is likely to include negative numbers. Finally, it would be helpful for students to understand that "measurement error" is the difference between the measured value and the actual value. Measurement error can come from natural variation in the measured data due to the precision limitations of the measurement device. For example, if the mass of a substance is measured three times using a balance with the precision of ± 0.1 g, the measurements might be 23.1 g, 23.0 g, and 23.2 g. There may also be systematic errors due to problems in the experiment such as poor measurements and spilling of substances.

Teaching Sequence
Materials (for Each Group)

- Epsom salt solution (teacher prepare Epsom salt solution by dissolving 15 g Epsom salt per 100 mL distilled H_2O)
- Household ammonia
- Water
- 50-mL beaker
- Spoon to stir
- Balance
- Eye protection
- 25-mL graduated cylinder

Instructions for Activity

- **(2 min) Frame the lesson:** Tell students that they will build on their knowledge of atoms to construct an argument for what happens to atoms in a chemical reaction.
- **(Length depends on the option you choose) Procedure:** Three data collection/provision options are provided as follows. If you are tight on time and have access to a balance, we

recommend Option 2 because the most important part of the activity is the conclusion; this is where students argue about the scientific idea.

Option 1: Have small groups of students collect data and pool the class data, as outlined in the student activity sheet.

Option 2: Demonstrate the procedure for students and collect data for the class. We recommend providing students with additional data/trials if you decide on this option.

Option 3 (if there is not access to a balance): Demonstrate the precipitation reaction and provide students with a set of data.

- **(20 min) Analysis:** Have students complete the analysis questions individually or in small groups. Optional: Remove the equations from the analysis questions and facilitate students' reasoning of the appropriate calculations. Compile the class data and share them with students. Then, facilitate a discussion of why the different groups' changes in mass were not the same (i.e., why is there variation in the data?). It is important to play devil's advocate that measurement error (random fluctuations in the measurements, spills during pouring, and evaporation) can account for changes in mass.
- **(15 min) Conclusion: This is the most important part because this is where the students argue about the scientific concept!**

1. Have students write a conclusion individually, in small groups, or as a class, as you see appropriate.

2. Facilitate an argument line for Question 2: "Do the class data support the law of conservation of matter?" It is important that students recognize that although there may have been a mean change in mass, the evidence supports the law of conservation of matter because measurement error can account for changes in mass. If students do not develop this idea on their own, make sure that you play devil's advocate and suggest it for them to consider. Likewise, in contrast, if students argue that the data are consistent with the law of conservation of matter, play devil's advocate by arguing that a decrease in mass is not consistent with the law of conservation of matter. Here is a suggested question:

   a. "What is your reasoning for how the class data do/do not support the law of conservation of matter?"

3. Note: It is common for students to have difficulty explaining the connection between claims and evidence. Suggested follow-up prompt: "You have cited evidence. To improve your argument and strengthen your reasoning, explain how the evidence 'the mass stayed the same' supports the law of conservation of matter."

   b. Prompt students to respond to each other's claims using talk moves such as, "Could someone restate what [student name] just said?" and "Do you agree/disagree with [student name's] idea? Explain your thinking." "What has someone else said that has changed your thinking?"

4. Following the argument line, have students revise their arguments.

Student Activity: Is Matter Always Conserved?

An electronic copy of this activity is available on the companion website at https://resources.corwin.com/OsborneArgumentation.

FIGURE A.23.1   Epsom Salt   **FIGURE A.23.2   Ammonia**

© San Francisco Salt Company

© Phanuwath | Dreamstime.com

Introduction

When some substances are mixed together, they produce different substances, which is a process known as a "chemical reaction." Epsom salt (Figure A.23.1) and ammonia (Figure A.23.2) are two household chemicals that react when they are mixed together. Some people dissolve Epsom salt in water and soak their bodies in the solution because they think it reduces stress or relieves pain. Ammonia is one of the most commonly produced chemicals in the world. It is used for many purposes, including cleaning and making medications. In this activity, you will determine if the mass of these substances changes during a chemical reaction.

Materials

- Epsom salt solution (teacher prepares Epsom salt solution by dissolving 15 g Epsom salt per 100 mL distilled H_2O)
- Household ammonia
- Water
- 50-mL beaker

- Spoon to stir
- Balance
- Eye protection
- 25-mL graduated cylinder

PART 1: Procedure

1. Find the mass of a 50-mL beaker and a 25-mL graduated cylinder and record them in your data table.

2. Using the 25-mL graduated cylinder, measure out 10 mL of Epsom salt solution, weigh it, and pour it into the 50-mL beaker. Rinse out the graduated cylinder.

3. Using the 25-mL graduated cylinder, measure out 20 mL of ammonia and weigh it.

4. Add the ammonia to the beaker.

5. Record what you observe for 5 minutes.

6. Weigh the beaker.

	g
Mass of 50-mL beaker	
Mass of 25-mL graduated cylinder	
Mass of cylinder and Epsom salt solution	
Mass of cylinder and ammonia solution	
Mass of 50-mL beaker and products	

PART 2: Analysis

1. Calculate the mass of the Epsom salt solution (before mixing) using the following equation. Show your calculation.

(Mass of graduated cylinder and Epsom salt solution – mass of cylinder = mass of Epsom salt solution)

2. Calculate the mass of the ammonia solution (before mixing) using the following equation. Show your calculation.

(Mass of graduated cylinder and ammonia solution – mass of cylinder = mass of ammonia solution)

3. Calculate the total mass of liquids before mixing using the following equation. Show your calculation.

(Mass of ammonia solution + mass of Epsom salt solution = total mass of liquids before mixing)

4. Calculate the mass of the substances after the reaction using the following equation. Show your calculation.

(Mass of 50-mL beaker and products − mass of beaker = mass of substances after the reaction)

5. Calculate the change in mass using the following equation. Show your calculation and **explain what the change in mass means.**

(Mass of substances after the reaction − total mass of liquids before mixing = change in mass)

6. Record the change in mass found by other groups.

Group	Change in Mass

7. What do you notice about the class data?

8. Why do you think groups found different changes in mass? In other words, why is there variation in the data?

9. What is the mean of the change in mass data? Show your work.

10. What is the range of the change in mass data? Justify your answer.

11. Why is it important to find the mean and range of the class data?

PART 3: Conclusions

1. Did the mass of the substances change during the chemical reaction? If so, how? Support your claim with evidence.

2. Scientists have found that matter is not created or destroyed, and they call this idea the law of conservation of matter. Do the class data support the law of conservation of matter? Justify your answer using evidence and reasoning.

3. Michelle says, "Mass decreases during some chemical reactions because some atoms disappear." Explain what is wrong with Michelle's idea.

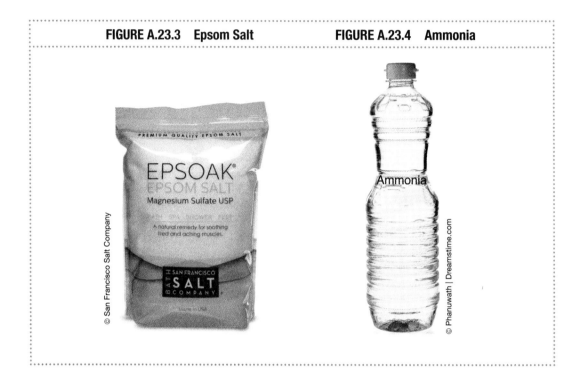

FIGURE A.23.3   Epsom Salt

FIGURE A.23.4   Ammonia

© San Francisco Salt Company

© Phanuwath | Dreamstime.com

PART 1: Procedure

6. Weigh the beaker.

	g
Mass of 50-mL beaker	41.23 g
Mass of 25-mL graduated cylinder	22.16 g
Mass of cylinder and Epsom salt solution	32.47 g
Mass of cylinder and ammonia solution	42.89 g
Mass of 50-mL beaker and products	72.25 g

PART 2: Analysis

1. Calculate the mass of the Epsom salt solution (before mixing) using the following equation. Show your calculation.

(Mass of graduated cylinder and Epsom salt solution – mass of cylinder = mass of Epsom salt solution)

32.47 g – 22.16 g = 10.31 g

2. Calculate the mass of the ammonia solution (before mixing) using the following equation. Show your calculation.

(Mass of graduated cylinder and ammonia solution –
mass of cylinder = mass of ammonia solution)

42.89 g – 22.16 g = 20.73 g

3. Calculate the total mass of liquids before mixing using the following equation. Show your calculation.

(Mass of ammonia solution + mass of Epsom salt solution =
total mass of liquids before mixing)

10.31 g + 20.73 g = 31.04 g

4. Calculate the mass of the substances after the reaction using the following equation. Show your calculation.

(Mass of 50-mL beaker and products – mass of beaker =
mass of substances after the reaction)

72.25 g – 41.23 g = 31.02 g

5. Calculate the change in mass using the following equation. Show your calculation and **explain what the change in mass means.**

(Mass of substances after the reaction – total mass of liquids
before reaction = change in mass)

31.02 g – 31.04 g = –0.02 g

The change in mass means the mass of the products is 0.02 g less than the mass of what we started with.

6. Record the change in mass found by other groups.

Group	Change in Mass
1	–0.02 g
2	–0.01 g
3	0.00 g
4	–0.04 g
5	+0.02 g
6	–0.23 g
7	+0.01 g
8	0.00 g

7. What do you notice about the class data?
The changes in masses are all close to zero, except for Group 6.

8. Why do you think groups found different changes in mass? In other words, why is there variation in the data?

We may have spilled when pouring the liquids from the graduated cylinder into the beaker, which would make the change in mass more negative than it would have been if we hadn't spilled. In addition, there is always a little bit of liquid that sticks to the surface of a container when you pour it out, and that would have the same effect on the results. Finally, natural variation in measurements affects the data. If we measured the masses over and over, it wouldn't be exactly the same every time.

9. What is the mean of the change in mass data? Show your work.

NOTE: We would advise asking Group 6 if they spilled or made an error in their calculations and then omit this group's change in mass in the calculation of the class mean.

$$(-0.02 \text{ g} + -0.01 \text{ g} + 0.00 \text{ g} + -0.04 \text{ g} + 0.02 \text{ g} + 0.01 \text{ g} + 0.00 \text{ g}) / 7 = -0.01 \text{ g}$$

10. Why is it important to find the mean of the class data?

It is important to find the mean of the class data because the mean change in mass is more likely to show what actually happens than just one of our measurements. Each measurement has random error, and finding the mean reduces random error.

PART 3: Conclusions

1. Did the mass of the substances change during the chemical reaction? If so, how? Support your claim with evidence.

Yes, the mass of the substances decreased a small amount during the chemical reaction. There was an average of a 0.01-g decrease in the mass of the substances.

2. Scientists have found that matter is not created or destroyed, and they call this idea the "law of conservation of matter." Do the class data support the law of conservation of matter? Justify your answer using evidence and reasoning.

The class data do support the law of conservation of matter. The average change in mass was –0.01 g. Because this measurement is very close to zero and there is measurement error, there is basically no change in mass. Matter has mass, and the mass of the substances doesn't change during the chemical reaction, so we can conclude that the amount of matter before the chemical reaction is the same as the amount of matter after the chemical reaction—matter was not created or destroyed!

3. Michelle says, "Mass decreases during some chemical reactions because some atoms disappear." Explain what is wrong with Michelle's idea.

We learned that the law of conservation is "matter cannot be created or destroyed." If atoms disappear, they would be destroyed, so Michelle's idea does not fit with this law. In addition, there was not a change in mass during the chemical reaction that cannot be explained by measurement error. If atoms disappeared in the chemical reaction, then the mass of the substances after the chemical reaction might have been less than the mass of the substances after the chemical reaction.

Additional Resources

Phet: Balancing chemical equations: https://phet.colorado.edu/en/simulation/balancing-chemical-equations

	Extension Activities
	Have students identify examples from their everyday lives where the mass of something changes. Then have them explain where the mass goes and how the example is consistent (fits) with the law of conservation of matter.

Acknowledgments

- This activity was adapted from http://www.cfep.uci.edu/cspi/docs/lessons_secondary/precipitate Lab.pdf
- San Francisco Salt Company generously permitted use of the Epsom Salt image.

Notes

_____

_____

_____

_____

_____

_____

_____

_____

_____

_____

_____

_____

Where Oh Where Have the Atoms Gone?

Learning Goals

The goals of this activity are for students to

- construct an argument for which model of atoms after a chemical reaction is best
- apply the law of conservation of matter to critique an alternative model of the atoms after a chemical reaction

NGSS References

MS-PS1-5

Develop and use a model to describe how the total number of atoms does not change in a chemical reaction and thus mass is conserved.

    Clarification Statement: Emphasis is on law of conservation of matter and on physical models or drawings, including digital forms, that represent atoms.

       Assessment Boundary: Assessment does not include the use of atomic masses, balancing symbolic equations, or intermolecular forces.

This activity would ideally follow the "household chemical reaction" activity, although it does not necessarily need to. The goal of this exercise is to build a deeper understanding of the idea that atoms rearrange and do not disappear during chemical reactions. You will demonstrate how there is a decrease in the mass of the system for the reaction of baking soda and vinegar. Then, students will engage in argument about which of competing models for the products of the chemical reaction is best.

Science Background

Content Knowledge

Scientists have found that matter is not created nor destroyed, and this principle is known as the "law of conservation of matter." In a chemical reaction, atoms rearrange to form new substances, and the total number of atoms does not change. If matter does not leave or enter the system, the total mass before and after the reaction is the same. However, if matter leaves the system, the mass of the products (i.e., the substances formed when a reaction is complete) is less than the mass of the reactants (i.e., the substances initially present in a chemical reaction). Matter leaves the system in this activity because when vinegar and baking soda react, carbon dioxide is produced and the bubbles are released into the surrounding air. Thus, an accurate representation of the products would show fewer atoms in the system compared to the reactants, the total number of atoms of each element as the same, and different molecules (i.e., different arrangements of the atoms).

Knowledge for Teaching

Students are provided with representations of atoms that compose substances before and after a chemical reaction. Specifically, there are representations of the molecules for the reaction of sodium bicarbonate (baking soda) and acetic acid (vinegar), which produces sodium acetate, water, and carbon dioxide as described in the following chemical equation.

$$NaHCO_3 + C_2H_4O_2 \rightarrow NaC_2H_3O_2 + H_2O + CO_2$$

sodium bicarbonate + acetic acid → ammonium acetate + water + carbon dioxide

One of the representations of the products in the chemical reaction (Jackson's model) is not consistent with the law of conservation of matter because there are more atoms in his representation than the number of atoms represented in the sodium bicarbonate and acetic acid representations. Savannah's model is consistent with the law of conservation of matter because the total number of atoms is the same as the reactants, but her model does not show atoms combining or rearranging to form new substances, and thus, Savannah's model is not consistent with the observation that a new substance is formed in the reaction. In addition, Savannah's model is not consistent with the evidence that the mass of the system decreases. Ethan's and Naomi's models are consistent with both the law of conservation of matter and the observation in the investigation. Ethan's representation is the "best" in that it accurately shows the products of the reaction. However, unless the chemical equation is provided to students and they understand how to interpret it, they do not have enough information to conclude whether Ethan's or Naomi's model is better.

Prior Knowledge for Students

Students need to know that atoms are the smallest fundamental particles of elements (i.e., subatomic particles compose atoms, but these particles are not in and of themselves elements). Molecules are two or more atoms bonded together. Students should also know that evidence for the conservation of matter in a chemical reaction is that the mass of substances before a chemical reaction (i.e., reactants) is the same as the mass of substances after a chemical reaction (i.e., products). It would be helpful for students to understand some purposes of scientific models: They represent a system (or parts of a system), explain phenomena, and communicate ideas to others. In addition, models are based on evidence, and they are modified when new evidence is uncovered that the models can't explain. As for the models in this activity, it would also be helpful if students have interpreted or constructed models of atoms using circles.

Teaching Sequence

- **(5 min) Elicit background knowledge:** If your students completed the household chemical reaction activity, ask them what they learned from it. If not, use questioning to elicit the idea that there is not a change in mass of substances in a chemical reaction (if there was a change in mass, it could not be accounted for by measurement error). Explain to students that they will build on their knowledge of conservation of matter and construct an argument for how to represent what happens to atoms in a different chemical reaction.
- **(5 min) Part 1: Predict:** Tell students that the class will collect data for the mass before and after the reaction of baking soda and vinegar. Ask students to predict what will happen to the mass and ask, "What is your reasoning?"
- **(5 min if you choose to demonstrate the reaction, longer if students collect data) Observe:** Use the following procedure to demonstrate and collect data (or have students collect data) for the mass of baking soda and vinegar before and after they react:

- ○ Set the balance to 0.
- ○ Fill a beaker with 20 mL of vinegar.
- ○ Add one spoonful of baking soda to the second beaker.
- ○ Place both beakers on the balance and record the starting mass.
- ○ Dump the baking soda into the beaker. Do not stir.
- ○ Place the empty beaker back on the balance. Record the ending mass, including both beakers.
- ○ Calculate the amount of mass changed.

- **(10 min) Explain:** Have small groups discuss why there was a decrease in the mass, elicit ideas as a full class, and facilitate students' response to each other's ideas. Then, tell students that scientists often use models to explain their data and they use evidence to argue which model is best, which is what they will do in the next part of the activity.
- **(10 min) Part 2: Models:** Students should count the number of atoms of each element represented in the vinegar and baking soda models and then complete the graphic organizer in small groups or individually. An optional scaffold would be to complete one box in each row as a class so students have a model response.
- **(10 min)** For Question 4, use a four corners structure, where each corner of the room corresponds to a student's model. It is important that students use the law of conservation of matter and evidence that there was a change in the substances in their arguments for which representation is best. Thus, we recommend asking questions, such as the following:

  - ○ "How does the law of conservation of matter support Ethan's/Savannah's/Naomi's/Jackson's model?"
  - ○ "How does the observation that a white substance formed in the reaction support Ethan's/Savannah's/Naomi's/Jackson's model?"
  - ○ Emphasize that both Ethan's and Naomi's models are consistent with the evidence and we need more information to determine which is best. Scientists also collect more data when they do not know which of their ideas is best.

- **(5 min)** For Question 5, students should critique an alternative model of their choice.

Student Activity: Where Oh Where Have the Atoms Gone?

An electronic copy of this activity is available on the companion website at https://resources.corwin.com/OsborneArgumentation.

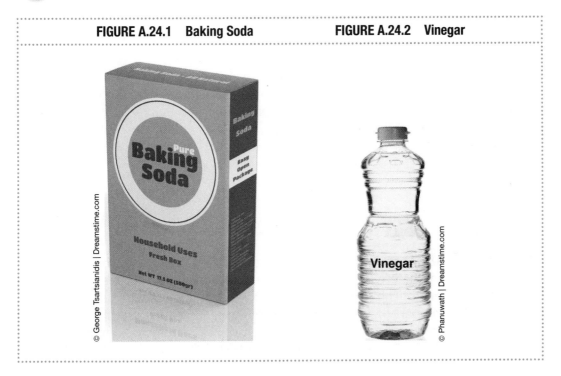

FIGURE A.24.1 Baking Soda   FIGURE A.24.2 Vinegar

Introduction

When some substances are mixed together, they produce different substances, which is a process known as a "chemical reaction." Baking soda (Figure A.24.1) and vinegar (Figure A.24.2) are two common ingredients used in cooking that react when they are mixed together. In this activity, you will construct an argument for which model of the atoms in the chemical reaction is best.

PART 1: Predict, Observe, Explain

1. **Predict** what will happen to the mass of the vinegar, baking soda, and materials when the vinegar and baking soda are mixed together. Will the initial mass increase, decrease, or stay the same? Support your answer using your knowledge and reasoning.

2. **Observe** the reaction and record the masses of the vinegar, baking soda, and measuring:

Initial mass: _____

Final mass: _____

Change in mass: _____

	Total Number of Atoms

3. **Explain** your observations using what you have learned about conservation of matter. Also, conclude whether your prediction was accurate or not and support your answer with evidence.

PART 2: **Models**

1. Figures A.24.3 and A.24.4 represent the atoms of the Epsom salt and ammonia solutions before the chemical reaction. Each symbol represents an atom of an element. The square box around the atoms represents the system, which is the part of the universe being studied. For this activity, the system includes the chemicals on the balance. Count the number of atoms of each element that are represented in both models and fill in the following table.

2. Savannah, Jackson, Ethan, and Naomi represent the atoms after the chemical reaction. Use the models (Figures A.24.3–A.24.8) to complete the table.

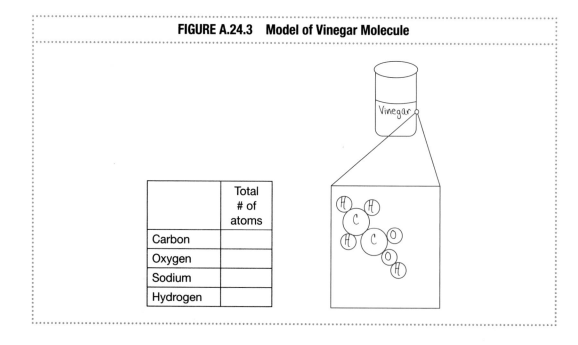

FIGURE A.24.3   Model of Vinegar Molecule

	Total # of atoms
Carbon	
Oxygen	
Sodium	
Hydrogen	

FIGURE A.24.4   Model of Baking Soda Molecule

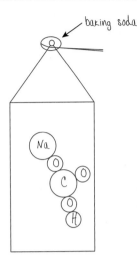

	Total # of atoms
Carbon	
Oxygen	
Sodium	
Hydrogen	

FIGURE A.24.5   Savannah's Model

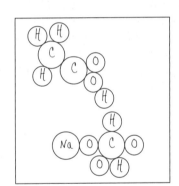

	Total # of atoms
Carbon	3
Oxygen	5
Sodium	1
Hydrogen	5

FIGURE A.24.6   Jackson's Model

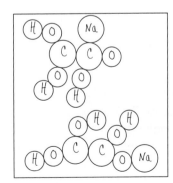

	Total # of atoms
Carbon	4
Oxygen	8
Sodium	2
Hydrogen	6

FIGURE A.24.7   Ethan's Model

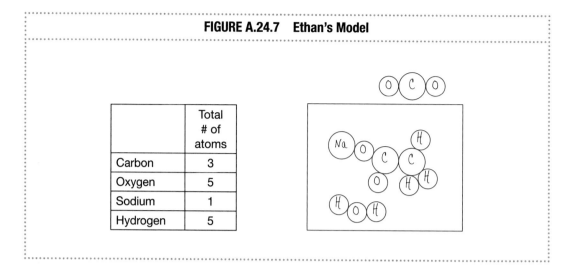

	Total # of atoms
Carbon	3
Oxygen	5
Sodium	1
Hydrogen	5

FIGURE A.24.8   Naomi's Model

	Total # of atoms
Carbon	3
Oxygen	5
Sodium	1
Hydrogen	5

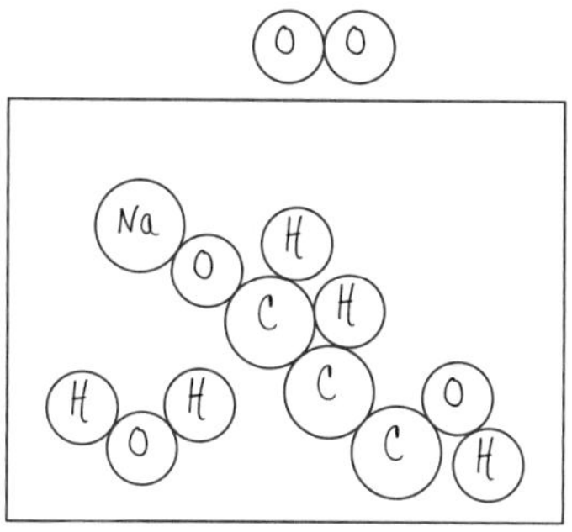

3. Complete the following table to compare and contrast the models of the substances before and after the chemical reaction.

	Savannah's Model	Jackson's Model	Ethan's Model	Naomi's Model
Are there any differences between the **total** number of atoms of each element in the students' models compared to the vinegar and baking soda models? If so, what are they?				

	Savannah's Model	Jackson's Model	Ethan's Model	Naomi's Model
Are there any differences between the **number of atoms in the system** in the students' models compared to the vinegar and baking soda models? If so, what are they?				
Are there molecules in the students' models that are different from the vinegar and baking soda molecules? (yes or no)				

4. Scientists have found that matter is not created or destroyed, and this idea is called the *law of conservation of matter*. Based on the law of conservation of matter and the above table, whose model do you think is best? Use evidence and the law of conservation of matter to support your claim.

5. Explain how one of the other models does not fit with the law of conservation of matter.

Suggested Responses

Beneath are an indication of the possible responses to this activity that would demonstrate a good understanding of the science.

PART 1: Predict, Observe, Explain

1. **Predict** what will happen when the vinegar and baking soda are mixed together. Will the initial mass increase, decrease, or stay the same? Support your answer using your knowledge and reasoning.

I think the mass will decrease because there are bubbles when vinegar and baking soda are mixed together. Since bubbles have mass and leave liquids to enter the surrounding air, the mass will go down.

2. **Observe** the reaction and record the masses of the vinegar, baking soda, and measuring equipment.

Initial mass: __155.4 g_____

Final mass: __154.7 g_____

Change in mass: _– 0.7 g_____

3. **Explain** your observations using what you have learned about conservation of matter. Also, conclude whether your prediction was accurate or not and support your answer with evidence.

PART 2: Models

1. Count the number of atoms of each element that are represented in both models and fill in the following table.

2. Complete the following graphic organizer to compare and contrast the models of the substances before and after the chemical reaction.

	Savannah's Model	Jackson's Model	Ethan's Model	Naomi's Model
Are there any differences between the **total** number of atoms of each element in the students' models compared to the vinegar and baking soda models? If so, what are they?	No	Yes, there is one more carbon atom, three more oxygen atoms, one more sodium atom, and one more hydrogen atom.	No	No

	Savannah's Model	Jackson's Model	Ethan's Model	Naomi's Model
Are there any differences between the number of atoms **in the system** in the students' models compared to the vinegar and baking soda models? If so, what are they?	No	Yes, in the system there is one more carbon atom, three more oxygen atoms, one more sodium atom, and one more hydrogen atom.	Yes, in the system there is one less carbon atom and two less oxygen atoms.	Yes, in the system there are two less oxygen atoms.
Are there molecules in the students' models that are different from the vinegar and baking soda molecules? (yes or no)	No	Yes	Yes	Yes

4. Scientists have found that matter is not created or destroyed, and this idea is called the *law of conservation of matter*. Whose model do you think is best? Use evidence and the law of conservation of matter to support your claim.

The law of conservation of matter says "matter cannot be created or destroyed" and Ethan's and Naomi's models show the same number of atoms after the reaction as before the reaction. If the number of atoms had changed, then matter would have been created or destroyed, which wouldn't fit with the law of conservation of matter. In addition, there were bubbles, which shows something new was formed in the chemical reaction, and Naomi's model shows different molecules than those shown before the reaction.

5. Explain how one of the other models does not fit with the law of conservation of matter.

Jackson's model does not fit with the law of conservation of matter because he shows fewer atoms than there were before the reaction. Matter is not created or destroyed, so the number of atoms of each element needs to be the same before and after the reaction.

Additional Resources

Phet: Balancing chemical equations: https://phet.colorado.edu/en/simulation/balancing-chemical-equations

Tips for modeling in science: https://www.cfa.harvard.edu/smg/Website/UCP/classroom/modeling.html

Tools for Ambitious Science Teaching: Models and modeling introduction: http://ambitiousscienceteaching.org/wp-content/uploads/2014/09/Models-and-Modeling-An-Introduction1.pdf

Investigation of burning steel wool (increase in the mass of the system)—see Lesson 14: Atoms in Equals Atoms Out—Rusting: http://newdirectionsscience.weebly.com/uploads/2/0/6/5/20652672/chemistry_that_applies_teachers_guide.pdf

Extension Activities

Have students argue whether the mass of the system would change if you react baking soda and vinegar in a closed bag. Then, collect data (or have students collect data) using the procedure below. Following the data collection, have students construct models and engage in argument about which model is best.

1. Fill a clean beaker with 30 mL of vinegar.
2. Add one spoonful of baking soda to a clean plastic bag.
3. Gently place the beaker with the vinegar in the plastic bag. DO NOT spill the vinegar!
4. Try to push all the air out of the bag, seal the bag, and place it on the balance without spilling the vinegar.
5. Record the initial mass.
6. Without opening the bag, tip the beaker, mixing the vinegar with the baking soda.
7. Still without opening the bag, record the ending mass of the contents of the plastic bag.
8. Calculate the amount of mass changed.

References and
Further Resources

Alexander, R. (2005). *Towards dialogic teaching*. York, UK: Dialogos.

Allchin, D. (2012). Teaching the nature of science through scientific errors. *Science Education, 96*(5), 904–926.

Ames, G. J., & Murray, F. B. (1982). When two wrongs make a right: Promoting cognitive change by social conflict. *Developmental Psychology, 18*, 894–897.

Asterhan, C. S. C., & Schwarz, B. B. (2007). The effects of monological and dialogical argumentation on concept learning in evolutionary theory. *Journal of Educational Psychology, 99*(3), 626–639.

Bachelard, G. (1968). *The philosophy of no* (G. C. Waterston, Trans.). New York, NY: Orion.

Barron, B. (2003). When smart groups fail. *The Journal of the Learning Sciences, 12*(3), 307–359.

Becker, C. B. (1986). Reasons for the lack of argumentation and debate in the Far East. *International Journal of Intercultural Relations, 10*(1), 75–92.

Berland, L. K., & Reiser, B. (2008). Making sense of argumentation and explanation. *Science Education, 93*(1), 26–55.

Billig, M. (1996). *Arguing and thinking* (2nd ed.). Cambridge, UK: Cambridge University Press.

Black, P., & William, D. (2006). *Inside the black box: Raising standards through classroom assessment.* London, UK: King's College.

Blatchford, P., Kutnick, P., Baines, E., & Galton, M. (2003). Toward a social pedagogy of classroom group work. *International Journal of Educational Research, 39*, 153–172.

Chi, M. (2009). Active-constructive-interactive: A conceptual framework for differentiating learning activities. *Topics in Cognitive Science, 1*, 73–105.

Coming to an office near you. (2014). *The Economist*. Retrieved from http://www.economist.com/news/leaders/21594298-effect-todays-technology-tomorrows-jobs-will-be-immenseand-no-country-ready

Common Core State Standards Initiative. (2010). *Common Core State Standards for Mathematics.* Retrieved from http://www.corestandards.org/

Crombie, A. C. (1994). *Styles of scientific thinking in the European tradition: The history of argument and explanation especially in the mathematical and biomedical sciences and arts* (Vol. 1). London, UK: Duckworth.

Dawkins, R. (1976). *The Selfish Gene*. Oxford: Oxford University Press.

Feynman, R. P., Leighton, R. B., & Sands, M. (2013). *The Feynman lectures on physics, desktop edition* (Vol. 1). New York, NY: Basic Books.

Ford, M. J. (2008). Disciplinary authority and accountability in scientific practice and learning. *Science Education, 92*(3), 404–423.

Gilbert, J. (2005). *Catching the knowledge wave? The knowledge society and the future of education.* Wellington, New Zealand: NZCER Press.

Halliday, M. A. K. (1993). *Towards a language-based theory of learning. Linguistics and Education, 5*(2), 93–116.

Harré, R. (1984). *The philosophies of science: An introductory survey* (2nd ed.). Oxford, UK: Oxford University Press.

Hattie, J. (2008). *Visible learning: A synthesis of over 800 meta-analyses relating to achievement.* London, UK: Routledge.

Hattie, J., & Timperley, H. (2007). The power of feedback. *Review of Educational Research, 77*(1), 81–112.

Howe, C. J., Tolmie, A., & Rodgers, C. (1992). The acquisition of conceptual knowledge in science by primary school children: Group interaction and the understanding of motion down an inclined plane. *British Journal of Developmental Psychology, 10*, 113–130.

Hynd, C., & Alvermann, D. E. (1986). The role of refutation text in overcoming difficulty with science concepts. *Journal of Reading, 29*(5), 440–446.

Keeley, P., Eberle, F., & Farrin, L. (2005). *Uncovering student ideas in science, Vol. I: 25 formative assessment probes.* Arlington, VA: NSTA Press.

Kuhn, D. (1992). Thinking as argument. *Harvard Educational Review, 62*(2), 155–178.

Kuhn, D., Wang, Y., & Li, H. (2011). Why argue? Developing understanding of the purposes and values of argumentive discourse. *Discourse Processes, 48*, 26–49.

Latour, B., & Woolgar, S. (1986). *Laboratory life: The construction of scientific facts.* Princeton, NJ: Princeton University Press.

Lemke, J. (1990). *Talking science: Language, learning and values.* Norwood, NJ: Ablex.

Longino, H. E. (1990). *Science as social knowledge.* Princeton, NJ: Princeton University Press.

Manz, E. (2015). Representing student argumentation as functionally emergent from scientific activity. *Review of Educational Research, 20*(10), 1–38.

Mercer, N., Dawes, L., Wegerif, R., & Sams, C. (2004). Reasoning as a scientist: Ways of helping children to use language to learn science. *British Educational Research Journal, 30,* 367–385.

Mercer, N., & Littleton, K. (2007). *Dialogue and development of children's thinking: A sociocultural approach.* London, UK: Routledge.

Mercer, N., Wegerif, R., & Dawes, L. (1999). Children's talk in the development of reasoning. *British Educational Research Journal, 25*(1), 95–111.

Mercier, H., & Sperber, D. (2011). Why do humans reason? Arguments for an argumentative theory. *Behavioral and Brain Sciences, 34*(2), 57–74.

National Research Council. (2012a). *Education for life and work: Developing transferable knowledge and skills in the 21st century.* Washington, DC: Board on Testing and Assessment and Board on Science Education, Division of Behavioral and Social Sciences and Education.

National Research Council. (2012b). *A framework for K–12 science education: Practices, crosscutting concepts, and core ideas.* Washington, DC: Committee on a Conceptual Framework for New K–12 Science Education Standards, Board on Science Education, Division of Behavioral and Social Sciences and Education.

Naylor, S., & Keogh, B. (2000). *Concept cartoons in education.* Sandbach, UK: Millgate House Publishers.

Newton, P., Driver, R., & Osborne, J. F. (1999). The place of argumentation in the pedagogy of school science. *International Journal of Science Education, 21*(5), 553–576.

Nisbett, R. E. (2003). *The geography of thought: How Asians and Westerners think differently.* New York, NY: Free Press.

Norris, S. P. (1997). Intellectual independence for nonscientists and other content-transcendent goals of science education. *Science Education, 81*(2), 239–258.

Osborne, J. (2011.) Science teaching methods: A rationale for practices. *School Science Review, 93*(343), 93–103.

Penney, K., Norris, S. P., Phillips, L., & Clark, G. (2003). The anatomy of high school science textbooks. *Canadian Journal of Science and Mathematics Education, 3–4,* 415–436.

Popper, K. (1963). *Conjectures and refutations: The growth of scientific knowledge.* London, UK: Routledge and Kegan Paul.

Resnick, L., Michaels, S., & O'Connor, C. (2010). How (well-structured) talk builds the mind. In J. Sternberg (Ed.), *From genes to context: New discoveries about learning from educational research and their applications* (pp. 163–194). New York, NY: Springer.

Rowe, M. B. (1974). Wait-time and rewards as instructional variables, their influence on language, logic and fate control: Part one. Wait-time. *Journal of Research in Science Teaching, 11*(2), 81–94.

Sadler, P., & Good, E. (2006). The impact of self- and peer-grading on student learning. *Educational Assessment, 11*(1), 1–31.

Sadler, P. M., Sonnert, G., Coyle, H. P., Cook-Smith, N., & Miller, J. L. (2013). The influence of teachers' knowledge on student learning in middle school physical science classrooms. *American Educational Research Journal, 50*(5), 1020–1049.

Sampson, V., & Clark, D. (2009). The impact of collaboration on the outcomes of scientific argumentation. *Science Education, 93*(3), 448–484.

Schwarz, B. B., Neuman, Y., & Biezuner, S. (2000). Two wrongs may make a right . . . if they argue together! *Cognition and Instruction, 18*(4), 461–494.

Siegel, H. (1988). *Educating reason: Rationality, critical thinking and education.* London, UK: Routledge.

Tamir, P., & Zohar, A. (1991). Anthropomorphism and teleology in reasoning about biological phenomena. *Science Education, 75*(1), 57–67.

Toulmin, S. (1958). *The uses of argument.* Cambridge, UK: Cambridge University Press.

Weiss, I. R., Pasley, J. D., Sean Smith, P., Banilower, E. R., & Heck, D. J. (2003). *A study of K–12 mathematics and science education in the United States.* Chapel Hill, NC: Horizon Research.

Wertsch, J. (1991). *Voices of the mind: A sociocultural approach to mediated action.* Cambridge, MA: Harvard University Press.

Zohar, A., & Nemet, F. (2002). Fostering students' knowledge and argumentation skills through dilemmas in human genetics. *Journal of Research in Science Teaching, 39*(1), 35–62.

Index

Note: Page numbers in *italic* refer to figures.

About the Authors

Jonathan Osborne holds the Kamalachari Chair in Science Education at the Graduate School of Education, Stanford University. Previously, he held the chair in Science Education at King's College London. He was a coauthor of the report *Beyond 2000: Science Education for the Future* and an adviser to the U.K. House of Commons Science and Technology Committee in 2002 for their report on Science Education. He was president of the U.S. National Association for Research in Science Teaching (2006–2007) and has won the association's award for the best research publication in the *Journal of Research in Science Teaching* twice (2003 and 2004). He was a member of the U.S. National Academies Panel that produced the *Framework for K–12 Science Education* that is the basis for the new Next Generation Science Standards. Currently, he is chair of the expert group that produced the framework for the science assessments conducted by the OECD Program for International Student Assessment (PISA) in 2015 and 2018. His research interests are in the role of argumentation in the teaching and learning of science and improving the teaching of literacy in science.

Brian M. Donovan is The John Evans Gessford Stanford Interdisciplinary Graduate Fellow in K–12 Education. He holds a BA in biology from Colorado College, an MA in teaching from the University of San Francisco, and an MS in biology from Stanford University and graduated from Stanford University with a PhD in science education in 2016. Before Stanford, he taught science in San Francisco middle schools and to "at-risk" high school youth in a wilderness therapy program. At Stanford, he has taught in the Stanford Teacher Education Program and worked on different I.E.S.-funded intervention research projects (both experimental and design based) in the Stanford Graduate School of Education and in the Stanford Department of Psychology. His scholarship explores how psychological essentialism interacts with biology education to affect the development of prejudice and stereotyping during adolescence. His scholarship has been published in a variety of journals, including *Science Education, The Journal of Research in Science Teaching, PLoS Biology,* and *Studies in the History and Philosophy of Science.* He recently received a 3-year fellowship from Stanford University to study how to teach about human difference to improve understanding of human genetic variation and increase motivations to confront racial prejudice.

J. Bryan Henderson received his PhD from Stanford University in science education. He is interested in the utilization of educational technology to facilitate peer-to-peer science learning via formative assessment techniques. His classroom-based research on peer learning intersects with multiple years of experience studying the learning of science through evidence-based argumentation. As a cofounder and research director of the *Braincandy* nonprofit, Dr. Henderson is working with teachers across the United States to make formative assessment materials and best practices freely accessible via cloud-based applications. His scientific background is in astrophysics, with research positions at major observatories in Arizona, Chile, and The Netherlands. He has over a decade of experience teaching statistics, learning theories, and physics at the college level. In addition to a PhD from Stanford, he also possesses three bachelor's degrees in physics, astronomy, and philosophy (with distinction) from the University of Washington and two master's degrees in physics and education from Portland State University. Dr. Henderson is currently a tenure-track assistant professor of learning sciences at Arizona State University, where he is a recipient of the ASU Centennial Professorship for outstanding teaching, leadership, and service.

Anna C. MacPherson received her PhD from Stanford University in science education. Her primary research interests are in developing new ways to assess complex scientific thinking, as well as understanding how students and teachers use such assessments in the classroom. Prior to beginning doctoral study, she taught high school biology and chemistry in the New York City public school system. She also has significant scientific research experience and several publications in the fields of ecology and neuroscience. She holds a BS in biology from Stanford and an MA in adolescent science education from Hunter College, CUNY. She is currently the manager of Educational Research and Evaluation at the American Museum of Natural History in New York City.

Andrew Wild is completing his PhD in science education at Stanford University. Prior to graduate school, he taught high school chemistry and conceptual physics in the San Francisco Bay Area. He is a graduate of the Stanford Teacher Education Program and he holds a BA in chemistry from Carleton College. His research interests include social norms for science teaching and equity in science education. He also has expertise in performance-based assessments and scientific argumentation. Andrew has mentored teachers in both California and Vermont, where he currently lives. He also conducts research for the Knowles Science Teaching Foundation, where he is a Senior Fellow.

CORWIN HAS ONE MISSION: to enhance education through intentional professional learning.

We build long-term relationships with our authors, educators, clients, and associations who partner with us to develop and continuously improve the best evidence-based practices that establish and support lifelong learning.

Solutions you want. Experts you trust. Results you need.

Author Consulting

Author Consulting

On-site professional learning with sustainable results! Let us help you design a professional learning plan to meet the unique needs of your school or district. www.corwin.com/pd

Institutes

Institutes

Corwin Institutes provide collaborative learning experiences that equip your team with tools and action plans ready for immediate implementation. www.corwin.com/institutes

eCourses

eCourses

Practical, flexible online professional learning designed to let you go at your own pace. www.corwin.com/ecourses

Read2Earn

Read2Earn

Did you know you can earn graduate credit for reading this book? Find out how: www.corwin.com/read2earn

Contact an account manager at (800) 831-6640 or visit **www.corwin.com** for more information.